•BATTLE COLORS•

Insignia And Aircraft Markings Of The US Army Air Forces In World War II

Volume VI

China/Burma/India & Western Pacific Theater Of Operations

Robert A. Watkins

Schiffer Publishing Ltd®

4880 Lower Valley Road • Atglen, PA 19310

THIS VOLUME IS RESPECTFULLY
DEDICATED TO ALL USAAF PERSONNEL WHO SERVED IN THE

CHINA-BURMA-INDIA
THEATER OF OPERATIONS

DURING WORLD WAR II

Book Design & Illustration: Robert A. Watkins

Other Schiffer Books by the Author:
Battle Colors Series I-V

Library of Congress Control Number: 2016961169

Type set in Times New Roman

ISBN: 978-0-7643-5273-7
Printed in China

Published by Schiffer Publishing, Ltd.
4880 Lower Valley Road
Atglen, PA 19310
Phone: (610) 593-1777; Fax: (610) 593-2002
E-mail: Info@schifferbooks.com
Web: www.schifferbooks.com

Table of Contents

Foreword

The Schiffer Publishing *Battle Colors* series by Robert A. Watkins provides an important contribution to the history of the United States Army Air Forces (USAAF) in WWII. There are many different books on a myriad of topics related to that conflict, ranging from histories of the various units or specific aircraft types, to generalized histories of the entire aerial campaign. Some books chronicle various "nose art" so common on aircraft during that era; others illustrate the squadron, group, and tactical markings used in different theaters of war, and still others describe the operating locations of various units involved. Many of these books are excellent, others less so, and some are not very good at all. Mr. Watkins has done a masterful job combining so much information into a single volume. As a retired Air Force historical officer, I find Watkins' work to be historically significant, fascinating, complete, and compelling.

One of my first memories was of my father—an infantryman—describing how his unit (Co. F, 2nd Battalion, 168th Infantry, 34th Inf. Div.) was guarding an airfield in North Africa when a battle-damaged B-24 bomber landed there. Another time, he observed a P-38 that landed on one engine. These stories brought the air war to life for me during my early years. In fourth grade, I first found a copy of Stephen Sears' American Heritage book, *Air War Against Hitler's Germany* in our school library. I must have checked it out five or ten times that year; I was hooked, and the air war became my focus. The history of WWII has been one of my favorite topics ever since. I joined the Civil Air Patrol in ninth grade, and in college I entered Air Force ROTC. I was commissioned in the Air Force in 1981, and became a missile launch officer. I served twenty-six years on active duty and as a reserve member. From 1989–2008, I served as a historical officer at Tinker AFB, Oklahoma; Hill AFB, Utah; and at the Air Force Historical Research Agency, Maxwell AFB, Alabama, until I retired as a lieutenant colonel.

When I purchased Watkins' first volume on the Eighth Air Force bomber units, I was very impressed with his scholarship and the amount of information in each entry. The Eighth is the best known and certainly the most written about of the USAAF numbered air forces in WWII, and this volume on the bomber units is excellent. Watkins lists the various stations for each group, as well as a map showing the station location, the squadrons assigned to each, and even the group and squadron emblems and codes. The group motto (if it had one) is listed, in Latin and in English. The unit's campaign history and even its call sign is included.

The highlights of the book are the excellent, full-color renditions of each unit's tactical markings and tail codes. In Volume II, he provides the same information on the Eighth Air Force fighter units. Volume III discusses the Ninth Air Force; the medium bomber and tactical fighter force based in England in late 1943 that moved on to the continent after D-Day. This volume put even more emphasis on the location of each unit, since they moved forward to keep pace with the Allied ground armies. In addition to the fighter and bomber units, it also covers troop transport, reconnaissance, and other units. Volume IV covered the Ninth Air Force in North Africa and the Fifteenth (the Italy-based strategic air force) and Twelfth (its tactical equivalent) Air Forces. After concluding with the European air war, Watkins turned to the Pacific Theater for Volume V, covering the Fifth, Seventh, Eleventh, and Thirteenth Air Forces. All these volumes build upon the successful formula set forth in Volume I and they are all excellent references. I am proud to have the entire set and I refer to the books regularly.

Because the other numbered air forces in WWII were not as well documented as the Eighth, I was especially pleased to read Watkins' work on lesser known air forces. His efforts are rewarding to any historian who wants a clear, easy-to-use reference book on an often misunderstood topic. I now eagerly await Bob's latest volume on the Tenth and Fourteenth Air Forces in the China-Burma-India Theater and the Twentieth Air Force based in the CBI and later in the Marianas. The markings of the various aircraft in the CBI are not well known, and some authors have simply guessed at those markings (if they attempt to address that theater at all). The Twentieth is well known and often discussed for its role in the massive firebombing campaign and its aerial mining of Japanese waters, as well as for the atomic bombing carried out by the 509th Composite Group. If the first five volumes of the series are a guide, Volume VI should be a fitting climax and a tremendous addition to every WWII history buff's library.

Watkins' contributions to the history of the Army Air Forces in WWII cannot be overstated. The *Battle Colors* books are a fascinating look at a critical time in our history and provide a gold mine of detail about not only the aircraft markings, but also about how each unit performed its mission during that great conflict. Mr. Watkins has done a tremendous service keeping alive the legacy of every USAAF veteran that served, and we who follow in their footsteps owe Bob a large debt of gratitude.

Mark W. Nelson
Lt. Col., USAFR (Ret.)

Introduction

China-Burma-India / The Forgotten Front

Remote locations, primitive operating and living conditions, limited supplies and personnel, and conducting operations with outdated and all too often battle weary aircraft. These factors pretty well sum up the situation the war in the CBI was conducted in from 1941 through 1945.

In reality, the battle for China dated earlier to 1931, when Japan—its own limited resources stretched to their absolute limits—took advantage of an internal civil war and invaded Manchuria as the first major step toward expanding its "Greater East Asia Co-Prosperity Sphere" (Japan's equivalent to Nazi Germany's *Lebensraum* ideology). On 18 February 1932, the Japanese established the Manchu State—the Manchuhuo puppet government—with Henry (Aisin-Gioro) Pu Yi—the last hereditary Emperor of China—installed by the Japanese at its head in an attempt to lend an aura of legitimacy to Japan's land grab policy. With a prevailing isolationist attitude at the time, the United States (and most of Europe) was not overly concerned with China's problems. Eventually, Japan's aggression in the far east began to cause increasing concern, as its expansionist policies began to closely mirror events developing in Western Europe. Trade embargoes imposed by the United States on exports of steel, scrap metal, and crude oil in 1940 in protest against Japan's aggression was a real game changer, a move that led to a series of events ultimately culminating with Japanese naval air units attacking the United States on Oahu, Hawaii, on 7 December 1941.

"The Gathering Storm"

When Japanese forces were attacking Pearl Harbor and the Philippines, official US presence in China consisted of the American Mission to China (AMMISCA). Established barely two months before the attack on Pearl Harbor, AMMISCA was something akin to a US Far East Lend-Lease program. Headquartered in Chungking, China, under the command of Brig. Gen. John Magruder, his organization's function was to advise and assist the Chinese government in matters relating to logistical support—a tall order under even ideal conditions. Gen. Magruder had to contend not only with an aggressive foreign invader, but internal civil conflict as well. The Kuomintang (KMT) nationalist forces of the Republic of China under Generalissimo Chiang Kai-shek and the Chinese People's Communist (CPC) forces under Mao Tse-tung had been at each other's throats since August 1927, long before adding invading Imperial Japanese troops into the mix.

Matters were helped to some degree when the KMT and CPC united in late 1937, to concentrate on combating the invading Japanese, but this was by no means a permanent arrangement; just a temporary cessation of hostilities allowing both factions to focus on the foreign invaders.This temporary truce made the organizational efforts of AMMISCA somewhat easier, but only somewhat.

Under far better conditions, the transition from a peacetime to wartime society is, as a rule, tumultuous, resulting in most initial attempts to organize into something resembling a cohesive fighting force being jumbled, awkward, uncoordinated, and counterproductive. A good analogy can be found by looking no further than the organizational wartime structure of something as relatively simple as a single squadron within our own AAF: the 528th Fighter Squadron of the 311th Bombardment (later Fighter-Bomber; Fighter) Group, Fourteenth Air Force. The 528th Fighter Squadron was originally constituted as the 382d Bomb Squadron (Light) on 28 January 1942. The squadron was redesignated the 382d Bombardment Squadron (Dive) on 27 July, the 528th Fighter-Bomber Squadron on 30 September 1937, and finally, the 528th Fighter Squadron on 30 May 1944. Such changes were not uncommon within the structure of the AAF during the war, and this organizational quandary involved just one fighter squadron of one fighter group—and our country was not engaged in a civil war compounded by a foreign invasion. Each of these transformations resulted in changes in training, maintenance, ordinance, and in some cases aircraft type. Multiply these factorized elements by quantum leaps by adding into the mix the vast expanses of the Asian continent coupled with a widely diverse assemblage of cultures, languages, and dialects, and obtaining any sense of a coordinated, cohesive effort on a vastly wider scale than a single squadron would appear to be an almost impossible goal. It was a complete and absolute logistical nightmare that did not even take into consideration the war in Europe.

This single example is set forth to better illustrate the enormity of the logistical ball of snakes that needed sorting out by all involved before the war could effectively be taken to the enemy, but somehow those assigned with solving just this seemingly unsolvable problem did in fact do just that—they solved it—but it took a lot of time.

Making Due with What Resources Were Available

This was the keystone to the success of Gen. Chennault's AVG; the *Jing Bao* (air raid) pole may best illustrate this policy. Lacking long range radio communication systems or any type of modern early warning radar equipment, Chennault adopted, refined, and greatly expanded this ancient Chinese method of communication into a highly efficient early warning air raid system.

One ball hoisted on a pole indicated an alert. Two balls was the signal to man battle stations: anti-aircraft gunners went to their assigned posts and pilots and ground crews stood by their respective aircraft. A third ball raised on a pole meant imminent danger. Flying Tiger fighters went airborne to attack the attackers in the air instead of being caught as helpless sitting targets on the ground, a common occurrence before Chennault's innovative Rube Goldberg early warning system.

The Supply Problem

Most readers are more than likely familiar with the Burma Road, the vital link providing desperately needed munitions and other supplies to Allied

forces engaged in fierce fighting with stubborn and determined Japanese forces. What may not be as well known to some is the *Aluminum Trail*, the nickname given to the AAF supply route over the Himalayas—an air route so treacherous and deadly that supply missions were credited the same as combat missions when tabulating airmen's rotation points. But more on this in the Air Transport Units Section.

Consolidating Command

Gen. Joseph W. Stillwell was appointed by the US War Department to act as chief of staff to Chiang Kai-shek, in addition to functioning as commanding general of the United States Army Forces in China, Burma, and India. In effect, Stillwell was to act as a liaison officer while trying to organize an effective fighting force in Asia. Stillwell was no Gen. Eisenhower, but in spite of his reputedly abrasive personality a consolidated Allied force took root.

On 22 June 1942, all units and personnel under Stilwell's command were relieved from assignment to Army Group, Washington, DC, and assigned to American Army Forces, India, China, and Burma. There followed a number of redesignations, consolidations, and re-shuffling before the formalized and collective designation China-Burma-India Theater came into being.

In the meantime, while all of these Allied organizational growing pains were taking place, Japanese ground and air forces were making continued advances in the planned expansion of their "Greater East Asia Co-Prosperity Sphere." All the while, the American Volunteer Group (AVG*) Flying Tigers of the Chinese Air Force (CAF), under the command of Gen. Claire Chaunault, were waging an effective defensive air campaign against the Japanese Air Force, operating on a shoestring budget with an inventory of war birds many considered obsolete and virtually unfit against more modern enemy fighters. Chennault and his Tigers were proving what a numerically outnumbered determined fighting force could accomplish using whatever resources were available, coupled with innovative combat tactics. Many of these tactics would later be incorporated by AAF and other Allied units. When the AVG was incorporated into the Fourteenth Air Force, there would be some conventionally minded fighter group commanders who turned up their noses at the "maverick" tactics employed by the AVG, all too often with disastrous results.

There was no question the Curtis P-40 Warhawk was slower and less maneuverable than many of its Japanese adversaries, but Chennault had studied his opponent's aircraft and fighting tactics, and consequently developed a system of "dog fighting" that proved highly effective against even the newest Japanese fighters.

Interim Transition and Long Term Reorganization

When the American Volunteer Group (AVG/CAF) was officially disbanded on 4 July 1942, it was reconstituted within the USAAF as the 23d Fighter Group. Plans were in the works for the creation of the Fourteenth Air Force, which would ultimately operate from China proper, and to which the newly formed 23d FtrGp would eventually be assigned. In the meantime, the 23dFS was organized within the structure of the newly formed China Air Task Force (CATF) and placed under the operational control of the Tenth Air Force. The collective command and subsequent official use of the China-Burma-India Theater was abolished on 24 October 1944, to be replaced with the following separate and distinct theaters:

US Forces-China Theater / US Forces-India-Burma Theater

The continued use of CBI remained common throughout the remainder of the war and beyond. In all but official communications, C.B.I. remained the accepted acronym when referring to all operations in that part of the world, a tradition that carries over even today when referring to US combat involvement on the Asian Continent post-October 1944. To eliminate the possibility of confusing the abbreviation AAF (American Army Forces) with the abbreviation Army Air Forces (AAF), it became accepted practice to use United States Army Forces, China, Burma, and India (USAF CBI).

Eastern Air Command (EAC)

On 15 December 1943, Supreme Allied Commander (in the newly-formed South East Asia Command) Admiral Lord Louis Mountbatten directed the integration of joint Allied air operations over Burma and formed the Eastern Air Command, originally charged with two primary objectives: (1) Protect lines of communication between the supply base India and the fighting Chinese front and (2) destroy the Japanese Air Force in Burma. This command operated continuously until 1 June 1945 under Maj.Gen. George E. Stratemeyer.

* The American Volunteer Group (AVG) was originally designated the 1stAVG, with planning and organization for the 2dAVN that was to be a tactical bombardment unit equipped with medium bombers and coastal reconnaissance aircraft; 33 Lockheed Hudson (A-28), 33 Douglass DB7 (A-20), 82 pilots, and 359 ground crewmen were actually assembled and scheduled to embark from San Francisco on 10 December 1941. The 3dAVG was designated as another fighter unit with pilots (Aviators for you Navy types) and ground maintenance personnel recruited from the US Navy and Marine Corps. Needless to say, the attack on Pearl Harbor 7 December 1942 brought all of this planning and preparation to a screeching halt.

Heraldry and the USAAF

Over the years numerous requests have been submitted regarding the background of AAC/AAF emblems. What exactly was the process required for the submission of a group/squadron unit emblem for approval? How long did the process take? Who designed these emblems?

These are a few of the questions that routinely come up, and the following official excerpt from the US Army Quartermaster Foundation should at least answer the first of these questions:

The Quartermaster Heraldic Section and The US Army Institute of Heraldry

"In 1920, the Army officially adopted heraldic coats of arms. This originated the use of distinctive unit insignia (more commonly called unit crests) to identify an individual soldier with his regiment. The purpose was to foster Army tradition and esprit de corps. The first unit to wear such an insignia was the 51st Artillery, Coast Artillery Corps, which received approval for wear from the War Department on 18 March 1922.

"Quartermaster (QM) Corps Assumes Responsibility:
"By 1924, heraldic responsibility was delegated to the Quartermaster General. The Heraldic Section of the Office of the Quartermaster General was responsible for the research, design, and development of distinctive unit insignia, shoulder sleeve insignia (patches), flags, medals, seals, coats of arms, and other heraldic items for the Army.

"The Heraldic Section painstakingly performed historical research of unit histories to determine design and redesign of coats of arms and distinctive unit insignia. It was also responsible for ensuring quality control of the manufacture of the insignia that it had designed.

"The Heraldic Section assisted the manufacturer in meeting its stringent specifications by inspecting all models and dies and requiring samples of completed work. Before final acceptance, the design and prototype were approved by the Quartermaster General during World War II.

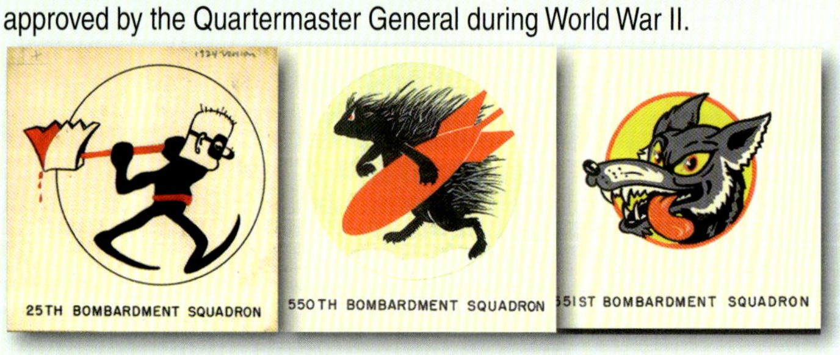

"The three images above are copies of original emblem design artwork as submitted to the Heraldic section for approval consideration. The actual image size could vary as long as it fit within the proscribed submission format. Each of these designs was subsequently approved for use."

The previous information answers the question who was responsible for AAF unit emblem approval. The matter of how emblem designs were submitted is best addressed by including excerpts from a letter dated 30 March 1944 from Headquarters, Army Air Forces, Washington, DC to all major AAF commands on the topic of squadron insignia:

"1] It has been brought to the attention of this Headquarters that squadrons authorized to have organizational insignia for aircraft marking have been adopting insignia not approved by this headquarters. In some instances, detachments not authorized unit insignia are using unofficial markings on trucks or other equipment. Under provisions of AAF Regulation 35-22, 2 August 1943, squadron insignia may be adopted only by organizations having aircraft assigned to them.

"2] Squadron insignia officially approved by this Headquarters have been given widespread publicity in *National Geographic* Magazine, in national magazine advertising, and through other publicity media. Such insignia are of considerable interest to the families and relatives of the men in the squadrons. Under the regulations, however, no publicity has been or will be given to squadron insignia not approved by this Headquarters.

"3] Organizations not having insignia and organizations using insignia not approved by this Headquarters are requested to forward their designs to the Asst. Chief of Air Staff, Personnel, Headquarters Army Air Forces, Washington 25 DD. If the designs conform to the provisions of AAF Regulation 35-22, official approval and registration will be made by this Headquarters, and the designs will be published when and wherever possible.

"4] It is requested that the above information be furnished to the commanding officers of all squadrons under your command eligible to have squadron aircraft markings."

AAF Regulation 35-22 deals with the dos and don'ts concerning recommended formats, and unacceptable and acceptable design elements that should or should not be incorporated within these designs.

Although the criteria for group and squadron designs was almost identical, these regulations were eased somewhat when it came to approval of squadron design submissions.

The turnaround from date of design submission to the review process of the design varied, but it appears that as the war progressed design submission turnaround time increased substantially, possibly as much as six to ten months. This can be directly attributed to many AAF unit designs not being officially approved before war's end. Many groups and squadrons were inactivated shortly after the end of hostilities, thus bringing to an immediate halt pending design approval applications.

The problem this poses for researchers is that official US Air Force policy mandated that any given group/squadron emblem from WWII that was not approved through the proper channel would not be recognized in the official histories of those respective units.

Compounding the approval process of unit insignia was War Department Circular/Number 226, dated 7 June 1944. This directive stated a temporary suspension on the processing of coats of arms and distinctive badges by HQ/AAF was hereby placed in effect. It is not certain just when this suspension was lifted, but any delay in processing must have proven problematic, given an already overloaded Heraldic Section.

The following are examples adopted by various AAF units during WWII, but for any variety of reasons were never processed through the official review procedure.

Some of these designs are on file with the Air Force Historical Agency with no final disposition on record. The reasons? The dates recorded as to when these particular designs were received closely corresponds with the moratorium date indicated in WD Circular/No.226. Was this action responsible for these designs never receiving approval? We will probably never know. What we do know is in spite of these and many other similar insignia being displayed and otherwise used within their respective units, they will never appear in any official unit histories until the USAF policy concerning unapproved group and squadron emblems during WWII is changed.

Another problem encountered by researchers concerning AAF group/squadron insignia has to do with personal preference.

There are a vast number of emblem designs that were originally approved at a unit level while those units were in transition training in the United States, only to be summarily discarded by a new commanding officer immediately following overseas deployment. The examples below serve to illustrate this point.

While it is known for certain that each of these three designs represented the same unit (356th Bomb Sqdn) at various times during WWII, only the far right image was ever properly approved, and is therefore the only insignia (for better or worse) found in the official USAF historical file when researching this squadron.

Emblem Patch Types

AAF group and squadron insignia were put to a wide variety of usage: including aircraft application, signage, printed material, etc. Topping this list would most certainly be that of uniform display. The following represent the most common methods used to affix these emblems to AAF uniform components.

• Chenille Stitching On Felt
Commercially manufactured during the war primarily by U.S. based companies.

Embroidered Cloth •
A wide range of quality were available, both machine produced and hand stitched.

• Incised and Dyed Leather
Many of the best examples were produced in Allied occupied Italy.

Printed Decal On Leather •
Wet transfer decals produced to fill orders placed by individual AAF units.

• Silk Screened Fabric
Inexpensive, affordable patches printed in quantity mainly by stateside suppliers.

Hand Painted Leather •
Many of these were generated in AAF units by personnel possessing a wide range of artistic skill.

• Dyed, Layered Leather
The best examples were often purchased from skilled indigenous craftsmen.

Hand Sewn, Layered Cloth •
Created by hand stitching carefully pre-cut fabric strips on felt; perhaps the least common type of AAF uniform patch.

• Bullion-Metallic Thread On Felt
Comparatively expensive, the finest examples were arguably produced in Great Britain during WWII.

• ASSIGNED: CHINESE AIR FORCE, C. NOV-1941 THRU JUL-4-1942 •

CAMCO
(CENTRAL AIRCRAFT MANUFACTURING CO.)
C. JUL-1941

C.A.F.
c. Nov-1941

ABOUT THE FLYING TIGERS EMBLEM

Col. Claire Chennault had this to say regarding this now legendary image: "How the term Flying Tigers was derived from the shark-nosed P-40s I never will know. It was not until just before the AVG was disbanded that we had any kind of group insignia." In March 1942 Disney Studios supplied these emblems as high quality, two-part dry transfer decals with adhesive backing, as opposed to the less resilient wet transfer type. The victory "V" portion of this design was developed as a separate decal but, consequently, often not applied to the AVG Hawks with the tiger image.

(1ST) AMERICAN VOLUNTEER GROUP

INSIGNIA/(UNOFFICIAL)
MOTTO: 'RETURN WITH HONOR'
SOBRIQUET: 'FLYING TIGERS' AKA 'FEI HU'
ORGANIZED: C. JULY-1941
DECOMMISSIONED: 4-JULY-1942

FIRST SQUADRON

SOBRIQUET: ADAM & EVES

ORGANIZED: C. NOV-1941
DISBANDED: 4-JUL-1942

SECOND SQUADRON

SOBRIQUET: PANDA BEARS

ORGANIZED: C. NOV-1941
DISBANDED: 4-JUL-1942

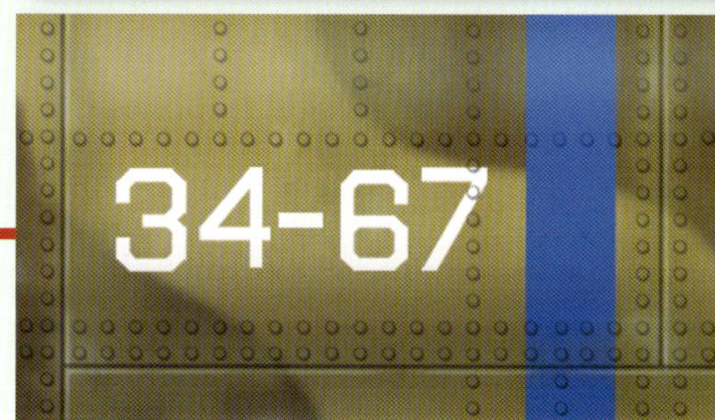

THIRD SQUADRON

SOBRIQUET: HELL'S ANGELS

ORGANIZED: C. NOV-1941
DISBANDED: 4-JUL-1942

Although the 1st American Volunteer Group was not officially connected with the AAC, this unit is considered too important not to be included due to the influence the Tigers had on future AAF tactics.

Tactical Paint/Serial Numbers:

The original Curtiss P-40s delivered to the AVG were actually Tomahawk Mk.IIBs originally built for the RAF (designated H81-A-2 Series). These Hawks were factory painted in colors that "approximated" a standard RAF Temperate Scheme. This tricolored aircraft camouflage actually called for Dark Earth and Dark Green on top surfaces accompanied with a Sky application to fuselage and wing undersurfaces, but the Curtiss factory results would not qualify as a "product match." It is not certain whether the RAF numerical codes normally applied with black paint toward the rear of the fuselage were affixed to any of the original AVG Hawks. Regardless, CAF codes consisting of a three-inch letter/number combination were applied mid-fin with white paint after assembly. For identification purposes the "last two" numbers of CAF ID numbers were often duplicated in larger sizes on either side of the fin or rudder surfaces.

National Markings:

There were no national markings of any kind applied to these aircraft, but after assembly, top and bottom wing surfaces were adorned with CAF roundels, each measuring approximately 36 in. in diameter. By mid-summer 1941, squadron aircraft codes were assigned, and these began appearing in the form of 21–24 in. high, white two-digit numbers applied to the rear fuselage. These numbers varied greatly, as no uniform stenciling pattern had yet been developed. With the exception of Second Squadron, the numbering sequences assigned to aircraft were not rigidly adhered to.

Squadron color codes were adopted late in 1941, and began appearing as 5–6 in. vertical bands encircling the rear fuselage just forward of the empennage proper.

• Squadron Emblems:

- First Squadron: The original concept for this insignia incorporated a "red" apple in the design until Col. Chennault pointed out that from a distance, especially in a combat situation, this design might well be mistaken as a Hinomaru, the standard Japanese meatball aircraft marking. Upon brief and prudent reflection it was decided the substitution of a "green" apple was a better choice. With this revision, the finalized emblem was adopted and began appearing on squadron aircraft fuselages approximately 24 in. in diameter until eventually replaced by the Disney tiger emblem.
- Second Squadron: Few ships of this unit displayed the unpopular Panda Bear emblem, instead adopting a mixture of individualized insignia designs.
- Third Squadron: First to apply emblems to aircraft; approximately 24 in. high with many variations. There never was a standard design established, accounting for the wide assortment of configurations depicted in wartime photos we see today.

• Shark Heads:

The AVG adopted shark heads based on a magazine cover of *Illustrated Weekly of India*, November 1941 edition. This cover image depicted Hawks of RAF No.112 Squadron operating in North Africa bearing a shark face motif applied to their aircraft. Members of No.112 Squadron had originally been inspired by earlier shark head applications to Me-Bf 110 twin engine fighters of Luftwaffe Stab II./ZG 76. Shapes of shark head applications among the AVG varied widely, as did colors, e.g. red, white, and black; red, white, blue, and black, etc. Within the AVG, 3rd Squadron heads tended to be the most elaborately executed.

• Flying Tiger:

Disney Studios not only designed this iconic emblem, but supplied left and right facing decals for aircraft application. Included with the decals was a supply of enameled brass sweetheart pins to be distributed among AVG personnel.

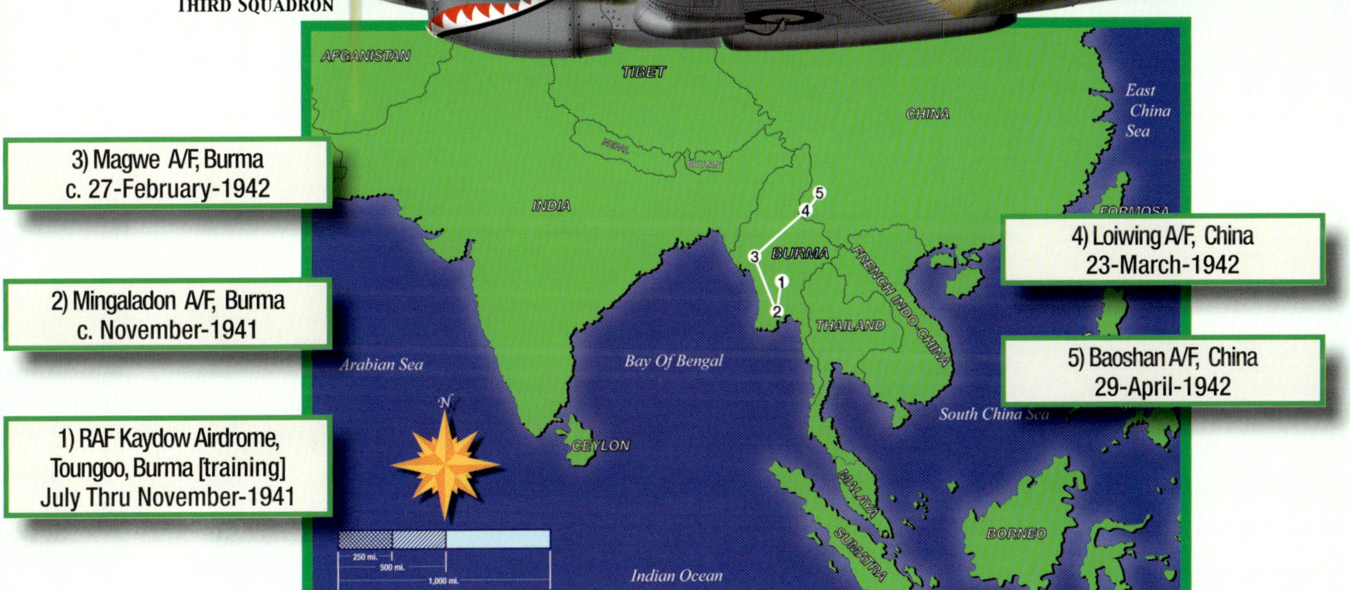

• Attached: Tenth AAF, July-1942 •

HQ/Tenth AF
Jul-1942
thru
Mar-1943

China Air Task Force (Prov) (CATF)

***Insignia:** (unapproved)*
***Motto:** (unknown)*
***Sobriquet:** Flying Tigers*
***Organized:** July 1942*
***Disbanded:** 10 March 1943*
***(Reorganized:** 23rdFtrGp, Fourteenth AF)*

* One of the first changes made in connecti with the newly formed CATF was the modific tion to the group's Flying Tiger emblem. T basic Tiger image was retained, but with a fe additions depicting the tiger jumping through Kuomintang national emblem, sporting an Unc Sam-style stars-and-stripes top hat, and shre ding a Japanese national flag with its forepaw In many instances the meatball flag was depi ed torn in half, while other versions displayed t flag in tatters but retaining a recognizable imag The wings adorning the original Tigers insigr were either reduced in size or eliminated al gether in later revised emblems.

**11th Bombardment Squadron (M)

Attached: TDY/CATF: September-1942

Assigned:
341st Bombardment Group (M)
15-September-1942

** Jiggs, the WWI emblem created by George McManus from the syndicated cartoon strip *Bringing Up Father* (see 341st BombGp, p. 90).

16th Fighter Squadron

Attached: TDY/CATF: July-1942

Assigned:
51st Fighter Group
15-Janurary-1941

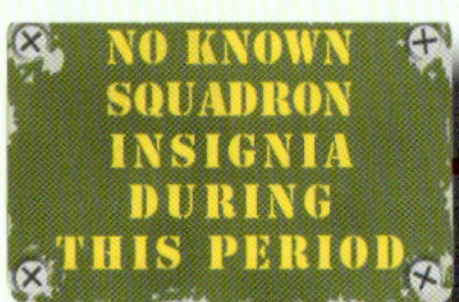

74th Fighter Squadron

Formerly: 1st Pursuit Squadron/AVG

Constituted:
74th Pur Sqdn (Incpt)/17-Dec-1941
Redesignated:
74th Ftr Sqdn/15-May-1942
Activated: 4-Jul-1942

75th Fighter Squadron

Formerly: 2nd Pursuit Squadron/AVG

Constituted:
75th Pur Sqdn (Incpt)/17-Dec-1941
Redesignated:
75th Ftr Sqdn/15-May-1942
Activated: 4-Jul-1942

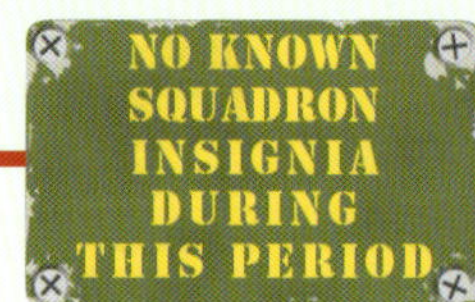

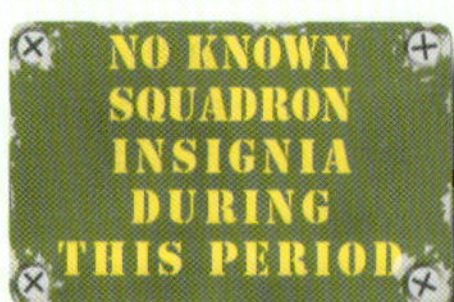

76th Fighter Squadron

Formerly: 3rd Pursuit Squadron/AVG

Constituted:
76th Pur Sqdn (Incpt)/17-Dec-1941
Redesignated:
76th Ftr Sqdn/15-May-1942
Activated: 4-Jul-1942

Emblem: China Air Task Force Era

The new China Air Task Force (CATF) was an interim combat organization pieced together in July 1942, after the disbandment of the AVG. Commanded by former AVG/CO Claire Chennault—recently reinstated into the USAAF and promoted to brigadier general—the CATF was placed under operational control of the Tenth Air Force based in New Delhi, India. The former 1st American Volunteer Group was absorbed into the 23d Fighter Group of the USAAF; although the newly formed 23d FtrGp retained few of the original pilots of the famed Flying Tigers, it did adopt a modified version of the now famous AVG emblem and the equally famous Shark Face nose art on its P-40 Warhawks.

Republic P-43 Lancer

By August 1942, the CATF was operating with an assortment of mostly hand-me-down aircraft—fifty-six B and E series P-40s carried over from earlier AVG days—while the 11th Bomb Squadron had a total of eight operational B-25C Mitchells; all of these were spread out over a wide geographical area. The only new aircraft operating with the CATF were P-43 Lancers "on loan" from the Chinese Air Force (CAF).

While retaining the Kuomintang emblems on the wings, this same device was overpainted on both sides of the Lancer fuselage and replaced with large white numerical codes, while the existing white Chinese Air Force tail fin aircraft identification serial numbers remained intact.

Individual aircraft tactical markings were sporadic at best during this somewhat chaotic period; on 19 March 1943, the CATF was officially disbanded and evolved into the new Fourteenth Air Force based in Kunming, China. During its brief nine-month existence, the CATF was credited with 149 Japanese aircraft shot down, with an additional 85 probables. Add to this a total 65 bombing missions dropping 311 tons of bombs on Japanese military targets and it amounts to a most impressive combat record for a unit with so brief a history. Total losses within the CATF amounted to 16 P-40s and one B-25 Mitchell. An equally impressive statistic, and as history records, a portent of things to come in the air war in the CBI over the next two years.

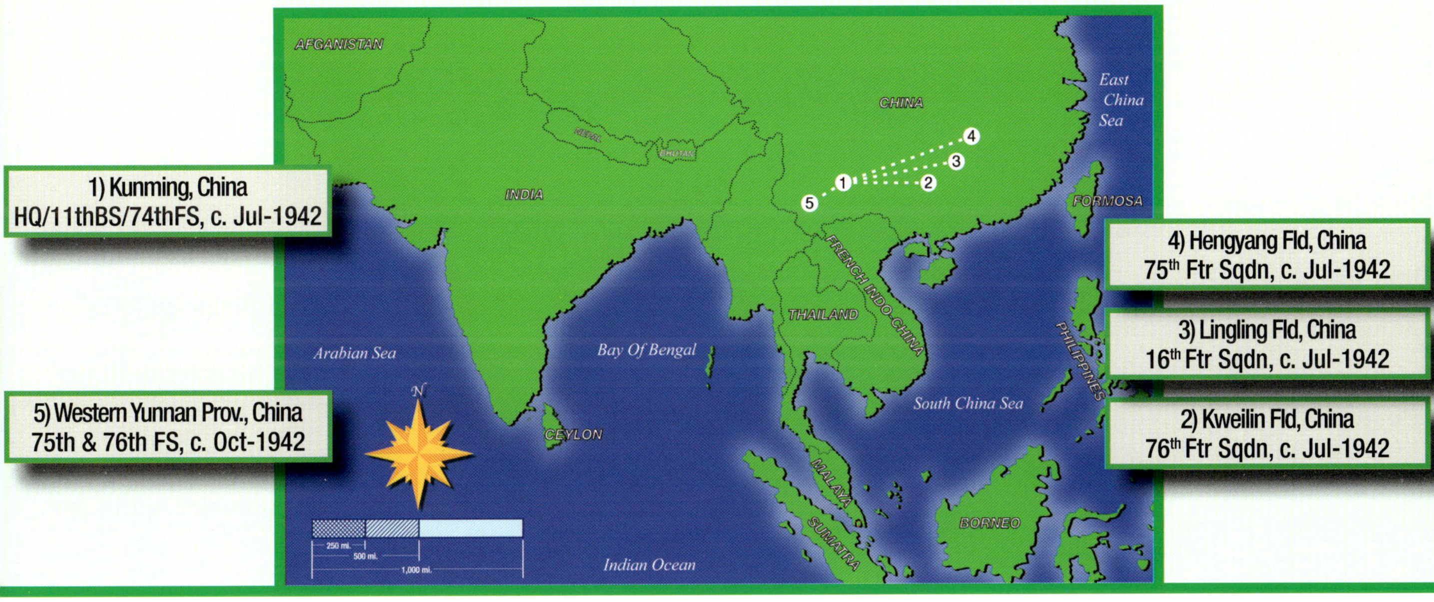

• Attached: Tenth AAF, October-1942 •

HQ/Tenth AF
Oct-1942
thru
Feb-1943

India Air Task Force (Prov) (IATF)

Insignia: (unknown)
Activated: 3-Oct-1942
**Disbanded:* c. Mar-1943

7th Bombardment Group (H)

Assigned: Tenth AF/ March-1942

Squadrons:
9th Bombardment Squadron (H)
436th Bombardment Squadron (H)
492d Bombardment Squadron (H)
493d Bombardment Squadron (H)

51st Fighter Group

Assigned: Tenth AF/ March-1942

Squadrons:
16th Fighter Squadron
25th Fighter Squadron
26th Fighter Squadron

341st Bombardment Group (M)

Assigned: Tenth AF/ September-1942

Squadrons:
11th Bombardment Squadron (M)
22d Bombardment Squadron (M)
490th Bombardment Squadron (M)
491st Bombardment Squadron (M)

* Last official After Action Report for the ITAF was 12 February 1943.

Activated at Dinjan Airfield under the command of Col. Caleb V. Haynes, the mission of the newly formed India Air Task Force was to support Chinese operations by hitting Japanese supply lines in central and southern Burma. All AAF combat units currently in India were placed under the operational control of IATF, consisting of the 7th Bombardment Group (H), 51st Fighter Group, and 341st Bombardment Group (Medium), all based at Karachi at that time.

The Paper Air Force: At the offset the IATF was faced with the following reality: in the 7thBG(H), the 9thBS was still operating in the MTO and the 436thBS was only beginning to receive its inventory of combat aircraft, while the 492d and 493d BS were comprised of administrative personnel only. Of the 341stBG's squadrons, the 11th was operating out of China, the 22d was still receiving its aircraft, and the 490th and 491st had no assigned combat aircraft.

This photo of a B-24 of the 9thBS(H) is typical of the absence of tactical markings other than the US national emblem. AAF ground crews had their hands full simply trying to keep the war birds in their care in operational status. Under these conditions there was little time or need for unit markings.

Of the three squadrons comprising the 51stFG, the 16thFS was operating in China and the 25thFS was still in training, leaving only the 26thFS in combat ready status.

All Allied airfields in western India were subject to constant air attacks by the Japanese, requiring an extensive effort to hide aircraft between missions. The photo above was once a P-40, and illustrates the consequences of not following elaborate camouflaging protocol.

The stations map below provides a fairly good idea of just how thinly stretched USAAF resources were during the early stages of combat operations in northwestern India. All available resources operated at maximum level in an effort to provide the fledgling Tenth Air Force with badly needed time to build and organize an effective air presence.

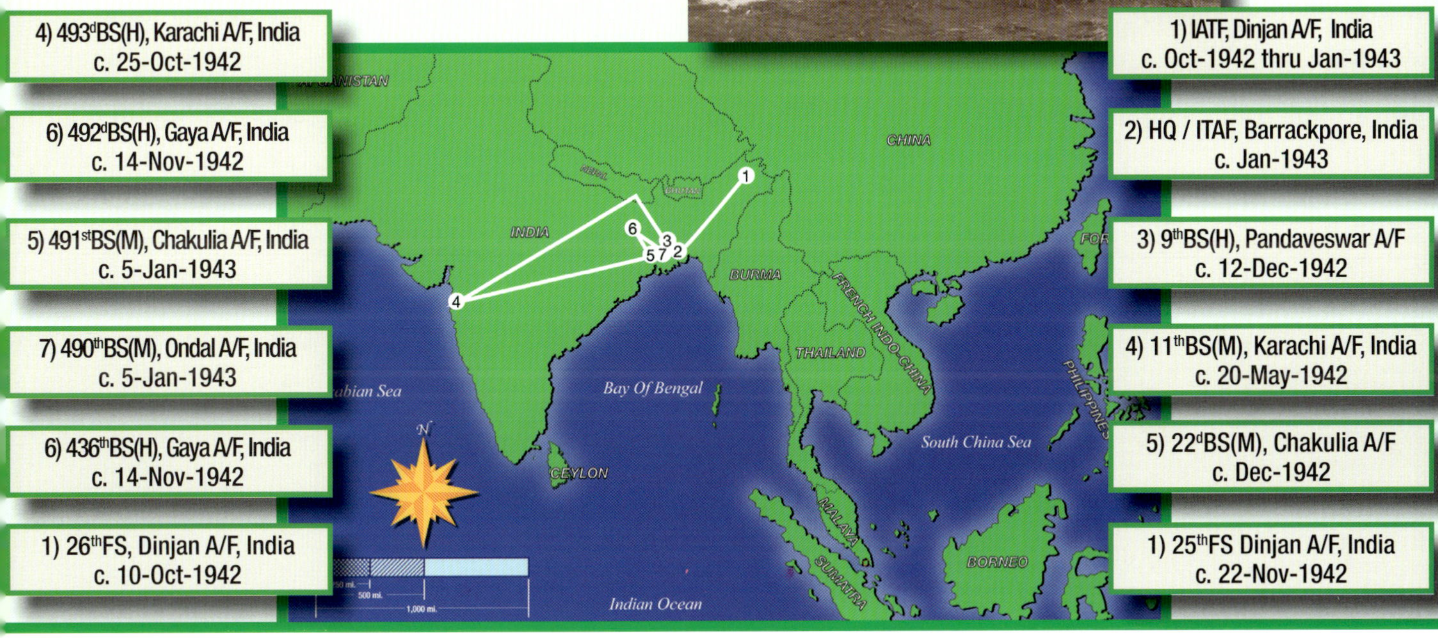

U.S.A.A.F. FIGHTER UNITS

CHINA-BURMA-INDIA THEATER OF OPERATIONS

Tactical Markings:

There was a love/hate relationship where fighter markings were concerned; they were loved by the folks back home, but mostly disliked by overworked ground crews responsible for keeping their charges in top fighting condition. Adding additional paint schemes—some quite intricate—into the mix was the last thing these men needed, but these devices were something that many in the AAF simply had to learn to live with. As to the men who flew their units' war birds into combat, some were indifferent, while others considered their aircraft markings a source of pride.

On the practical side, aircraft tactical markings evolved from a very real need to reduce friendly fire losses, while at the same time providing a means for pilots to recognize good guys from bad guys in combat situations. Being able to quickly identify one's flight or squadron leader could literally mean the difference between life and death in an aerial combat situation, a fact fully recognized and appreciated by most veteran pilots.

Then there was the public relations factor. Those AAF commanders who possessed the ability to see beyond the realm of immediate combat operations were keenly aware of a simple fact: photographers—whether AAF personnel, but most especially those who worked for civilian news services—would always gravitate toward colorfully adorned aircraft. These same photos invariably ended up in front of the American public, the same public the US government relied heavily on to buy War Bonds during the course of WWII. So important was the War Bond campaign that highly publicized fighter pilots joined with other equally famous wartime heroes making coast-to-coast guest appearances at well attended War Bond drives. These drives were highly beneficial to helping the US prosecute the war; replicas of airmen's combat aircraft, and in some cases the actual ships flown in battle, were centerpieces of these events. The more colorfully ornate the airframe the greater the crowd appeal and the more War Bonds were sold.

Another factor recognized by more astute group and squadron commanders was the esprit de corps, the morale-building factor inherent as a side benefit of necessary tactical markings. Receiving a letter informing the recipient that his squadron was featured in a local, regional, or national publication was a tremendous morale booster. Copies of these articles, often featuring a profile of one or more unit aircraft resplendent in tac markings, often ended up posted on bulletin boards and reprinted, or at the least mentioned in group/squadron newsletters. Seeing their unit mentioned in this manner at home was a shot in the arm to men serving so far from home.

All of this may not have helped alleviate the additional burden these markings imposed on ground crews responsible for their application and maintenance, but it is worth noting the importance these devices played in the war.

Group/Squadron Emblems:

Group and particularly squadron emblems, while not necessarily a critical tactical marking device, were an important morale building element in many AAF units.

There are some societies and military that discourage the use of individual team or unit symbols, preferring instead a collective, organizational pride. The Soviet Army adhered to such a policy. A collective pride in Mother Russia was the prevailing doctrine mandated within the entire Soviet military, while displays of individual unit affiliation were discouraged, if not stringently forbidden. Things were and always have been different in the United States. While love of country was always the foundation upon which all else rested, American fighting men have been raised on playing fields where team colors and mascot images play an important part in their day-to-day growth. Virtually all team sports adopted images and colors serving as banners under which contestants competed. It was only natural then that this same tradition would follow them into battle when the time came, and in many cases a group and/or squadron emblem would become an enduring source of pride for the remainder of the lives of those individuals that served under those symbols.

This concept of image identity may seem trite and difficult to understand by later generations of Americans, but for those that grew up before the age of electronic computer games and the internet, team symbols and mascots were an important component of formative years on the playing field and a source of unity and pride.

As with everything in life, the unit emblems featured in the *Battle Colors* series had widely varying degrees of significance during the war.

Not all AAF personnel felt the same degree of esprit de corps as others, and there seems to be one argument that sports involvement may have played a determining factor in just how fervently an airman felt about his unit emblems. Those young men that were involved in some particular organized sports activity during their formative years seem to have had a greater affinity toward their squadron's insignia than others who may not have been involved in extracurricular sports in school.

While it is interesting today to attempt to analyze our Greatest Generation's attraction toward the galaxy of various images they affixed to their flight jackets, aircraft, etc., the important thing to remember is these designs were of importance to this generation of Americans, military and civilian alike. Ironically, the US airman had more in common with the German Luftwaffe where this subject is concerned than with some of our own allies.

• ASSIGNED: SEVENTH AF, MAY-1942 THRU JUL-1945 / USAAF-TWENTIETH AF, JUL-1945 THRU V-J DAY •

7TH FTR CMD
MAY-1942

7TH INCPT CMD
23-JAN-1942

14TH PUR WG
1-DEC-1940

USAAF
16-JUL-1945

VII FTR CMD
5-AUG-1945

15TH FIGHTER GROUP

INSIGNIA: APPROVED/ 5-OCT-1942
MOTTO: I PURSUE WITH WINGS
CONSTITUTED: 15TH PURGP(FTR)/ 20-NOV-1940
ACTIVATED: HAWAII/ 1-DEC-1940
REDESIGNATED: 15TH PURGP(INTCP)/12-FEB-1942
15THFTRGP/ 15-MAY-1942

78THFTRSQDN
INSIGNIA VARIATION

Although the insignia shown below was the official emblem of the 78thFS dating to 1933, the image depicted above was universally adopted within the squadron for most of the war, and was the design applied to most of the squadron's aircraft and A-2 flight jackets.

45TH FIGHTER SQUADRON

INSIGNIA: APPROVED/24-AUG 1944
SOBRIQUET: TRAIL BLAZERS

CONSTITUTED: 45T PUR SQDN (FTR)/22-NOV-1940
ACTIVATED: 1-DEC-1940
REDESIGNATED:
45TH PUR SQDN/15-MAY-1942
45TH FTR SQDN/15-MAY-1942

47TH FIGHTER SQUADRON

INSIGNIA: APPROVED/19-SEP-1944
SOBRIQUET: TUR-NIP TERMITES

CONSTITUTED: 47THPUR SQDN (FTR)/22-NOV-1940
ACTIVATED: 1-DEC-1940
REDESIGNATED: 47THPUR SQDN (INCPT)/12-FEB-1942
47THFTR SQDN/15-MAY-1942

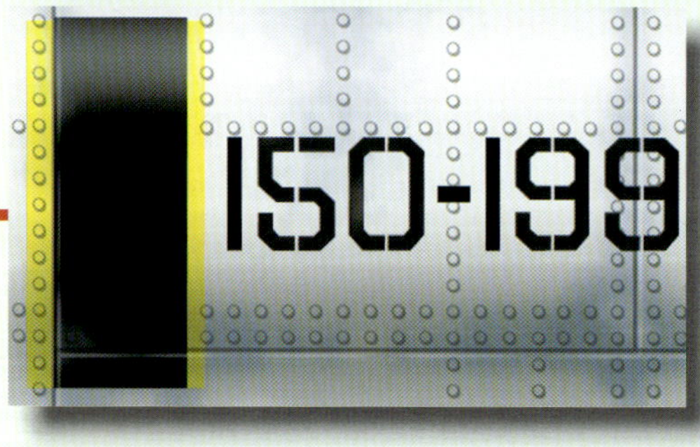

78TH FIGHTER SQUADRON

INSIGNIA: APPROVED/14-SEP-1933
SOBRIQUET: BUSHMASTERS

ORGANIZED: 78THAERO SQDN/28-FEB-1918
CONSTITUTED: 78THOBS SQDN/18-OCT-1927
REDESIGNATED: 78THPUR SQDN/8-MAY-1929
ACTIVATED: 1-APR-1931
REDESIGNATED: 78THPUR SQDN (INCPT)/22-DEC-1939
78THFTR SQDN/15-MAY-1942

Having suffered heavy losses during the attack on Pearl Harbor on 7 December 1941, the 15th Fighter Group operated with a wide assortment of whatever single and twin engine warbirds the US government could spare at the time, including A-12s, OA-9s, B-12s, P-36s, P-39s, and P-40s.

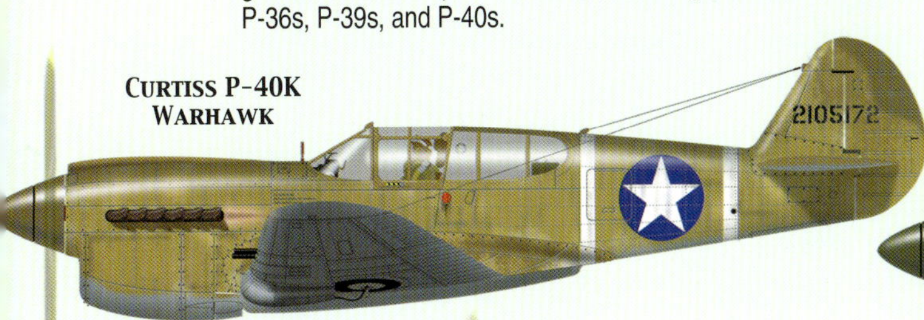

Curtiss P-40K Warhawk

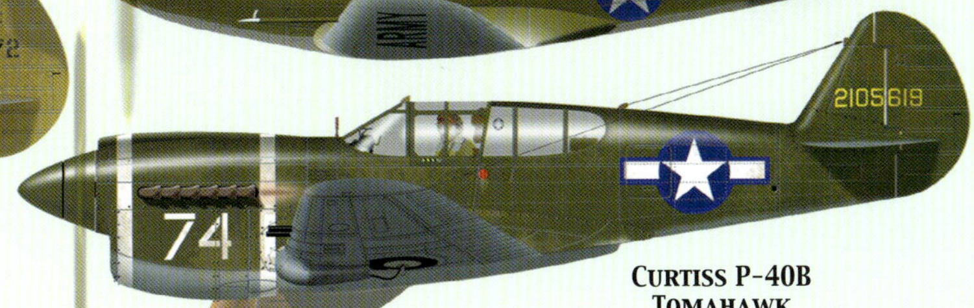

Curtiss P-40B Tomahawk

The prewar numerical designators displayed by the 45th, 46th, and 47th FS were temporarily discarded in the early months of the war but later resurrected, while at the same time standardizing mid-fuselage as the location for these markings.

Bell P-39 Airacobra

The assortment of airframe colors and insignia changes that affected the 15thFG in its first year of combat resembles a patchwork quilt. Beginning with a standard prewar, two color camouflage paint job, later group inventories included desert paint schemes on aircraft diverted from shipments to North Africa. A coral and light blue camouflage concoction was apparently whipped up using available limited paint supplies when detachments from the 15th Fighter Group were detached for combat operations sortied from Canton Island Airfield.

Timeline: Full Roster Of 15th Fighter Group Squadron Assignments

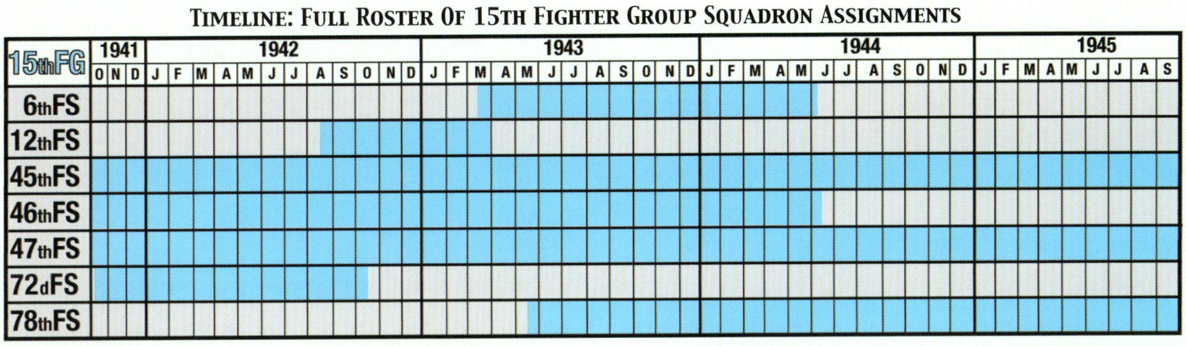

6th NgtFtrSqdn
(Refer to 18thFtrGp)

12th FtrSqdn
(Refer to 18thFtrGp)

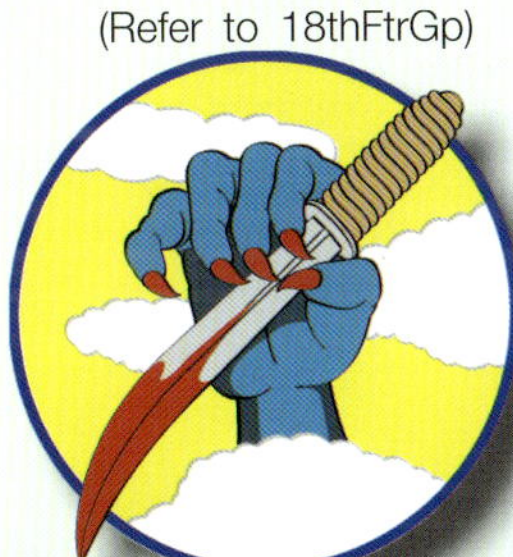

49th FtrSqdn
(Refer to 21stFtrGp)

72d FtrSqdn
(Refer to 21stFtrGp)

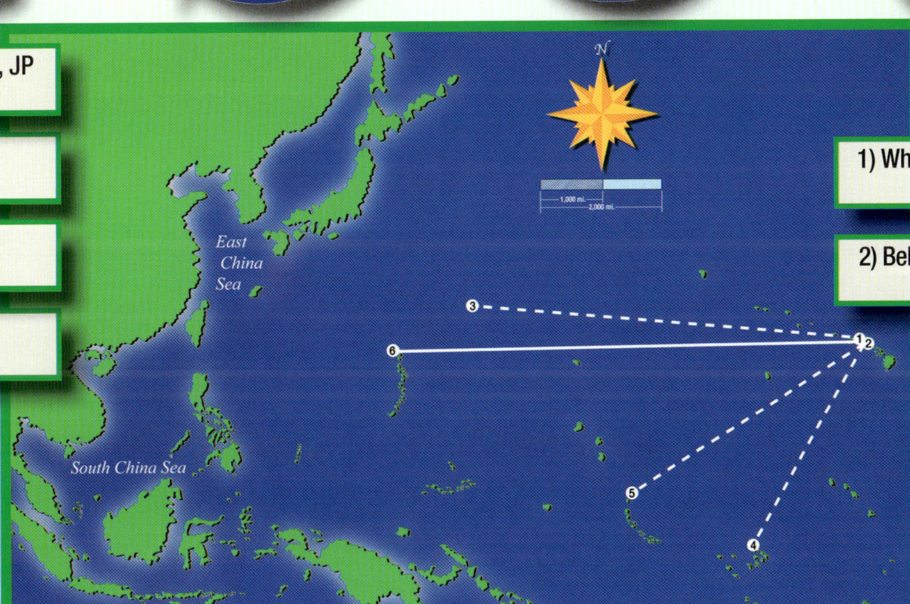

1) Wheeler AAF, Oahu, TH/US
1-Dec-1940

2) Bellows Field, Oahu, TH/US
3-Jun-1944

3) Midway Is., US
1943

4) Canton Is., UK/US
1942-1944

5) Makin Is., UK
1942-1944

6) South Field, Iwo Jima, JP
6-Mar-1945

Note: Detachments from the 15thFG operated temporarily from an assortment of airfields on numerous islands and atolls principally situated on Midway, Canton, and Makin. Additional duty stations included airfields on Baker, Nanumea, and Abemama Islands.

Note: 15thFG squadrons were dispersed throughout the islands at different times, including the following airfields:

- Haleiwa Field
- Barking Sands Field
- Mukuleia Field
- Kaneohe Field
- Stanley Field
- Hilo Field

15TH FTRGP
c. 1942 THRU JUL-1943

15TH FTRGP
c. JUL THRU DEC-1943

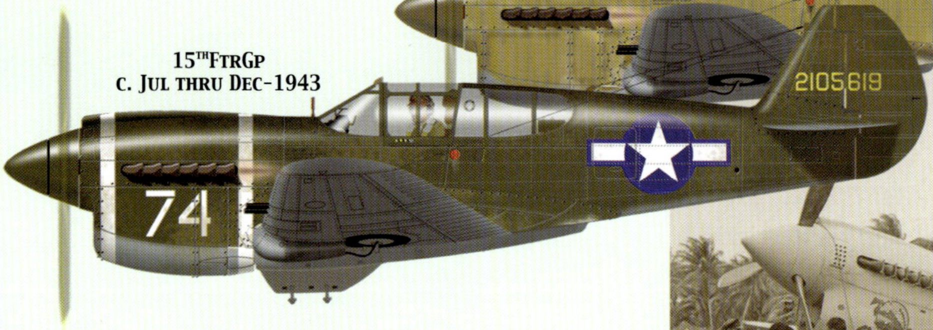

During the campaigns in the Gilbert and Marshall Islands, the 45th FtrSqdn displayed no unit markings, except for some ships with their squadron insignia affixed to both sides of the engine cowlings.

At the onset of WWII, 15thFG P-40 markings consisted of little more than dual white vertical fuselage bands affixed fore and aft the national insignia. In the summer of 1943, these devices were relocated to the forward fuselage between a two, white number-in-squadron code designator.

Before converting to the P-51 Mustang at the end of 1944, the 15thFG trained for extreme long-range bomber escort missions operating with the P-47 Thunderbolt. It was during this period that individual squadron tactical markings began to be standardized within the entire group.

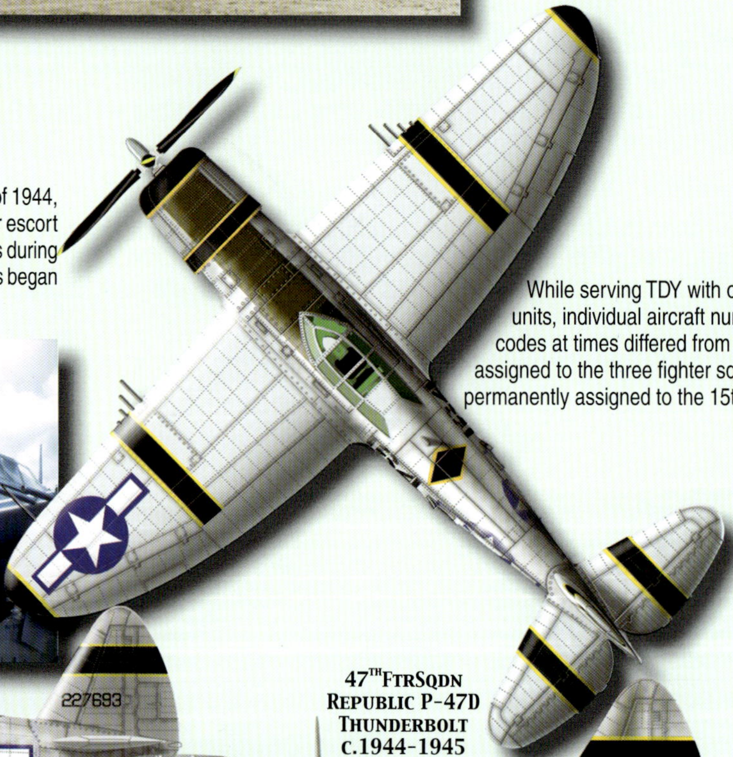

While serving TDY with other units, individual aircraft numerical codes at times differed from those assigned to the three fighter squadrons permanently assigned to the 15thFG.

47TH FTRSQDN
REPUBLIC P-47D
THUNDERBOLT
c.1944-1945

78TH FTRSQDN
REPUBLIC P-47D
THUNDERBOLT
c.1944-1945

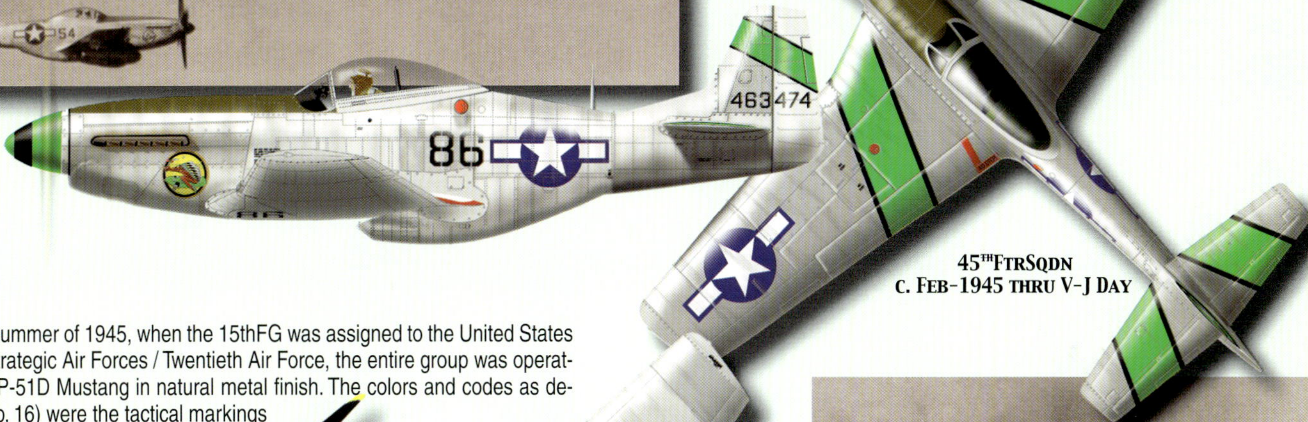

45th FtrSqdn
c. Feb-1945 thru V-J Day

By the summer of 1945, when the 15thFG was assigned to the United States Army Strategic Air Forces / Twentieth Air Force, the entire group was operating the P-51D Mustang in natural metal finish. The colors and codes as depicted (p. 16) were the tactical markings applicable during the 15thFG's tenure with the USAAF/Twentieth Air Force in the closing months of WWII. Respective squadron code numbers were applied with black paint to each side of the fuselage immediately forward the national insignia and generally measured between 18 to 20 in. high. These very same number-in-squadron codes were additionally applied in black paint to the landing gear covers of both the 47th and 78th FS.

47thFtrSqdn
c. Feb-1945 thru V-J Day

Each of the three squadrons adopted a unique tactical marking pattern that included the almost universal application of each squadron's respective insignia to the forward section of the aircraft fuselage. The 45thFS maintained their light green base color with added thin black borders, while the 47thFS elected to go with black bands bordered with yellow. 78thFS ships displayed equal amounts of black and yellow on the wing, horizontal stabilizer, and tail tips. Propeller spinners were painted in respective squadron colors, sometimes with an additional contrasting accent stripe thrown in.

78th FtrSqdn
c. Feb-1945 thru V-J Day

• ASSIGNED: SEVENTH AF, C.APR-1944 THRU JUL-1945 / TWENTIETH AF, C. JUL-1945 THRU V-J DAY •

7TH FTR CMD
MAY-1942

7TH INCPT CMD
23-JAN-1942

14TH PUR WG
1-DEC-1940

USAAF
16-JUL-1945

VII FTR CMD
5-AUG-1945

21ST FIGHTER GROUP

INSIGNIA: (UNOFFICIAL)

CONSTITUTED: 21ST FTR GP/31-MAR-1944

ACTIVATED: 21-APR-1944

©Walt Disney

This emblem was designed by Disney Studios in 1942, on behalf of the 58th Bombardment Squadron (Light). After a number of unit re-designations, it ultimately ended up the 531st Fighter Squadron displayed the insignia as depicted below.

46TH FIGHTER SQUADRON

INSIGNIA: APPROVED/11-MAR-1942

CONSTITUTED: 46TH PUR SQDN (INTCP)/22-NOV-1940
ACTIVATED: 1-DEC-1940
REDESIGNATED:
46TH PUR SQDN (INTCP)/12-FEB-1942
46TH FTR SQDN/15-MAY-1942

200-249

©Walt Disney

72D FIGHTER SQUADRON

INSIGNIA: APPROVED/19-JUN-1943
SOBRIQUET: THE SCALPERS

CONSTITUTED: 72D PUR SQDN (INTCP)/4-OCT-1941
ACTIVATED: 5-OCT-1941
REDESIGNATED: 72D FTR SQDN/15-MAY-1942

250-299

531ST FIGHTER SQUADRON

INSIGNIA: APPROVED/7-JUL-1944
SOBRIQUET: STRIKE AND RETURN

CONSTITUTED: 58TH BOMB SQDN (LT)/22-NOV-1940
ACTIVATED: 1-JAN-1941
REDESIGNATED:
58TH BOMB SQDN (DIVE)/19-OCT-1942
531ST FTR BMR SQDN/14-AUG-1943
531ST FTR SQDN/18-FEB-1944

300-349

All 21stFG squadrons were originally equipped with P-39 Airacobras which apparently bore no distinctive unit markings. The P-39s were quickly replaced with the P-38 Lightning. The earlier tactical markings of the squadrons comprising the 21stFG while serving with the Seventh Air Force are addressed in *Battle Colors / Volume V.* By the summer of 1945, when the 15thFG was assigned to the United States Army Strategic Air Forces / Twentieth Air Force, the entire group was operating with the P-51D Mustang.

Upon deployment to Iwo Jima for combat operations, all squadrons adopted a fairly uniform system of tactical markings. Each squadron was assigned a color that was applied to spinners, tail sections, and the tips of both wings and rear horizontal stabilizers, accented with the addition of a black bordering stripe.

46TH FTRSQDN
C. JAN-1945 THRU V-J DAY

72D FTRSQDN
C. JAN-1945 THRU V-J DAY

The only variations appear to have been the occasional lack of this bordering stripe on some wing and RHS applications, but these proved to be exceptions rather than the rule.

A series of three digit codes (see facing page) were additionally assigned to each squadron respectively.

531ST FTRSQDN
C. JAN-1945
THRU V-J DAY

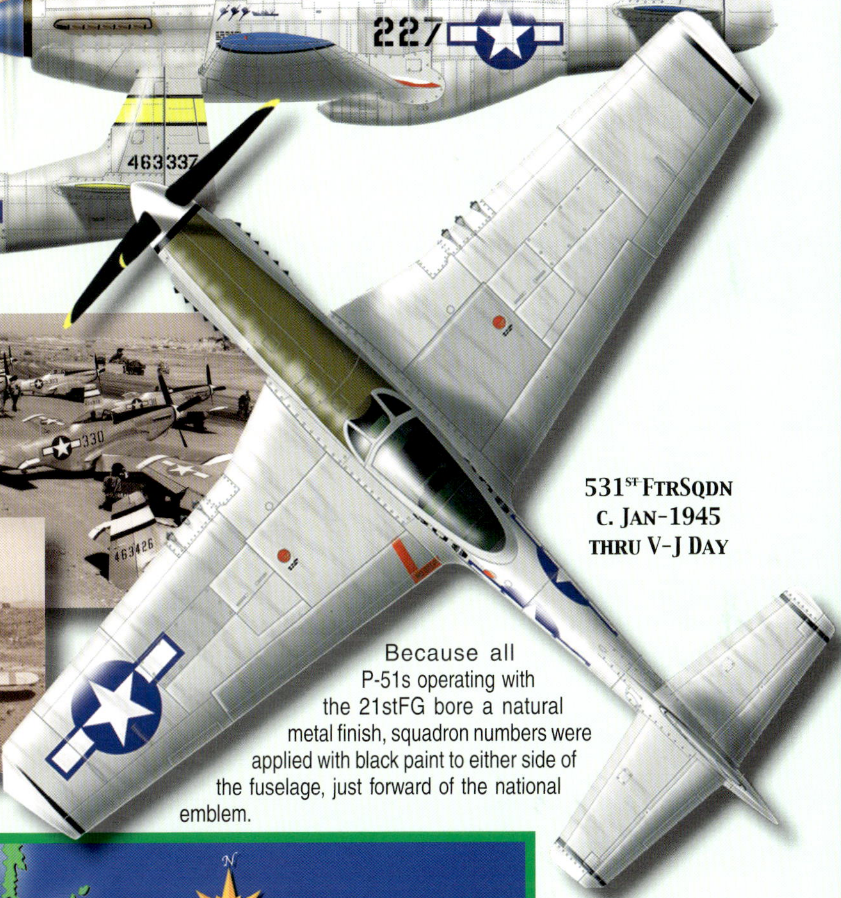

Because all P-51s operating with the 21stFG bore a natural metal finish, squadron numbers were applied with black paint to either side of the fuselage, just forward of the national emblem.

6) South Fld., Iwo Jima
16-Jul-1945

5) Central Fld., Iwo Jima
26-Mar-1945

*4) Makin Island
c. Dec-1943

*3) Canton Island
c. Mar-1943

* Note: Detachments from all three squadrons of the 21stFG operated temporarily from airfields on Canton and Makin Islands.

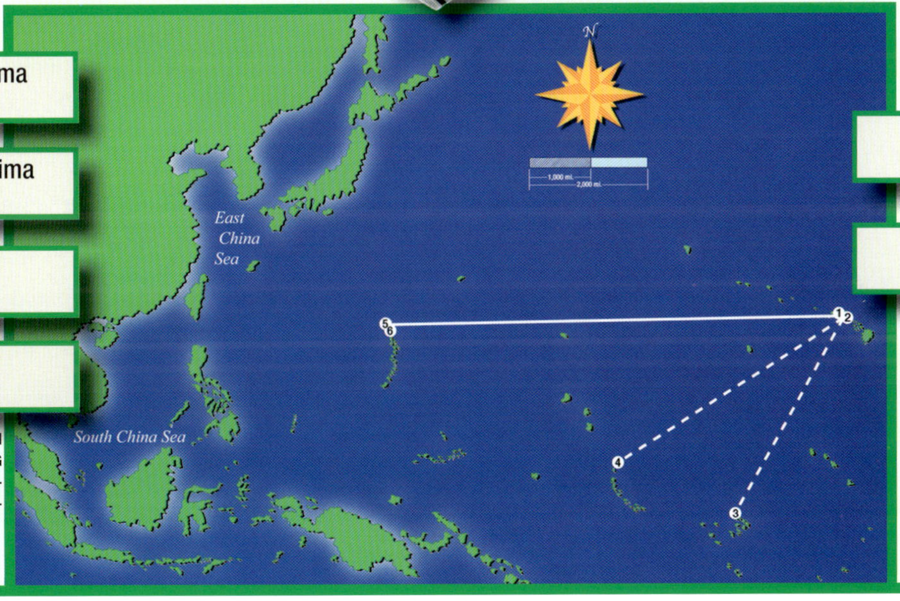

1) Wheeler Fld., Oahu
21-Apr-1944

2) Mokuleia Fld., Oahu
13-Oct-1944

Note: While headquarters of the 21stFG remained at Wheeler or Mokuleia respectively, its squadrons were dispersed throughout the islands at different times:

- Hickam Field • Hilo Field
- Mukuleia Field • Kaneohe Field
- Haleiwa Field • Bellows Field
- Kuoloa Field

• Assigned: Tenth AF, Jul-1942 thru Mar-1943 / Fourteenth AF, Mar-1943 thru V-J Day •

68th Comp Wg
1943-1945

China Air Task Force
Jul'42-Mar'43

23d Fighter Group

Insignia: (unofficial)
Motto: Return With Honor
Sobriquet: The Flying Tigers
Constituted: 23d PurGp(Intep)/ 17-Dec-1941
Redesignated: 23d FtrGp/ May-1942
Activated, China: 4-Jul-1942

•The Tigers Emblem•

Although never officially sanctioned during WWII, this famous Disney Studios designed insignia was later approved for display by the 74th Ftr Intcp Sqdn on 24 Sep 1952. On 21 Jan 1957, the 23dFG officially reclaimed their iconic emblem in the slightly modified format depicted above.

74th Fighter Squadron

**Insignia:* Submitted/ April-1944
Sobriquet: Gorilla Squadron

(Originally: 1st PurSqdn, AVG)
Constituted: 74th PurSqdn(Intcp)/ 17-Dec-41
Activated: 4-Jul-42
Redesignated: 74th FtrSqdn/ 15-May-42

c.1942-1944 — c.July 1942 thru 1944: 11-50
c.1945 — 1945 thru V-J Day: 1-40

75th Fighter Squadron

Insignia: (unapproved)
Sobriquet: 'Tiger Sharks'/'Black Tailed Bastards'

(Originally: 2d PurSqdn, AVG)
Constituted: 75th PurSqdn(Intcp)/ 17-Dec-41
Activated: 4-Jul-42
Redesignated: 75th FtrSqdn/ 15-May-42

c.1942-1944 — c.July 1942 thru 1944: 150-199
c.1945 — 1945 thru V-J Day: 40-80

76th Fighter Squadron

Insignia: Approved/ 24-Jul-44
Sobriquet: 'Vanguards'/'Pontiac Squadron'

(Originally: 3d PurSqdn, AVG)
Constituted: 76th PurSqdn(Intcp)/ 17-Dec-41
Activated: 4-Jul-42
Redesignated: 76th FtrSqdn/ 15-May-42

c.1942-1944 — c.July 1942 thru 1944: 100-149
c.1945 — 1945 thru V-J Day: 100-140

*Walt Disney Productions granted permission for use of this design by the 74thFS on 18 April 1944.

Attached Units

16th Fighter Squadron

Assigned: 51stFtrGp: 15-January-1941
Attached: 23dFtrGp: c. July 1942-Oct 1943
Numbers: c. Jul-1942: 10-39
Numbers: c. Oct-1943: 350-400

118th Tactical Reconnaissance Squadron

Assigned: AAF/India-Burma Sector: January-1944
Attached: 23dFtrGp: c.16-Jun-1944 thru 15-Aug-1945
Numbers: 500-600 c. June-1944
Numbers: 150-199 c.Feb-1945

449th Fighter Squadron

Assigned: 51stFtrGp: 26-Aug-1943
Attached: 23dFtrGp: c. 26-Aug-1943 thru Oct-1943
Numbers: none assigned while TDY

74th Fighter Squadron

The Lost Guerilla Squadron Emblem

• The images below depict an unofficial replacement insignia adopted by the 74thFS when the unit was reequipped with the P-51 Mustang and assigned to supply air support to Chinese guerrilla forces fighting the Japanese. This design apparently enjoyed wide use on uniforms, aircraft, buildings, and squadron signage. In spite of this usage, few quality examples of actual applications exist today. The recreation of this design is based on what little detail was gleaned from several soft focus wartime snapshots. Hopefully one day a pristine example of this forgotten emblem will surface.

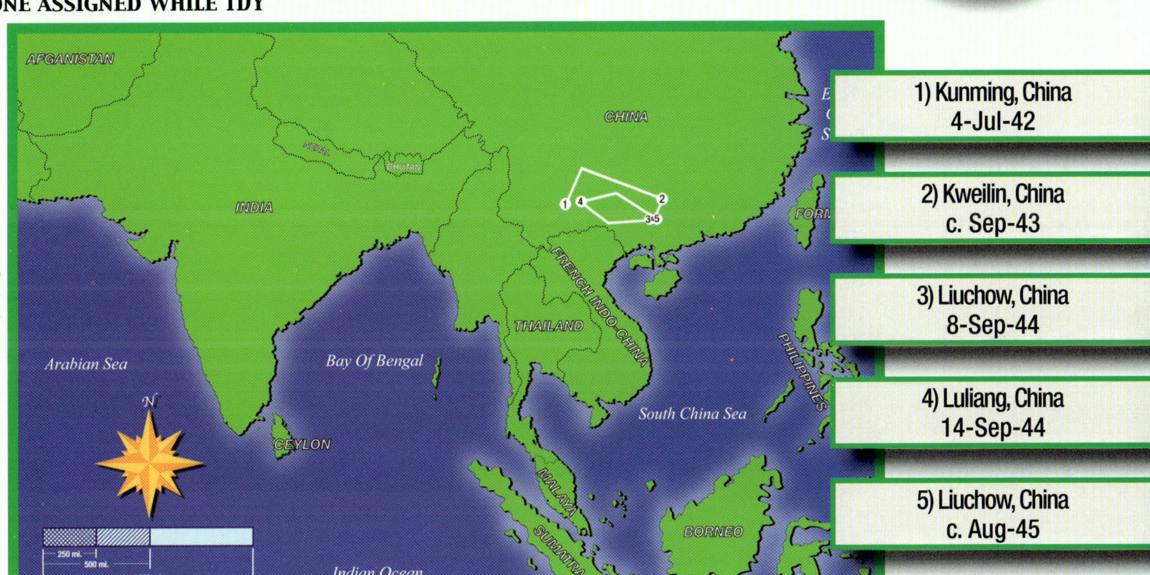

Note: Station assignments represent locations of HQ/23dFtrGp only. Detachments served in various other locations far too numerous to list.

118th Tactical Reconnaissance Squadron

• It is uncertain precisely when the 118thTacRcnSqdn adopted unit markings for their aircraft, but applications of the striking orange and black thunderbolt on the squadron's combat aircraft were in effect at least by early 1945. These applications began at the leading nose edge, running almost the entire length of the fuselage and terminating just forward the intersection point with the rudder. By the time these markings were adopted the primary aircraft used by the 118th were the P-51 and F-6, but the squadron was also equipped with a number of P-40s and L-5s. Whether any of the latter two aircraft types bore the squadron's thunderbolt tactical markings is unknown.

• Empennage: Factory serial numbers were replaced with large, black three-digit numerical squadron assigned codes ranging from 550–600 from June 1944. These numbers were officially changed in 1945 to 150–199, but the specific date this numerical change became effective is unknown. A smaller version of the thunderbolt design was also affixed toward the top of the fin/rudder; this same pattern was often duplicated on upper and lower outer tip surfaces of wings and tail stabilizers.

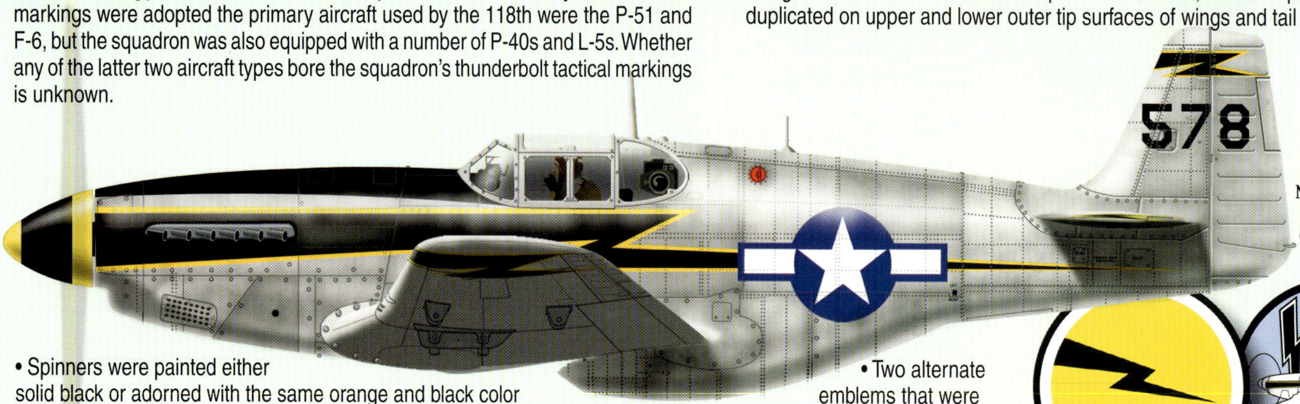

118th TacRcnSqdn North American P-51C c. Winter, 1944

• Spinners were painted either solid black or adorned with the same orange and black color combination used to apply the thunderbolts. A wide black band was applied vertically to the entire central portion of the spinner surface.

• Two alternate emblems that were adopted (both unofficially) and date from late 1944 to war's end.

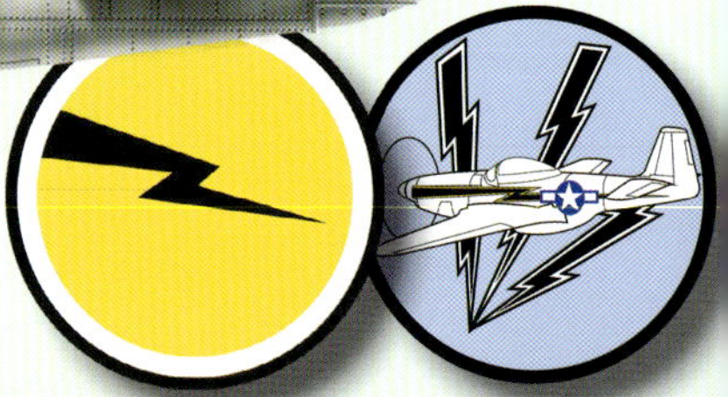

74th Fighter Squadron

Curtiss P-40 Warhawk

• Former AVG/CAW Hawks were transferred and put to work with little change in paint or tactical markings, except for the removal of the CAF Kuomintang emblem from the wings. The US star and bar on the fuselage continued to be replaced with an assigned two-digit aircraft number-in-squadron. The modified AVG Tiger image continued to be displayed mid-fuselage on former CAW Tomahawks until late 1943.

74th FtrSqdn/Curtiss P-40N c.1944

• In the fall of 1943, US emblems began appearing on fuselages of the 74thFtrSqdn. The number-in-squadron that had earlier occupied this location was relocated to the lower fin area in white; it was not uncommon for factory serial numbers to be removed entirely from the tail section, but there were some instances where the numbers applied on the rudders remained intact.

North American P-51 Mustang

• Assigned individual aircraft squadron numbers (1–40) were applied in black on the lower section of both sides of fin surfaces.

• Entire nose section of NMF P-51s were painted black with a scallop motif sweeping back, terminating at a point slightly aft the windscreen. Spinners were generally painted in a matching solid black. Some aircraft in the squadron were known to have displayed the Gorilla Squadron emblem mid-fuselage.

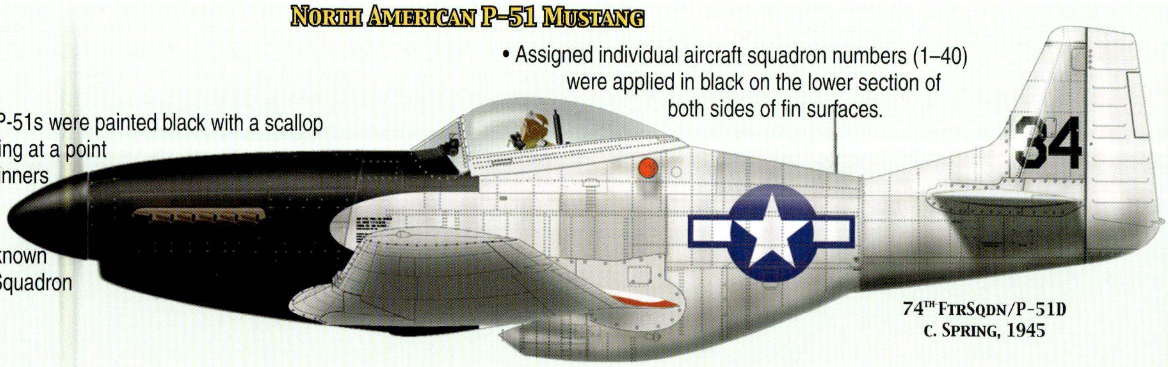

74th FtrSqdn/P-51D c. Spring, 1945

75TH FIGHTER SQUADRON

• When the 75th FS began combat operations with former AVG Hawks they incorporated an aircraft numbering system in the one hundred range, but apparently in no particular order. These numbers were applied in white toward the rear of the fuselage until late 1943, when these numerical codes were relocated to the lower fin area in a smaller size, also applied in white. As with the other original AVG squadrons, the vertical color recognition stripes to the rear of the fuselage were retained, as were the iconic AVG shark faces.

75TH FTRSQDN/CURTISS P-40K
c. FALL, 1942

75TH FTRSQDN/CURTISS P-40M
c. WINTER, 1943

• The Flying Shark emblem of the 75th FS was painted on both sides of the fin, but was removed when the aircraft numbers were relocated from the fuselage to the fin surfaces. During this time the US national emblem also began to be applied to the prescribed rear fuselage.

• The 75th began receiving P-51s in NMF in late 1944, but the squadron's new tail markings did not begin appearing on the Mustangs until early 1945. When applied, these markings consisted of the entire empennage being painted black, accompanied by a thin black stripe on an angle running from top to bottom.

75TH FTRSQDN/P-51B
c. SUMMER, 1944

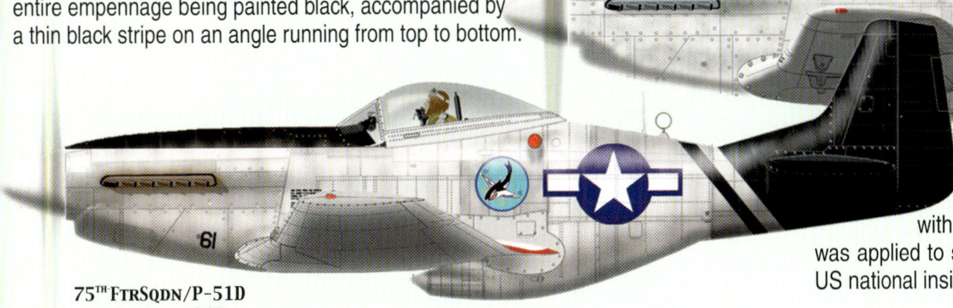

75TH FTRSQDN/P-51D
c. SPRING, 1945

• The black tails were originally accompanied with white, three-digit identification numbers ranging from 150–199. These numbers were later changed to 40–80, relocated to the lower front fuselage, just forward the wing root, and applied with black in a significantly smaller size. The 75th Squadron insignia was applied to some NMF Mustangs, positioned mid-fuselage just forward the US national insignia.

76TH FIGHTER SQUADRON

• The 76th FS was the first within the 23d FG to receive replacement aircraft in the form of P-51As c. November 1943. These were all painted in the standard AAF two-color scheme of Olive Drab over Neutral Gray and most were painted with a downward arching shark face. Spinners were painted yellow, and a white three-digit squadron number in the 100 range replaced the original factory applied serial number, which was usually reapplied to the central rear fuselage area, just aft the US national emblem.

76TH FTRSQDN/P-51A
c. FALL, 1943

76TH FTRSQDN/P-51B
c. SPRING, 1944

•When P-51B models began arriving at the 76th FS red eventually replaced the yellow spinners and the shark face design was also modified. Tail markings remained the same as with the earlier P-51A series, but none of these applications were carried over to the later NMF P-51As; the reapplication of serial numbers on the rear fuselage area appears to have been phased out by late 1944.

• By wars end, the 76th FS had adopted a large Indian silhouette, resplendent with war bonnet and painted in black on the tails of their NMF Mustangs. A number-in-squadron was also applied in black to the tail fin, immediately below and slightly forward the Pontiac Indian image. Spinners were generally painted either in a solid black or black divided vertically with a wide white color band.

76TH FTRSQDN/P-51D
c. WINTER, 1945

• Assigned *Twelfth AF, Nov-1942 • Tenth AF, Feb-1944 • Fourteenth AF, Apr-1944 • Tenth AF, Sep-1944 thru V-J Day •

Fourteenth AF
c.Apr-1944

Tenth AF
Feb-1944

Twelfth AF
Nov-1942

Tenth AF
Sep-1944

*33d Fighter Group

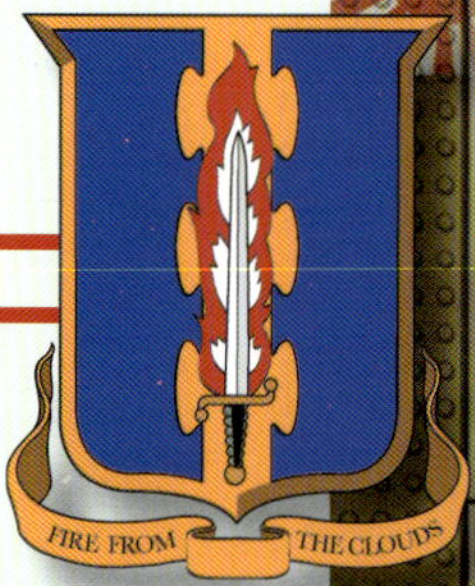

Insignia: Approved/ 21-Feb-1944
Motto: Fire From The Clouds
Sobriquet: The Nomads
Constituted:
33d PurGrp(Intep)/20-Nov-1940
Redesignated:
33d FtrGrp/May-1942

• 459th Fighter Squadron •
Transferred from the 80th FG 12 May 1945 through V-J Day. The 459th FS reportedly displayed aircraft numbers 30–81 painted in black on the outward facing radiator housings of their later NMF P-38 J and L models.

58th Fighter Squadron

Insignia: Approved/18-Jan-1944
Sobriquet: The Gorillas

Constituted: 74th PurSqdn(Intcp)/ 20-Nov-1940
Activated: 15-Jan-1941
Redesignated: 58th FtrSqdn/15-May-1942

Aircraft Numerical Codes In 800 Series: All Squadrons

59th Fighter Squadron

Insignia: Approved/ 24-Jul-1944
Sobriquet: Proud/Roaring Lions

Constituted: 59thPurSqdn(Intcp)/ 20-Nov-1940
Activated: 15-Jan-1941
Redesignated: 59thFtrSqdn/ 15-May-1942

Aircraft Numerical Codes In 800 Series: All Squadrons

60th Fighter Squadron

Insignia: Approved/ 15-May-1942
Sobriquet: 'Fighting Crows'

Constituted: 60th PurSqdn(Intcp)/ 20-Nov-1940
Activated: 15-Jan-1941
Redesignated: 60th FtrSqdn/ 15-May-1942

Aircraft Numerical Codes In 800 Series: All Squadrons

* Previously served in combat with the Twelfth AF in the MTO; refer to *Battle Colors-Vol. IV*

• When the 33d FG transferred from the Twelfth to the Fourteenth AF in early 1944, the unit began a series of transfers that earned the 33d its nickname, "The Nomads." Unit markings within the group structure was the assignment of three digit aircraft-in-squadron codes within the 800 series. These numbers were painted white mid-fuselage, just forward the US national emblem, with numbers varying 18–24 in. in height.

58TH FtrSqdn/P-47D
c. Fall, 1944

•There are no records indicating the use of color codes adopted by each squadron while serving in the MTO was discarded, and existing photographic evidence of this period indicates the prop bosses of each squadron's Thunderbolts were painted in the same colors adopted by the 33d FG while serving with the Twelfth AF.

• When originally affixed to 33dFtrGp olive drab over neutral grey P-47s, the white EAC Stripes were full wrap-around applications; the directive modification in February 1945 instructed not to have them applied to any control surfaces. The two wing elevations at left and the tail of P-38 #850 below clearly illustrate the effect of this modification. What is unclear today is the reasoning behind this modification. Similar identification stripes were used in virtually every theater of operation with no reported problems, so the logic behind the EAC Stripes modification is a mystery.

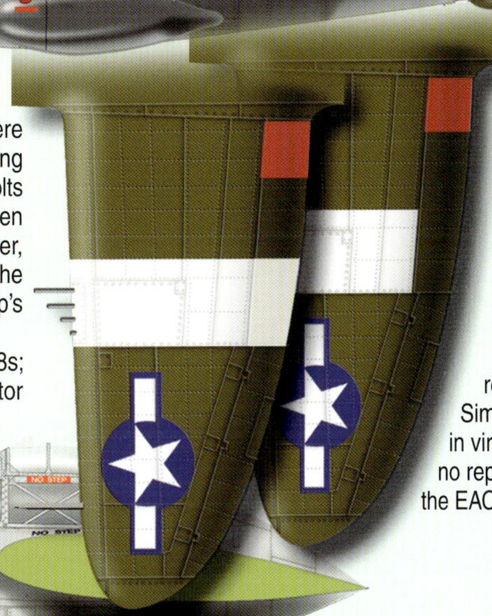

• Shortly after its second posting to the Tenth AF, all of the group's P-47s were adorned with EAC Theater markings adopted by all Allied units in India operating P-38s, P-47s, or P-51s. By the time the 33dFtrGp began to replace its Thunderbolts with P-38s in NMF, the original field order pertaining to EAC Stripes had been modified (February 1945); this modification excluded these markings on rudder, elevator, and aileron surfaces. As a result, none of the P-38s assigned to the 33dFtrGp bore full wrap-around EAC Stripes. The color used on all of the group's Lightnings was either black or Insignia Blue.
• The number-in-squadron identification was retained with replacement P-38s; these numerals were painted on the outboard facing surface of the radiator housings.
• Squadron colors were often applied to the spinners and nose tip of the fuselage.
• The 33dFtrGp emblem was known to have been affixed to the forward fuselage nose area of some of the group's P-38s, but the extent of such applications is unknown today.

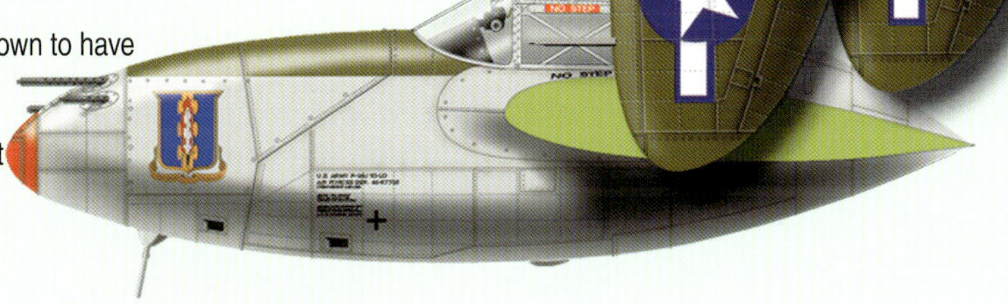

33D FtrGp/P-38J
c. Spring, 1945

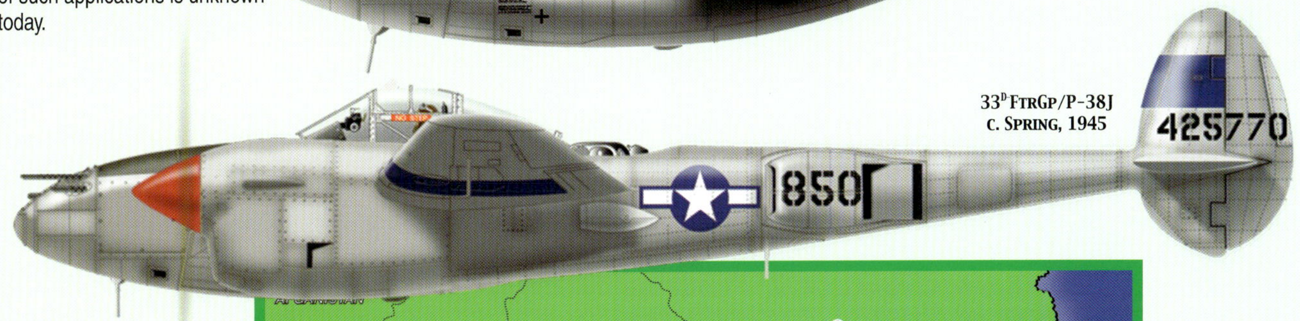

1) Karachi, India
Feb-1944

2) Shwangliu, China
Feb-1944

3) Pungchacheng (Quizhou), China
9-May-1944

4) Nagaghuli, India
3-Sep-1944

5) Sahmaw, Burma
25-Dec-1944

6) Piardoba, India
5-May-1945

• Assigned Tenth AF, Mar-1942 : Fourteenth AF, Oct-1943 thru V-J Day •

69TH Comp Wg
Oct-1943

51ST Fighter Group

Insignia: Approved/ 5-Feb-1942
Motto: Deftly And Swiftly
Sobriquet: Flying Horse Group
Constituted:
51ST Pur Gp (Intcp) / 20-Nov-1940
Redesignated:
51ST Pur Gp (Ftr) / Mar-1941
51ST Ftr Gp / May-1942

Early 449th FtrSqdn
The 449th FS changed its emblem after transferring to the Fourteenth AF, feeling the image of a tiger astride a P-38 was more appropriate than a duck—even Donald.

16TH Fighter Squadron

Insignia: (unapproved)
Sobriquet: The Great Wall In The Air (Sky)

Constituted:
16TH Pur Sqdn (Intcp)/ 20-Nov-1940
Activated: 15-Jan-1941
Redesignated:
16TH Pur Sqdn (Ftr)/ 12-Mar-1941
16TH Ftr Sqdn/ 15-May-1942

25TH Fighter Squadron

Insignia: (unapproved)
Sobriquet: Assam Dragons

Constituted:
25TH Pur Sqdn (Intcp)/ 20-Nov-1940
Activated: 15-Jan-1941
Redesignated:
25TH Pur Sqdn (Ftr)/ 12-Mar-1941
25TH Ftr Sqdn/ 15-May-1942

26TH Fighter Squadron

Insignia: Approved/ 20-Mar-1945
Sobriquet:
Flying Horse Squadron

Constituted:
26TH Pur Sqdn (Intcp)/ 20-Nov-1940
Activated: 15-Jan-1941
Redesignated:
26TH Pur Sqdn (Ftr)/ 12-Mar-1941
26TH Ftr Sqdn/ 15-May-1942

449TH Fighter Squadron

Insignia: Approved/ 31-Oct-1944
Sobriquet: Lightning Tigers

Constituted:
449TH Ftr Sqdn/ 2-Aug-1943
Activated: 26-Aug-1943

16th Ftr Sqdn

Insignia/(unapproved)
Sobriquet: "The Great Wall In The Air" is a reference to the Great Wall of China, a series of fortifications built over many generations whose primary purpose was to defend Chinese dynasties against attacks from nomadic hordes of the Eurasian Steppes.

Early 26th FtrSqdn (pre P-51s)

Insignia/(unapproved)
Sobriquet: "China Blitzers" was a play on the German word blitz, a noun describing a sudden, intensive military attack.

25th FtrSqdn

Insignia/(unapproved)
Sobriquet: The "Assam Dragons" emblem reflected the squadron's saber tooth shark faces adopted by the squadron and painted on the noses of their P-40s.

16th Fighter Squadron Assignments:
1] Karachi, India, 12 Mar 1942
2] Kunming, China, 27 Jun 1942 (detachment operated from Lingling, China, 10 Jul Aug 1942)
3] Chungking, China, 17 Aug 1942
4] Kweilin, China, 27 Oct 1942
5] Chenyi, China, 29 Nov 1942 (detachment operated from Yunnani, China, 26 Dec 1942–Mar 1943);
6] Kweilin, China, 31 Mar 1943
7] Hengyang, China, 20 Sep 1943
8] Chengkung, China, 25 Nov 1943 (detachments operated from Tsuyung, China, 25 Nov 1943–Apr 1944
9] Nanning, China, Feb 1944
10] Szemao, China, Apr 1944
11] Yunnani, China, May–Jul 1944
12] Liangshan, China, 16–31 Dec 1944
13] Kwanghan, China, 24 Dec 1944-30 Jan 1945
14] Laohokow, China, 1 Jan–16 Mar 1945
16] Poseh, China, 1 Feb–13 Apr 1945
17] Pakhoi, China, 7–19 Aug 1945
18] Nanning, China, 19 Aug 1945

16TH FIGHTER SQUADRON

• Retained and applied to all replacement aircraft were the same style shark face designs displayed on the older aircraft, first adopted while serving with the 23d FtrGp.
• Spinners were painted either a solid olive drab or divided vertically with stripes of varying color band widths of white and red, while others were an overall olive drab.
• Squadron Emblem: Some P-40s were known display the squadron's Great Wall insignia positioned mid-fuselage in the form of dry-transfer decals.

16TH FTRSQDN/P-40N
c. LATE-1942

• Fuselage aircraft codes were initial albeit briefly, a carry over from the 16th FtrSqdn's service with th 23dFtrGp (c. July 1942–October 1943) and were two-digit numbers in the 10–3 range. New codes were assigned to the 16th shortly after returning the 51st FtrGp. These were three-digit numbers in the 350–399 rang and were relocated—still in white—from the fuselage to the lowe one-third of the vertical fins.

• In early 1944, P-51B and C Mustangs began to supplement the squadron's inventory of P-40s. Originally delivered in a standard AAF two-color paint scheme, 16th FtrSqdn aircraft numbers remained on the lower third of the vertical fin in white numerals approximately 18–24 in. high.
• Early model P-51s were also adorned with the shark face of their P-40 predecessors, but these applications were gradually abandoned.

16TH FTRSQDN/P-51C
c. MID-1944

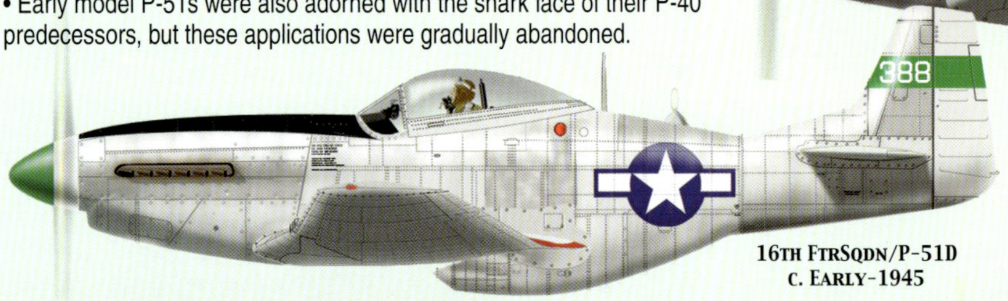

16TH FTRSQDN/P-51D
c. EARLY-1945

• With the arrival of later NMF Mustangs, assigned squadron aircraft numbers were again applied to the fin surface, only now in black. Many applications incorporated a horizontal green color band applied mid-fin in a full wrap-around pattern, including rudder surfaces. Numbers were applied in white.
• Spinners were either a solid O.D. or a combination the white and green colors applied to the tails.

25TH FIGHTER SQUADRON

•The 25th FtrSqdn displayed arguably one of the most recognizable tactical nose markings in the CBI with their distinctive saber tooth shark face design applied to virtually the entire inventory of the squadron's P-40 Warhawks.

25TH FTRSQDN/P-40
c. FALL, 1942

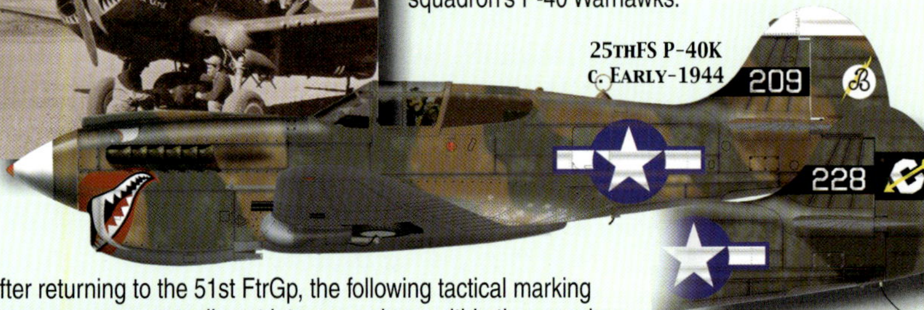

25THFS P-40K
c. EARLY-1944

•The Hawk profile above depicts the 25th FtrSqdn "in-squadron" tact markings while serving with the 23d FtrGp and operating from Dinj China. The assigned numerical series are said to have ranged from 4– but to date no definitive documentation has surfaced concerning particular tail marking sequence. Wartime combat footage and still pho on file confirm the use of single and double digit aircraft numbers positio mid-fin during the 25th FtrSqdn TDY service with the 23d FtrSqdn. So of these aircraft also retained their original RAF numbers applied just the fuselage emblem.

After returning to the 51st FtrGp, the following tactical marking changes were eventually put into general use within the squadron.
• Spinners varied from one aircraft to another. Some were painted a solid white, while others might use alternating Insignia Blue and white to divide the surface area vertically. Still others might be solid O.D. or a combination of O.D. and white applied equally to divide the spinner surface vertically.
• Aircraft numbers were applied in white, often accompanied by a blue or black horizontal band positioned on the lower fin area.

• One-of-a-kind rudder markings, in addition to the varied use of white on the top edge of tail sections, suggest these applications may have indicated flight and/or squadron leader recognition markings within the 25th.

25TH FTRSQDN/P-51C
c. EARLY-1945

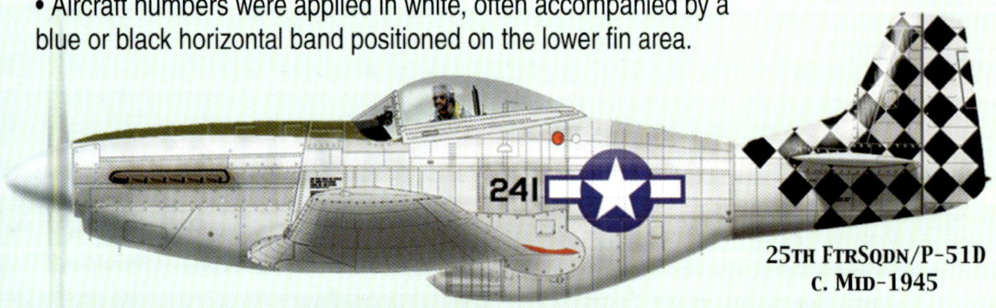

25TH FTRSQDN/P-51D
c. MID-1945

•The tactical markings after the 25th began receiving P-51 Mustangs entaile applying a checkerboard pattern to the entire empennage, the exception bein the horizontal stabilizers. These patterns varied from one application to another but the relocation of the aircraft number to just forward the fuselage nationa emblem was consistently adhered to within the squadron. All markings were applied using black paint on NMF airframe surfaces.

• Spinners on P-51s were generally either solid white or black, with the forward two thirds of the spinner painted white. Some ships in this squadron did display white spinners with a red tip, while others were painted in an alternating series of equal vertical bands of blue-white-blue.

26th Fighter Squadron

26th FtrSqdn/P-40K
c. Late-1943

• When the 51st FtrGp was reassigned to China and the Fourteenth AF, the 26th FS' originally assigned 18 in. tall white aircraft numerical codes were changed from 70–99 to 250–299. The location and size for these new codes was also modified. These slightly smaller numbers—still white—were relocated from the upper fin/rudder to the lower vertical fin surface.

• The squadron's P-40s still bore the iconic AVG Shark Face but with an additional element: applied on each side to the center of the mouth area was a self-adhesive backed transfer emblem of the squadron's China Blitzer emblem. The leading edge (12–14 inches) of the nose area was also painted a solid yellow.
• Spinners were painted a solid ANA Olive Drab or Insignia Red.

• The 26th began receiving C.D. P-51B/C Mustangs around March 1944. Aircraft numbers remained white on the vertical fins until October, when these same numbers were set against a black horizontal stripe bordered top and bottom with smaller yellow color bands, each with a thin black outside border stripe. Aircraft serial numbers were sometimes reapplied below this marking device using the same yellow paint.

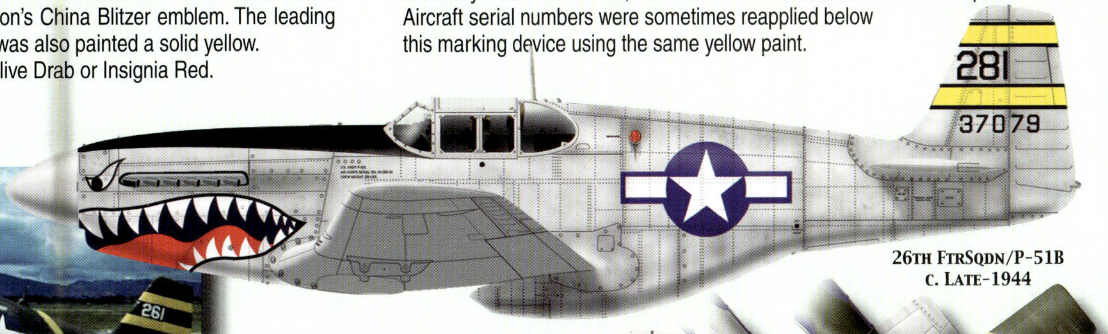

26th FtrSqdn/P-51B
c. Late-1944

26th FtrSqdn/P-51D
c. Early-1945

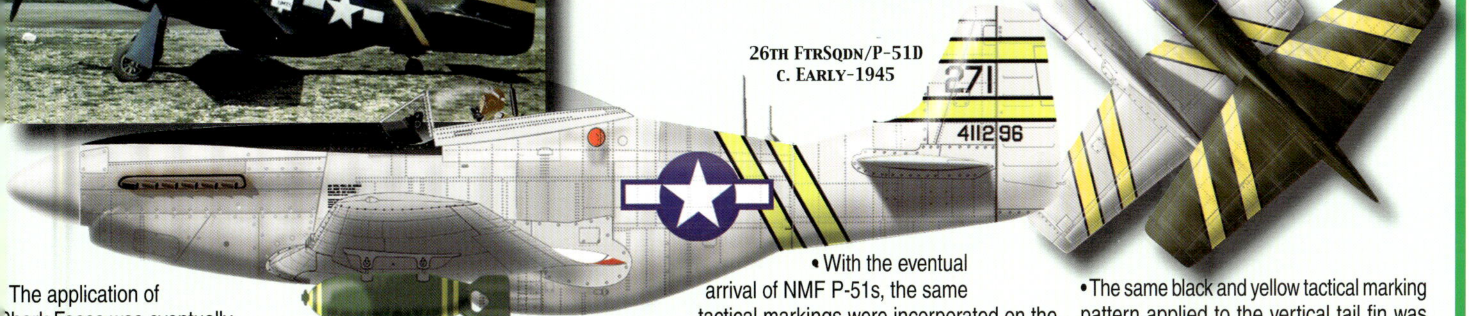

The application of
hark Faces was eventually
hased out on NMF P-51s. Existing
hotographic evidence indicates the
pplication of color to the spinners was also
ventually discarded.

• With the eventual arrival of NMF P-51s, the same tactical markings were incorporated on the newer Mustangs, with the exception of the center black band on the tail. This area was left unpainted except for the assigned aircraft number, now painted black on the NMF. Diagonal fuselage flight/squadron leader stripes were applied to painted and NMF Mustangs.

• The same black and yellow tactical marking pattern applied to the vertical tail fin was duplicated diagonally on both rear horizontal stabilizers. Individual aircraft numbers were not displayed on these applications.

449th Fighter Squadron

449th FtrSqdn/P-38H
c. Late-1943

449th FtrSqdn/P-38J
c. Early-1945

Unlike the other three squadrons comprising the 51st FtrGp, there appear to have been very few distinctive tactical markings employed by the 449th.
• Aircraft squadron numbers ranged from 300–399, applied to the outside radiator housings as white numbers painted on early camouflaged airframes and later in black on NMF surfaces.
• Factory applied aircraft serial numbers were retained as originally applied.
• Spinners were originally painted a solid Olive Drab, but were later given an overall coat of ANA Insignia Red.

• Assigned Tenth AF, June-1943 thru V-J Day •

May-1943
Dec-1945

80th Fighter Group

Insignia: Approved/ 14-Oct-1942
Motto: Angels On Our Wings
Sobriquet: The Burma Banshees
Constituted:
80th Pur Gp (Incpt)/ 13-Jan-1942
Activated: 9-Feb-1942
Redesignated:
80th Ftr Gp/ May-1942

Sluggo
Here is an actual WWII era embroidered uniform patch of the first unit emblem designed and displayed by the 90th Fighter Squadron

88th Fighter Squadron

Insignia: Approved/ 18-Jan-1942

Constituted:
88th Pur Sqdn (Intcp)/13-Jan-1942
Activated: 9-Feb-1942
Redesignated:
88th Ftr Sqdn/15-May-1942

10-39

89th Fighter Squadron

Insignia: Approved/ 5-Jun-1944

Constituted:
89th Pur Sqdn (Intcp)/13-Jan-1942
Activated: 9-Feb-1942
Redesignated:
89th Ftr Sqdn/15-May-1942

40-69

90th Fighter Squadron

Insignia: Approved/ 19-Jan-1945

Constituted:
90th Pur Sqdn (Intcp)/ 13-Jan-1942
Activated: 9-Feb-1942
Redesignated:
90th Ftr Sqdn/ 15-May-1942

70-99

459th Fighter Squadron

Insignia: Approved/ 28-Nov-1944
Sobriquet: Twin Dragon Squadron

Constituted:
90th Pur Sqdn (Intcp)/ 13-Jan-1942
Activated: 9-Feb-1942
Redesignated:
90th Ftr Sqdn/15-May-1942

No color assigned

100-126
1-19
30-81

88th Fighter Squadron / Flight C

This interesting emblem was reputedly the insignia originally belonging to Flight C of the 88th FtrSqdn; this design is the subject of yet another source of controversy among WWII historians. While there is little doubt this insignia did in fact originate with Flight C, there are those that maintain this design became so popular within the 88th Fighter Squadron that it was adopted as the unofficial replacement for the squadron's actual approved design. Such unauthorized emblem replacements were not uncommon within the structure of deployed AAF units during WWII, but no evidence has as yet surfaced that confirms or dispels the possible use of this design by the 88th Fighter Squadron.

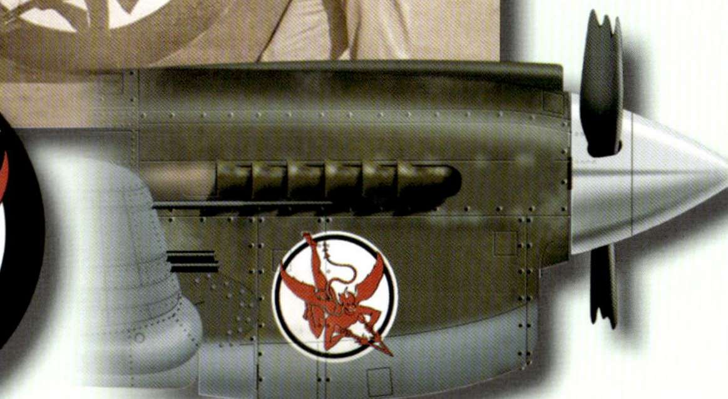

Original 90th Fighter Squadron Emblem

This emblem (above) represents the 90th FtrSqdn's original unit insignia developed prior to the squadron's overseas deployment. There is nothing on file to indicate this design was ever submitted for official approval, but we do have numerous period examples (above) that validate the existence and use of this insignia during the course of WWII.

The reasons for replacing the Sluggo image with the later Boxing Bear design are unknown. What we are certain of is the Bear image officially became the approved emblem of the 90th FtrSqdn in January 1945.

459th Fighter Squadron

Although the design depicted on the facing page was the official emblem for the 459th FtrSqdn, the variation at left was often seen affixed to the forward area of numerous aircraft assigned to this squadron. Although close-ups of this application have not yet surfaced, these appear to have been applied to the fuselage nose using a stencil. Hand-cut stencils were a viable solution often used by ground service personnel in the absence of pre-printed self-adhesive unit emblems that were unavailable, or simply not in a unit's budget allocation.

88TH FIGHTER SQUADRON

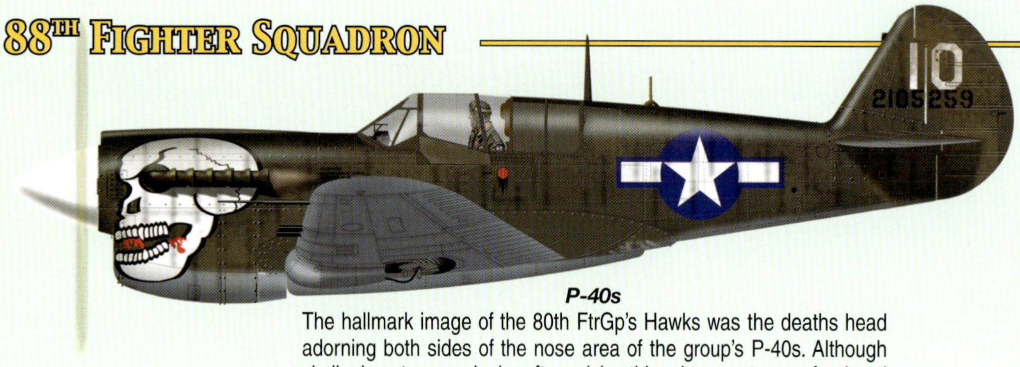

Two digit aircraft number-in-squadron were applied to the vertical tail section utilizing fin and rudder surfaces; they were normally around 16 in. high and ranged between 10–39. On some applications these numbers were applied considerably larger, and in such cases the aircraft serial number was removed.

P-40s

The hallmark image of the 80th FtrGp's Hawks was the deaths head adorning both sides of the nose area of the group's P-40s. Although similar in nature, each aircraft receiving this adornment was a freehand application. No stencils for this design existed, so each individual aircraft application varied slightly. Spinners of the 88th FtrSqdn were painted white (the assigned color for this squadron).

P-47s

With the group's transition to the P-47, the death's head was replaced with the simple painting of the cowling ring in squadron color with the respective two digit number-in-squadron applied with black to each side of the cowling ring. Some prop hubs were also painted white to match the cowling, but this practice was apparently random on the P-47s.

Wings, horizontal stabilizers, and tail sections displayed EAC Stripes: white on camouflaged surfaces, Insignia Blue on later all metal finishes. Aircraft fin serial numbers were retained. Two digit number-in-squadron codes approximately 22 in. high were relocated from the tail section to the mid-fuselage area—white on painted surfaces, black on metal finishes.

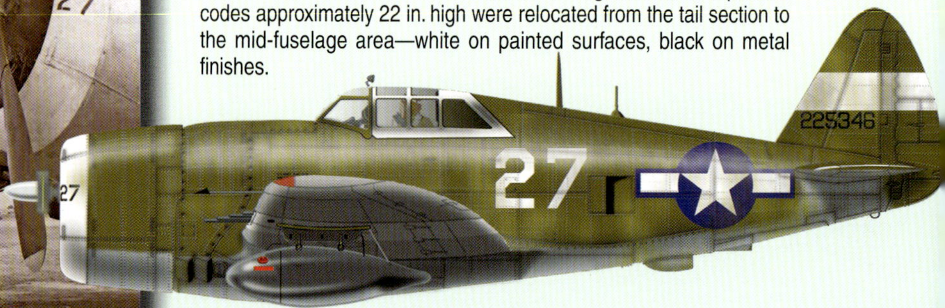

89TH FIGHTER SQUADRON

P-40s

Displaying the same distinctive 506th FtrGp white and black deaths head profile on both sides of the nose area, the distinguishing characteristics of the 89th FtrSqdn were the prop spinners painted in the 89th's assigned red color. The tail numbers (40–69) also served to identify Warhawks serving with the 89th FtrSqdn. Retention of the aircraft serial number was a hit or miss proposition.

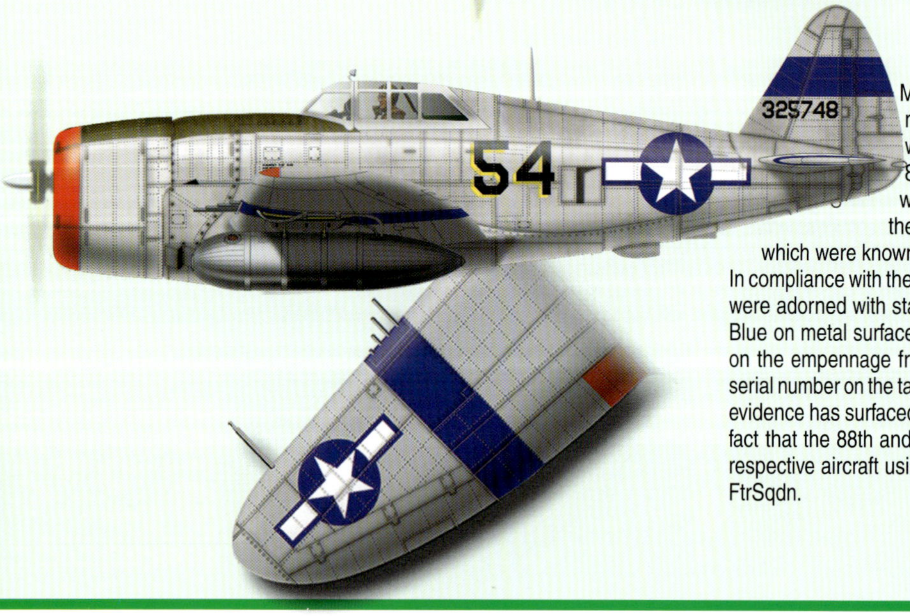

P-47s

Medium red cowling rings and the same 40–69 number-in-squadron codes applied mid-fuselage were the distinguishing characteristics of the 89th FtrSqdn. These latter devices were applied as white on the few early camouflaged airframes within the squadron and black on natural metal finishes, some of which were known to have featured a yellow drop shadow for accent. In compliance with the Tenth Air Force directive, all P-47s assigned to the squadron were adorned with standard EAC stripes: Insignia white on camouflage, Insignia Blue on metal surfaces. In spite of formal EAC standards to the contrary, stripes on the empennage frequently extended to control surfaces. The factory applied serial number on the tail fins were retained. At the time of publication no photographic evidence has surfaced regarding the use of red color coded cowling rings, but the fact that the 88th and 90th FtrSqdn did employ these very devices on their own respective aircraft using their own colors strongly suggests their use by the 89th FtrSqdn.

90th Fighter Squadron

As was the case with the other two squadrons in the 80th FtrGp operating Hawks, the basic design for the nose marker was the same: a white skull consisting of a heavy black outline with white details. Some applications of this design motif in the 80th featured the addition of red blood drops around the mouth, but this modification to the design varied considerably from one aircraft to another. Number-in-squadron codes were painted on the vertical tails in sizes varying from 16–22 in., the latter numeral sizes overprinting factory applied serial numbers. The reason for the particular size variance concerning these tail codes is unknown. Spinners were painted in the assigned squadron blue.

P-47s

The approved emblem of the 90th FtrSqdn was applied to a number of the squadron's P-47s. These applications were in the form of self-adhesive dry transfer decals and were positioned just below the forward area of the cockpit windscreen. The application of an earlier squadron emblem is addressed in greater detail on p. 35.

The tactical markings for the 90th FtrSqdn's Thunderbolts corresponded with markings in the 80th FtrGp. Individual aircraft call numbers were applied mid-fuselage, immediately forward the national emblem. These were approximately 22 in. high and were applied with black on the NMFs. Smaller versions of the two digit fuselage codes were duplicated on the cowling rings in white. The use of drop shadows with these devices on fuselage applications within the 90th FtrSqdn is unconfirmed. Tenth AF EAC markings were added in compliance with the directive mandating the application of these friendly forces markings to all P-47s operating in the Tenth AF area of operations. The 18 in. wide empennage and 28 in. wide chordwise wing stripes matched the engine cowling rings of the squadron's Bolts, ANA 502 Insignia Blue being the 90th's assigned color.

459th Fighter Squadron

P-38s

After being assigned to the 80th FtrGp, the 459th FtrSqdn developed a striking dragon motif that was applied to inboard and outboard surfaces of the twin booms of their assigned F series Lightnings; it served as a squadron tactical marking. There were no stencils used in these applications, resulting in slight variations from one aircraft to another. The colors used for these dragon markings were various shades of green outlined with a series of yellow dashes to give the painted image a bit better deification against the camouflaged airframes.

The faces on these applications were all similar and consisted of a black mouth outlined red, with a red tongue and a large white fang, surmounted by a white and black eye.

Assigned aircraft numbers were originally white on the outfacing vertical tails c. late 1943, ranging between 100–126. These numbers were replaced with the numerals 1–19—also white—in early 1944, and remained unchanged until the squadron was permanently reassigned to the 33d FtrGp on 12 May 1945. Factory applied serial numbers were rarely retained with the dragon applications.

• Assigned *Twelfth AF, Jan-1943 • Fourteenth AF, May-1944 thru V-J Day •

312th Ftr Wg
May-1944

*81st Fighter Group

Insignia: Approved/ 2-Mar-1943
Motto: The Name, The Arms, Loyalty
Constituted:
81st PurGrp(Intep)/13-Jan-1942
Redesignated:
81st FtrGrp/ May-1942

312th Fighter Wing Emblem
Approved 28 April 1945, this was the only official AAF Wing insignia of similar units assigned to the CBI.

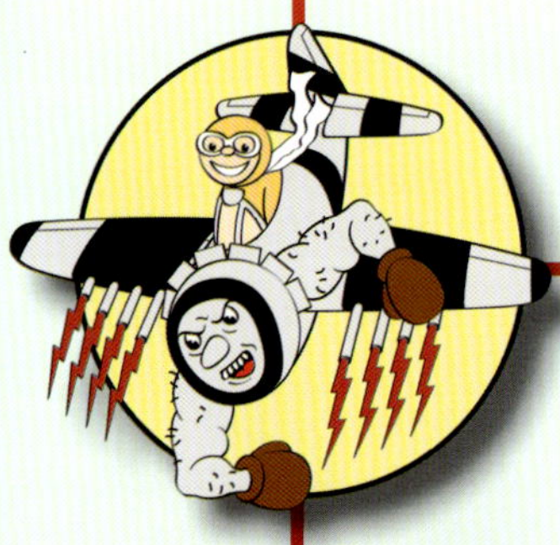

91st Fighter Squadron

Insignia: (unapproved-CBI)

Constituted:
91st Pur Sqdn (intcp)/ 13-Jan-1942
Activated: 9-Feb-1942
Redesignated:
91st Ftr Sqdn/ 15-May-1942

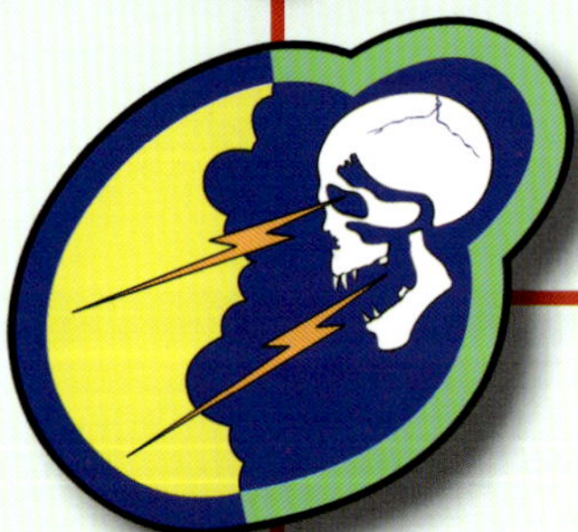

92d Fighter Squadron

Insignia: Approved 30-Jun-1945

Constituted:
92d Pur Sqdn (intcp)/ 13-Jan-1942
Activated: 9-Feb-1942
Redesignated:
92d Ftr Sqdn/ 15-May-1942

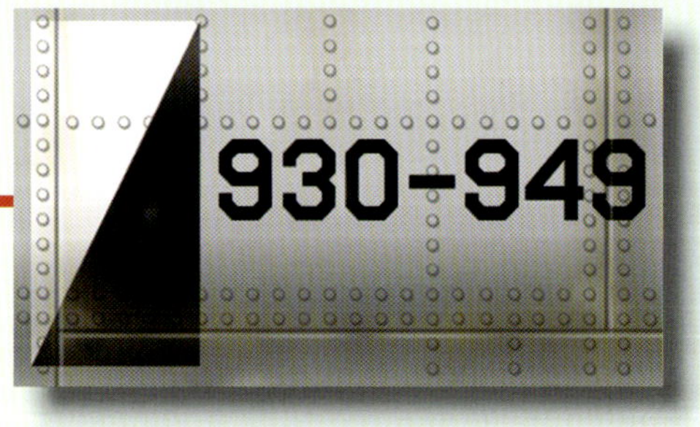

93d Fighter Squadron

Insignia: (unapproved-CBI)
Sobriquet: Thunder Jugs

Constituted:
93d Pur Sqdn (intcp)/ 13-Jan-1942
Activated: 9-Feb-1942
Redesignated:
93d Ftr Sqdn/ 15-May-1942

* Previously served in combat with the Twelfth AF in the MTO, refer to *Battle Colors-Vol. IV*

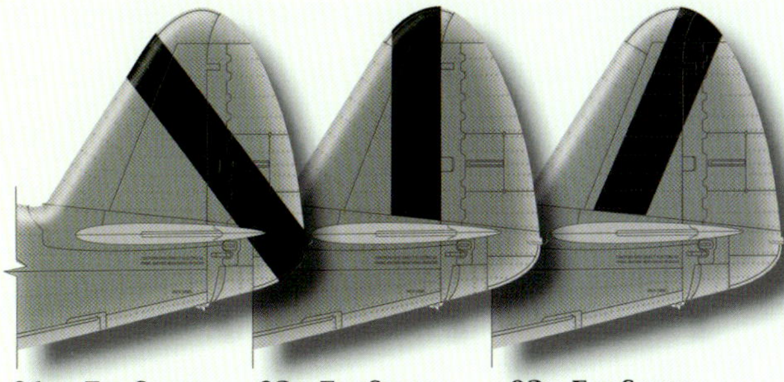

91st FtrSqdn 92d FtrSqdn 93d FtrSqdn

81st Fighter Group

Although this unit employed a variety of different tactical markings during its combat tour in the CBI, the one constant were the tail markings. There is even a running debate regarding the squadron's numerical sequences, but there is no debate where the tails are concerned (with the exception of the exact width of these devices). Virtually all historians tend to agree about the location and configuration of each of these three devices. The most obvious stumbling block encountered when researching the 81st FtrGp is the almost total lack of wartime photographs available within the traditional historical archives while this unit was deployed in the CBI.

91st FtrSqdn/P-47
c. Mid-1944

Engine Cowlings

Applying paint to the leading cowling ring appears to have been an on-again-off-again proposition, with specific time frames for their use being a mystery. What is known is that when this tactical device was utilized within the 81st FtrGp, it entailed white paint on camouflaged airframes, black on NMFs.

92d FtrSqdn/P-47
c. Late-1944

Fuselage Stripe

During their initial deployment in the CBI, the P-47s of the 81st FtrGp applied a vertical stripe to the fuselage of a width matching the tail stripe. This device was applied just forward the national emblem.

Squadron Numbers

Applied approximately midway to both sides of the fuselage, these devices were utilized by all three squadrons—white on olive drab, black on NMF surfaces. Although a field directive relating to these markings has not yet surfaced, the numerical height appears to have varied between 24–30 in.

Wing Markings

Chordwise stripes were applied to 91st and 92d FtrSqdn wings on camouflaged and NMF surfaces: white in the former instance, black in the latter. Wing tips were also known to have been similarly treated, but the extent of the use of this treatment within the squadrons and a specific time frame of usage is uncertain.

93d Fighter Group: Exception to the Rule

The 93dFS was apparently exempt from complying with the various tactical markings depicted above. This squadron entered combat in the CBI during August 1944, but was withdrawn from action, and from October until war's end functioned as an in-theater training unit operating out of their base in *Gushkara, India. The diagonal tail bar and fuselage number-in-squadron were the only known tactical devices employed by this squadron.

93d FtrSqdn/P-47
c. Mid-1944

* The 93d FS was withdrawn from combat after being operational in the CBI for about a month and was stationed at Gushkara A/F, where it was to serve as a training unit for the remainder of the war.

• Assigned Tenth AAF, Jul-1943 : Fourteenth AAF, Jul-1944 thru V-J Day •

312TH FTR WG
JUL-1944

The image above is what historical unit researchers love coming across. In spite of the often less-than-portrait photographic quality, wartime photos such as this one of the 529th FS design (dated August 1944, Dinjan, India) reinforce the existence and actual use of these unapproved emblems during WWII.

311TH Fighter Group

Insignia: Approved/ 13-Nov-1942
Motto: Strikes as Lightning
Constituted:
311TH Bomb Gp (Lt)/ 28-Jan-1942
Activated: 2-Mar-1942
Redesignated:
311TH Bomb Gp (Dive)/ Jul-1942
311TH Ftr-Bmr Gp/ Sep-1943
311TH Ftr Gp/ May-1944

385TH Bombardment Squadron (Dive)

Insignia: Approved/ 20-Oct-1942
Sobriquet: Bomberwockeys

Constituted:
385TH Bomb Sqdn (Lt)/28-Jan-1942
Activated: 2-Mar-1942
Redesignated:
385TH Bomb Sqdn (Dive)/27-Jul-1942
Disbanded: 30-Sep-1943

NO KNOWN SQUADRON COLOR OR CODES ASSIGNED

528TH Fighter Squadron

Insignia: (Unapproved)
Sobriquet: The Dragon Flies

Constituted:
382D Bomb Sqdn (Lt)/28-Jan-1942
Activated: 2-Mar-1942
Redesignated:
382D Bomb Sqdn (Dive)/27-Jul-1942
528TH Ftr-Bmr Sqdn/30-Sep-1943
528TH Ftr Sqdn/30-May-1944

*Aircraft No's. / India
10-39
*Aircraft No's. / China
1010-1039

529TH Fighter Squadron

Insignia: (Unapproved)
Sobriquet: Golden Tigers

Constituted:
383D Bomb Sqdn (Lt)/28-Jan-1942
Activated: 2-Mar-1942
Redesignated:
383D Bomb Sqdn (Dive)/27-Jul-1942
529TH Ftr-Bmr Sqdn/30-Sep-1943
529TH Ftr Sqdn/30-May-1944

*Aircraft No's. / India
40-69
*Aircraft No's. / China
1040-1069

530TH Fighter Squadron

Insignia: (Unapproved)
Sobriquet: Yellow Scorpions

Constituted:
384TH Bomb Sqdn (Lt)/28-Jan-1942
Activated: 2-Mar-1942
Redesignated:
384TH Bomb Sqdn (Dive)/27-Jul-1942
530TH Ftr-Bmr Sqdn/30-Sep-1943
530TH Ftr Sqdn/30-May-1944

*Aircraft No's. / India
70-99
*Aircraft No's. / China
1070-1099

* These numbers are based upon the standard AAF numerical assignment of squadron codes. Some evidence suggests the following code assignments may have actually been used:

528thFS / 01-32 • 529thFS / 33-59 • 530thFS / 60-90

The problem with this numerical allocation is all three squadrons would have been assigned an uneven distribution of aircraft. Until such a time that documentation relating to this subject surfaces, researchers are once again left with a best guess scenario as to actual squadron codes assigned.

Tenth Air Force Spinner Colors

Spinners often displayed respective squadron colors, a subject still open to debate to this day; as a rule, it is generally accepted that the colors depicted on the facing page were those used by each squadron, although some variations during this period are known to exist.

North American/A-36 Apache
c. Late-1944

Tactical Markings/Original

Large two digit numbers applied in white to the group's aircraft was the method adopted by the 311th FtrGp as tactical markings for each of its assigned squadrons. These devices were on the tail section with one digit affixed to the tailfin proper; the second digit was on the rudder surface. The original factory applied serial number was removed from the tail and reapplied in black to the rear fuselage, just aft the national emblem.

384TH Bombardment Squadron (Dive)

The squadron's original emblem was approved 16 April 1943, and was displayed on a number of the unit's A-36 Apache dive bombers. This good gremlin came in the form of printed, self-adhesive backed decals applied just aft the engine exhaust ports.

528TH Fighter Squadron

One of the 528th FtrSqn's more important operations was providing air support to Merrill's Marauders (5307th Composite Unit (Prov) / Galahad) involved in long range incursion operations into Burma c. February–August 1944. The code name used by the 528th communicating with ground personnel of the Marauders was Dragonfly Flight. The image depicted (left and facing) was originally designed as a special mission emblem for those members of the squadron directly participating in these operations. The dragonfly is an important symbol in Chinese lore, and when the 311th FtrGp was reassigned to the Fourteenth AF the 528th decided to adopt the former special operations emblem to represent the squadron, albeit unofficially, possibly due to the impact of War Department Circular No. 226 / Section III dated 7 June 1944, which placed a moratorium on Distinctive Insignia applications. Uniform patches of this design were originally available as embroidered silk and later supplied as wet transfer decals affixed to 5¼ in. circular leather disks.

530TH Fighter Squadron

A variation of this squadron's unapproved emblem. This particular image was used as the cover art for a published postwar unit history c. 1946. This is yet another example of the lack of continuity inherent with unit designs that, for whatever reason, failed to be approved by the Quartermaster Corps Heraldic Section.

Tenth Air Force Spinner Colors

The subject of both squadron colors and their subsequent application to propeller spinners is an ongoing debate among historians. The colors attributed to each respective squadron are best guesses based upon scrutiny of countless period photographs. Several factors have led to this confusion, including the exchange of aircraft between squadrons, in addition to sharing new and used replacement components. The underlying issue is the complete lack of even a fragmentary field order in connection with this topic.

North American/P-51 Mustang

528TH FtrSqdn c.Mid-1944

529TH FtrSqdn c. Late-1944

530TH FtrSqdn c. Early-1945

Tactical Markings/Revised

The application of dual tail stripes as tactical marking bands began to appear shortly after the 311th FtrGp's transfer to the Tenth AF, and were applied as depicted above. The serial numbers continued to be applied aft the national emblem, with the assigned numerical codes applied immediately forward this same device. In the case of the latter, it would appear from photographic evidence each squadron retained the two digit codes assigned while serving with the Tenth AF, with the addition of the number 10 in front of these original codes.

382D Bombardment Squadron (Light)

The Winged Death emblem (left) as it appeared in the December 1944 issue of *National Geographic*, and the original unit design of the 382d BombSqdn, which would later be redesignated the 528th FtrSqdn. In spite of this insignia's origins, this pattern was used by the squadron until replaced by the Dragon Flies design in mid-1944.

Squadron Assignments
The Station Listing shows the primary locations of 311th FG/HQ. As was the case with many units operating in the CBI, component squadrons at times operated from forward airfields that are not indicated on this map.

• Assigned: Twentieth AF, c. April/May-1945 • Eighth AF, Aug-1945 thru V-J Day •

301st Ftr Wg/1945

Twentieth AF 1945

413th Fighter Group

Insignia: (unknown)
Constituted:
413th FtrGp/5-Oct-1944
Activated: 15-Oct-1944

1st Fighter Squadron

Insignia: Approved/ 1-Mar-1945

Constituted: 1st FtrSqdn/ 5-Oct-1944
Activated: 15-Oct-1944

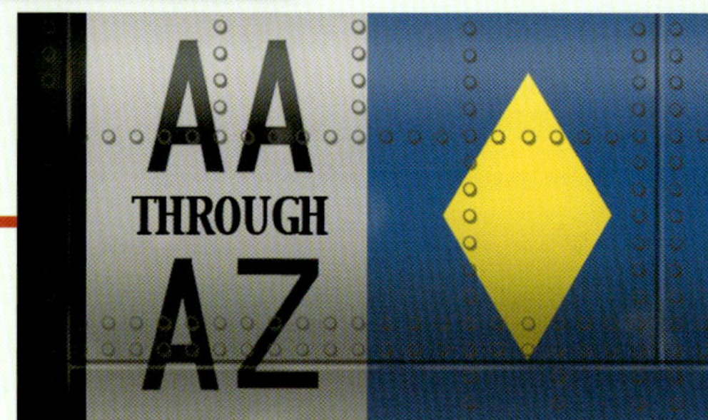

21st Fighter Squadron

**Insignia:* Approved/ 5-Jan-1946

Constituted: 21st FtrSqdn/5-Oct-1944
Activated: 15-Oct-1944

34th Fighter Squadron

**Insignia:* Approved/ 9-Nov-1945

Constituted: 24th FtrSqdn/ 5-Oct-1944
Activated: 15-Oct-1944

* Both squadrons adopted their respective designs during their brief combat tour of duty in the Western Pacific; none received official approval until after war's end.

Squadron Insignia
As of this writing, the 1st FtrSqdn is the only unit within the 413th FtrGp with period photographic evidence that confirms the applied use of the squadron emblem to assigned aircraft. (Note the 1st FtrSqdn black wing tip marking in the top photo.)

1st FtrSqdn/P-47N
First Pattern/c. Spring-1945

1st FtrSqdn/P-47N
Second Pattern/c. Summer-1945

Tactical Markings / First Pattern
Initial markings entailed the painting of rudder and cowling rings with respective squadron colors and playing card icons affixed as depicted. During this period factory-applied aircraft serial numbers on the fin area were retained.

The yellow cowling ring paint applications in the 21st and 34th FtrSqdn were bordered with a thin vertical black stripe, while 1st FtrSqdn cowlings were painted a solid black, as well as the wing tips of their assigned aircraft.

Assigned aircraft call letters were applied to both sides of the fuselage, just forward the national emblem. The size and positioning of these letter codes remained unchanged regarding first and second pattern applications.

21st FtrSqdn/P-47N
First Pattern/c. Spring-1945

21st FtrSqdn/P-47N
Second Pattern/c. Summer-1945

Tactical Markings / Second Pattern
The entire empennage was painted in adopted squadron colors as shown in the accompanying illustrations (Medium Blue in the case of the 1st FtrSqdn, Identification Yellow for the 21st and 34th Squadrons). Each application called for a thin black vertical stripe to be applied between the painted and unpainted area of the tail sections. Each respective squadron icon was relocated to the lower fin area, with the exception of the 1st FtrSqdn, which elected to straddle their diamond icon midway between the fin and rudder. In all cases the factory applied serial numbers were over painted and not reapplied.

34th FtrSqdn/P-47N
First Pattern/c. Spring-1945

34th FtrSqdn/P-47N
Second Pattern/c. Summer-1945

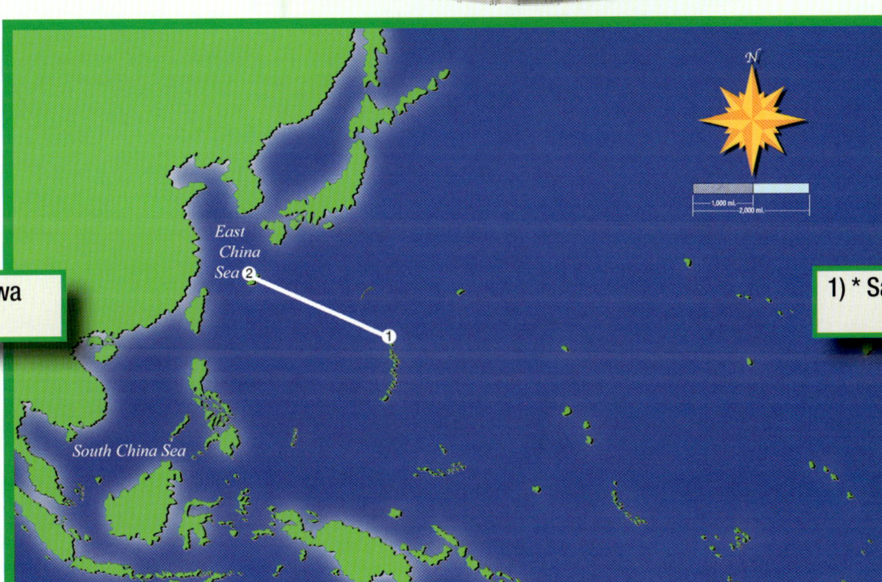

* The squadrons of the 413th FG conducted several strafing missions against Japanese installations on the Truk Islands prior to being formerly assigned to Ie Shima Airfield.

• Assigned: Twentieth AF, c. Jun/Aug-1945 thru V-J Day •

301st Ftr Wg/1945

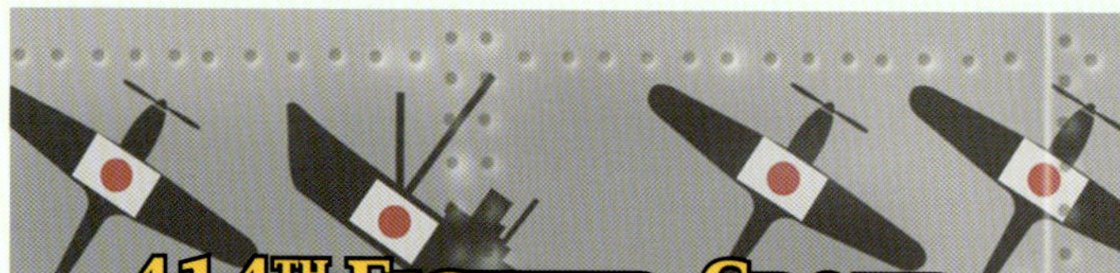

414th Fighter Group

Insignia: (unknown)

Constituted:

414th FtrGp/5-Oct-1944

Activated: 15-Oct-1944

413th Fighter Squadron

Insignia: (unapproved)

Constituted: 413th FtrSqdn/ 5-Oct-1944

Activated: 15-Oct-1944

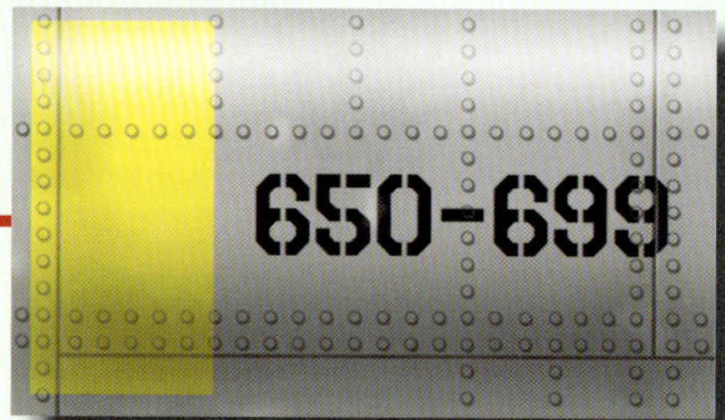

437th Fighter Squadron

Insignia: Approved/ 7-Mar-1945

Constituted: 437th FtrSqdn/ 5-Oct-1944

Activated: 15-Oct-1944

456th Fighter Squadron

Insignia: Approved/ 21-Mar-1945

Constituted: 456th FtrSqdn/ 5-Oct-1944

Activated: 15-Oct-1944

413TH FTRSQDN/P-47N
C. MID-1945

437TH FTRSQDN/P-47N
C. MID-1945

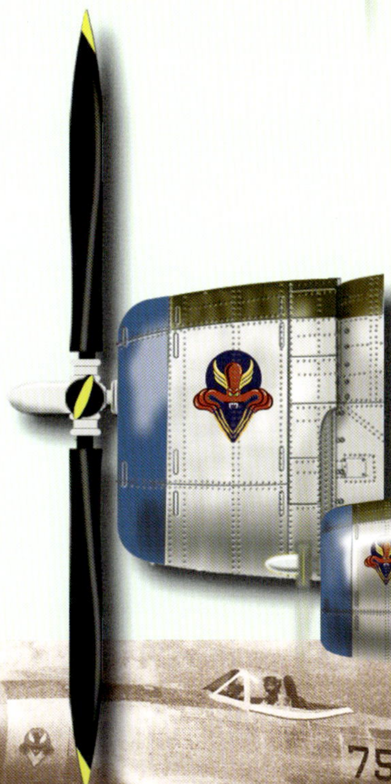

Squadron tactical markings within the 414th FtrGp consisted of a black 18 in. vertical band applied at the point separating the empennage from the main fuselage. The entire tail area, including control surfaces, was painted in respective squadron pattern/colors as depicted on the facing page. Engine cowling rings were similarly treated. Aircraft serial numbers were retained by either block masking prior to paint application or reapplied after painting was completed. Number-in-squadron codes were applied with black paint on both sides of the fuselage, immediately forward the national emblem. Although there exist wartime photos showing the application of the 456th FtrSqdn's emblem to engine cowlings, no similar evidence was discovered during research for this work indicating similar use by the other two squadrons.

456TH FTRSQDN/P-47N
C. MID-1945

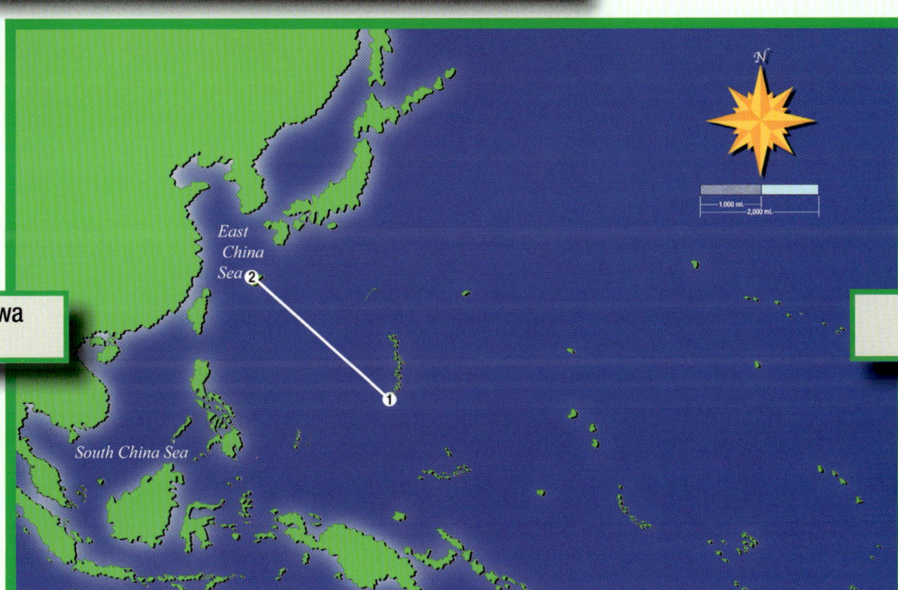

2) Ie Shima A/F, Okinawa
c. Jul-1945

* 1) North Field, Guam
c. Jul-1945

* The squadrons of the 414th FG conducted several strafing missions against Japanese installations on the Truk Islands prior to being formerly assigned to Ie Shima Airfield.

• Assigned: Twentieth AF, c. February/April-1945 thru V-J Day •

301st Ftr Wg/1945

*506th Fighter Group

Insignia: *Submitted/ 14-Jun-1945
Motto: Ad Caelum Ad Victoriam
(Skyward To Victory)
Constituted:
506th FtrGp/ 5-Oct-1944
Activated: 21-Oct-1944

• *The 506th FtrGp Emblem •

Although received by the Heraldic Secti too late in the war for final approval (t 506th was inactivated 16 December 194 the emblem depicted at left wa nonetheless adopted and displayed b this unit during its WWII oversea deployment. The visual componen feature Mt. Fujiyama representing the a offensive against Japan, while the hors represent P-51 Mustangs, the comb aircraft used by all three squadron assigned to the 506th FG. The styliz Zodiac symbol in the center of the shie represents the anniversary of the grou activation.

457th Fighter Squadron

Insignia: Approved/ 20 Jan 1945

Constituted:
457th FtrSqdn/ 5-Oct-1944
Activated: 21-Oct-1944

458th Fighter Squadron

Insignia: Approved/ 14 Apr- 1954
from WWII design

Constituted:
458th FtrSqdn/ 5-Oct-1944
Activated: 21-Oct-1944

462d Fighter Squadron

Insignia: Approved/ 12-Feb-1945

Constituted: 462d FtrSqdn/ 5-Oct-1944
Activated: 21-Oct-1944

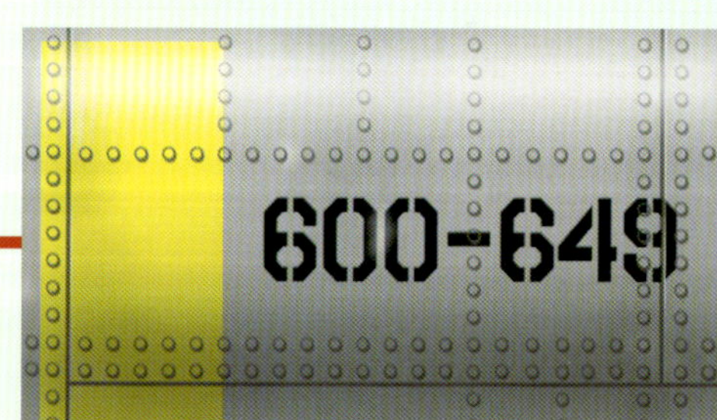

506th FtrGp/P-51D's
First Pattern Markings—c. Spring 1945

When the 506th FtrGp's air echelon was initially deployed to Tinian Island, each squadron was instructed to paint the empennage of their P-51s (except for the control surfaces, rudder, trim tab, and elevators) with a striped diagonal pattern, each in their respective assigned colors. Serial numbers were retained, and combat aircraft were assigned a number-in-squadron to be applied in black on the fuselage sides, just forward the national insignia.

506th FtrGp/P-51D's
Second Pattern Markings—c. Summer 1945

Squadron emblems were often applied to the Mustangs of all three squadrons in the form of dry transfer decals. Placement of these devices varied, with the 458th and 462d FtrSqdn electing to position their insignia mid-fuselage, just below the cockpit windscreen. The 457th FtrSqdn chose to position their emblem immediately aft the engine exhaust port cut-out.

While replacement aircraft received the new color pattern as directed, the order apparently did not affect existing inventory, as many aircraft in the three squadrons continued to carry the original striped pattern for some time following the change order.

Shortly after the 506th FtrGp's transfer to Iwo Jima it was concluded the tail stripes were far too time consuming to apply, and a change order went out directing that all non-control surfaces be painted with solid squadron colors instead.

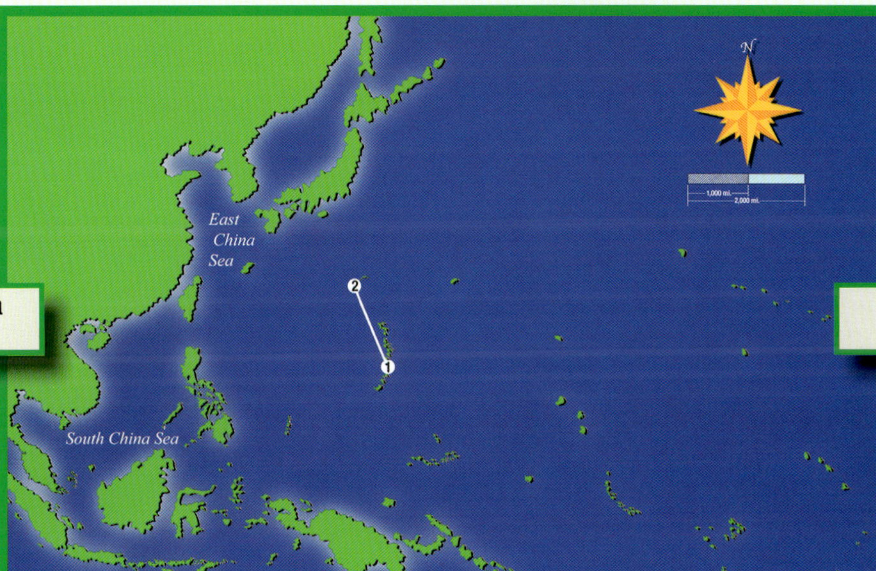

2) Central Field, Iwo Jima
c. 11-May-1945

*** 1) North Field, Tinian**
c. Mar/Apr-1945

* The air echelon of the 406th FG conducted several combat patrols operating TDY from Tinian Island prior to rejoining the rest of the group awaiting them at their permanent duty station on Iwo Jima.

• Assigned: Twentieth AF, c. April/May-1945 • Eighth AF, Aug-1945 thru V-J Day •

301st Ftr Wg/1945

507th Fighter Group

Insignia: (unknown)
Motto: (unknown)
Sobriquet: The Rainbow Group
Constituted: 507th FtrGp/5-Oct-1944
Activated: 12-Oct-1944

463d Fighter Squadron

Insignia: (submitted; never officially approved)

Constituted: 463d FtrSqdn/5-Oct-1944
Activated: 12-Oct-1944

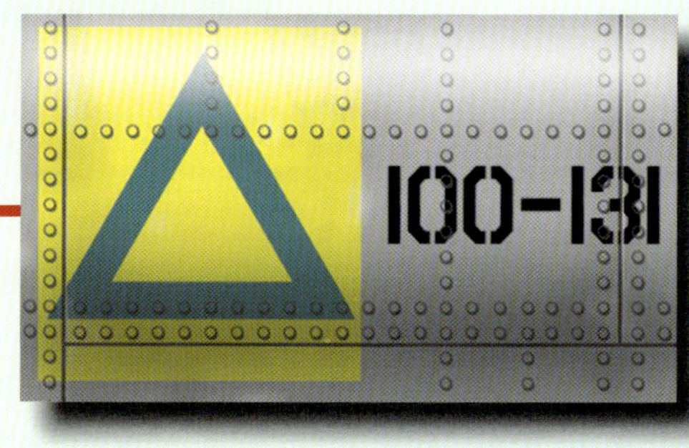

464th Fighter Squadron

Insignia: Approved/6-Mar-1945

Constituted: 464th FtrSqdn/5-Oct-1944
Activated: 12-Oct-1944

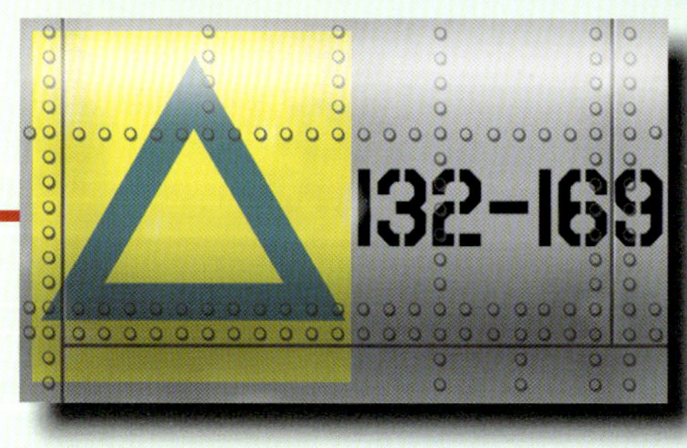

465th Fighter Squadron

Insignia: (unofficial)

Constituted: 465th FtrSqdn/5-Oct-1944
Activated: 12-Oct-1944

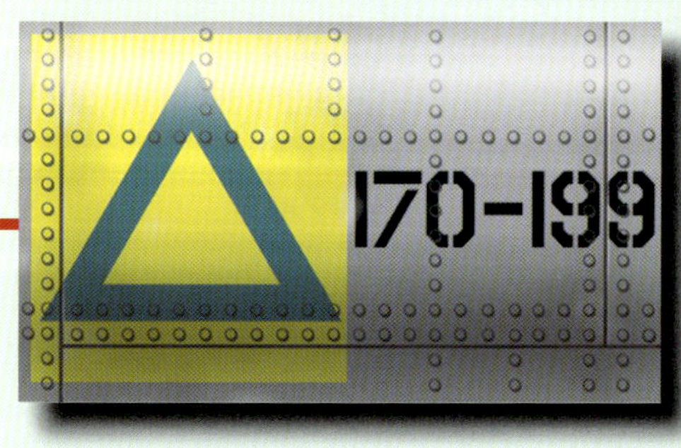

507th FtrGp-Squadron Emblem Applications

Based on period photographic evidence such as the above image, it is certain the 453th and 456th Fighter Squadrons applied their respective emblems near the cockpit area on the right side of the mid-fuselage area via large dry transfer decals. It is unknown whether these images were similarly applied to the right fuselage. It is also unknown whether the 463d FtrSqdn adopted this same practice.

507th FtrGp-Tactical Markings

507th FtrGp markings consisted of the entire empennage—including horizontal stabilizers—being painted with what appears to be ANA 505/Identification Yellow. Equilateral triangles were affixed to either side of the tail fin/rudder assembly with a paint that comes close to matching QM 23/Light Blue. Solid yellow stripes were applied to upper and lower wing surfaces, intersecting the location of the aircraft's wing mounted machine guns. Number-in-squadron codes were painted forward the national insignia on either side of the fuselage and were apparently most often affixed without filling the stencil break lines.

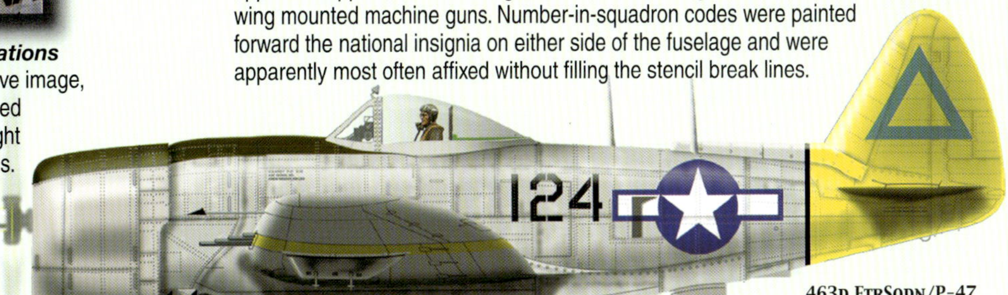

463d FtrSqdn/P-47
c. Late-1945

507th FtrGp-Tail Markings

In addition to an equilateral triangle positioned on either side of the vertical tail, a similar device was applied to the upper surface of the left horizontal stabilizer (LHS). There are some contemporary ıstrations and models of the 507th FtrGp' P-47s depicting the application the triangle device as being applied to both the upper right RHS and ɔth under surfaces as well, but period photos to date fail to show ʼidence indicating additional applications beyond those depicted ı this page.

Former 465th FtrSqdn Thunderbolt

This postwar photo (c. 1946) depicts a P-47 of the 51st Fighter Group (identified by the B5 fuselage code). All other tactical markings, including the emblem affixed just below the forward windscreen, originally belonged to the 465th FtrSqdn. Of particular interest are the black outline stripes applied to the yellow wing and tail tactical markings. This raises speculation as to just how widespread this particular outlining practice was within the 507th FtrGp during the war.

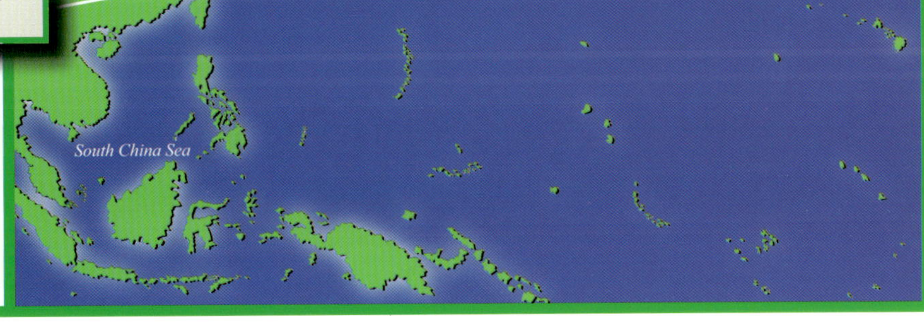

• Assigned China-Burma-India, c. Jun-1944 thru V-J Day •

AAF/India-Burma
22-Aug-1944

Tenth AF
11-Jun-1944

Fourteenth AF
Nov-1944

312th Ftr Wg (Attchd)
Feb-1945

426th Night Fighter Sqdn

Insignia: Approved/ 8-Jun-1944
Motto: (unknown)
Sobriquet: (unknown)
Constituted:
426th NgtFtrSqdn/ 8-Dec-1943
Activated: 5-Nov-1945

Northrop P-61 Black Widow
1944-1945

The 426th NgtFtrSqdn P-61s were painted overall with ANA 622 Jet with the serial number applied to the aft section of the tail booms with ANA 509 Insignia Red. Squadron aircraft displayed no distinctive unit markings on their P-61s, although individual aircraft names were commonly applied to the nose.

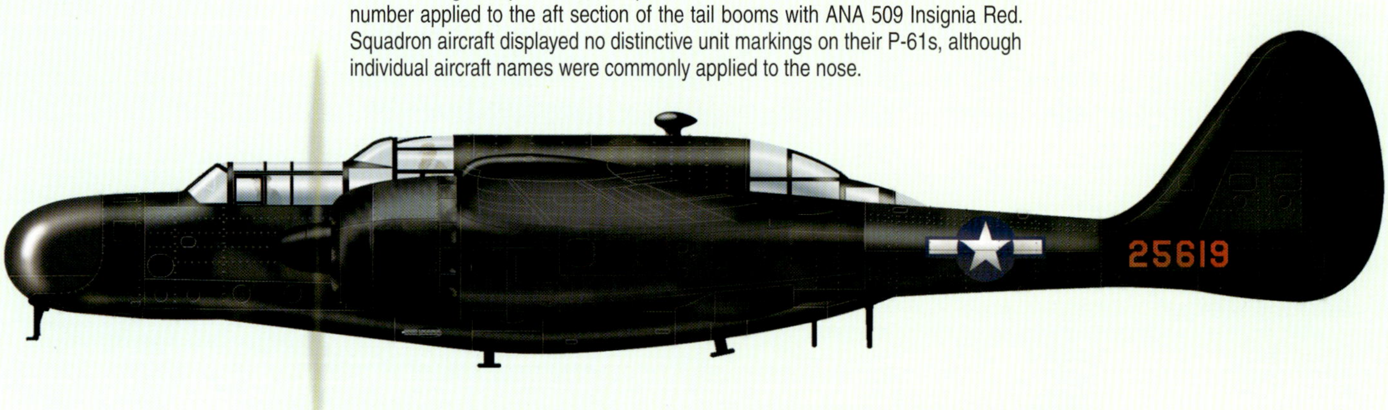

*** 1) Madhaiganj A/F, India**
9-Aug-1944

* The 436th NFS was non-operational while at this station.

*** 2) Chengtu A/F, China**
5-Nov-1944

* Detachments operated TDY from:
- Kunming A/F, China: 25 Nov–c. Dec 1944
- Hsian A/F, China: 27 Nov 1944–17 Aug 1945

*** 3) Shwangliu A/F, China**
C. Mar-1945

* Detachments operated TDY from:
- Liangshan A/F, China: c. Apr–Aug 1945
- Ankang A/F, China: c. Apr–Aug 1945

• Assigned Tenth AF, 11-Jun-1944 • Twelfth AF, c. Sep-1944 • AAF/India-Burma, 2-Oct-1944 •
• Tenth AF, 13-Dec-1944 • Fourteenth AF, 24-Aug-1945 thru V-J Day •

427th Night Fighter Sqdn

Insignia: Approved 30-Apr-1945
Motto: (unknown)
Sobriquet: (unknown)
Constituted:
427th NgtFtrSqdn/19-Jan-1944
Activated: 1-Feb-1944

Northrop P-61 Black Widow
1944-1945

As with the 426th, the 427th NgtFtrSqdn P-61s were painted in overall ANA 622 Jet, the serial numbers applied to the aft section of the tail booms with ANA 509 Insignia Red. Names were painted on the nose area of numerous squadron P-61s, but the unit never adopted tactical unit markings.

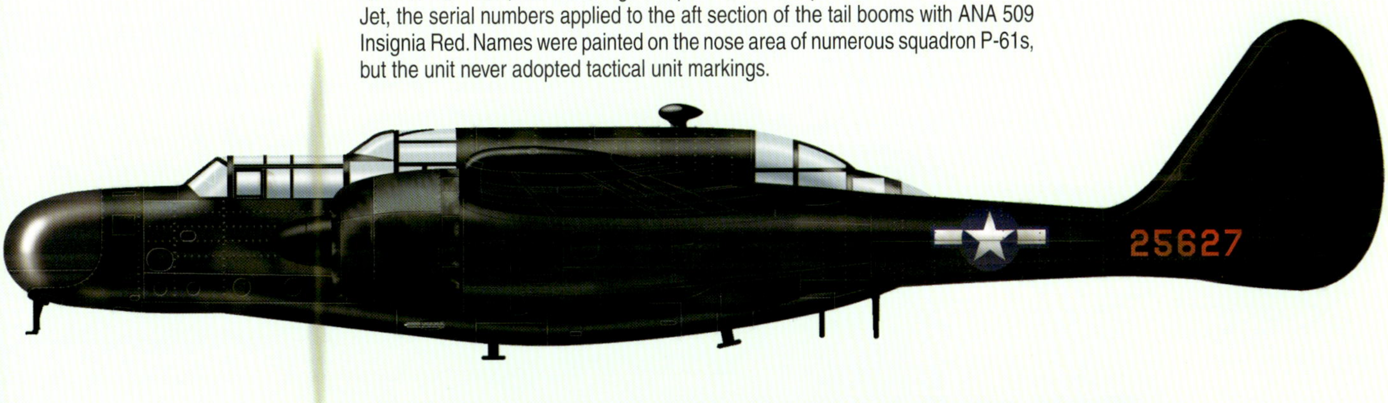

*** 3) Dinjan A/F, India**
25-May-1945

*Detachments operated TDY from: Chengkung A/F, China: 29 Jun–16 Aug 1945

*** 2) Myitkyina A/F, Burma**
c. Dec-1944

*Detachments operated TDY from: Kunming A/F, China: 18 Dec 1944–28 Jun 1945

*** 1) Pandaveswar A/F, India**
31-Oct-1944

*Detachments operated TDY from: Myitkyina A/F, Burma: 13 Nov–Dec 1944

5) Liuchow A/F, China
13-Aug-1945

4) Nanning A/F, China
26-Jul-1945

U.S.A.A.F. TRANSPORT UNITS

CHINA-BURMA-INDIA THEATER OF OPERATIONS

Tactical Markings

Because air transport units did not operate in massed air formations like the bombardment units, the need for high visibility aircraft markings was minimal at best. The few such markings adopted and depicted in the following section reflect personal rather than tactical needs. The painting on transport airframes such as *Smiley's Fleet*, *The Great SNAFU Airlines*, and others were for esprit de corps in one's group and not of any actual tactical value whatsoever—and it was effective.

From the jungles of India to the mountains of China, AAF transports moved everything from munitions to mules, and were credited as the deciding factor in the ultimate outcome of several battles and campaigns conducted by Allied forces in the CBI during WWII.

The men who flew these indispensable supply and replacement missions in the CBI were fully aware of the contributions they were making to the war effort, and their pride was reflected in the nicknames painted on the sides of their aircraft. Who wouldn't be proud to be a member of a unit known as "The Great SNAFU Fleet?"

Perhaps the most important and dangerous of these missions were flown "over the Hump." These continuous flights over the Himalayan Mountains were considered so hazardous the Air Force logged each Hump flight—coming and going—as a combat mission. This mission status was allocated to these operations not so much because of direct contact with the Japanese Air Force, but because the Himalayan air route was considered one of the most potentially dangerous in the world, rivaled only by flight operations over the Bering Sea in the northern Pacific Ocean. The Hump route ultimately earned the nickname the Aluminum Trail due to the high number of broken transports littering its mountainous route, but these flights were critical in the persecution of the war effort. Japanese ground forces closed the Burma Road in 1942, and it was not reopened to Allied supply convoys until completion of the Ledo Road in January 1945.

As with most units operating in the CBI, especially in the early years of the war, little was wasted. Even war weary aircraft was clipped of its wings and converted into everything from living space to classrooms.

India-Burma
Aug-1944

1st Combat Cargo Group

Insignia: (Unofficial)
Motto: (Unknown)
Sobriquet: (Unknown)
Constituted:
1stCmbtCrgoGp/11-Apr-1944
Activated: 15-Apr-1944

1stCmbtCrgoGp/Emblem

As is the case with so many images connected with units that served in the CBI during WWII, there is almost nothing official that can be attributed with the 1stCCG's rabbit design depicted at left. All we have are reminiscences of veterans who attest to the existence and use of this insignia by the 1stCCG during the war. Lacking any empirical evidence to the contrary, and preferring to err on the side of caution, the aforementioned emblem has been included in this text as a possible unapproved unit insignia.

1st Combat Cargo Squadron

Insignia: Approved/ 17-Jul-1944
Sobriquet: The Great SNAFU Fleet'

Constituted:
1st Combat Cargo Squadron:
11-Apr-1944
Activated: 15-Apr-1944

2d Combat Cargo Squadron

Insignia: Approved/ 17-Jul-1944

Constituted:
2d Combat Cargo Squadron:
11-Apr-1944
Activated: 15-Apr-1944

3d Combat Cargo Squadron

Insignia: Approved/ 28-Jul-1944

Constituted:
3d Combat Cargo Squadron:
11-Apr-1944
Activated: 15-Apr-1944

4th Combat Cargo Squadron

Insignia: Approved/ 17-Jul 1944

Constituted:
4th Combat Cargo Squadron:
11-Apr-1944
Activated: 15-Apr-1944

Alternate 2[D] Combat Cargo Squadron Emblems

Although the 2d CmbtCrgoSqdn had an official emblem, these two designs came into play during the squadron's deployment in the CBI. Whether these were mission emblems or unapproved replacement squadron designs is another unanswered question. To date, no historical documentation regarding either of these insignia has yet to be discovered, if in fact anything resembling a Field Order relating to either of these designs was ever issued at all.

Other than individual aircraft names painted on the nose area of some aircraft, none of the C-47 Skymasters that served with the 1st CmbtCrgoGp are known to have adopted any formal distinctive tactical unit markings. The 1stCmbtCrgoSqdn was known to have painted cabin windows olive drab on their outside surfaces. This procedure does not fall into the tactical markings category. The 3d CmbtCrgoSqdn was known to apply a number "3" enclosed by a horseshoe pattern in white on the mid-fin section of at least some of its C-47s. Just how extensive the use of this marking was within the squadron is uncertain due to the lack of any wartime documentation relating to this application.

Douglas C-47 Skytrain
1[ST]CmbtCrgoGp, c. 1944-1945

Douglas C-46 Commando
1[ST]CmbtCrgoSq, c. 1945

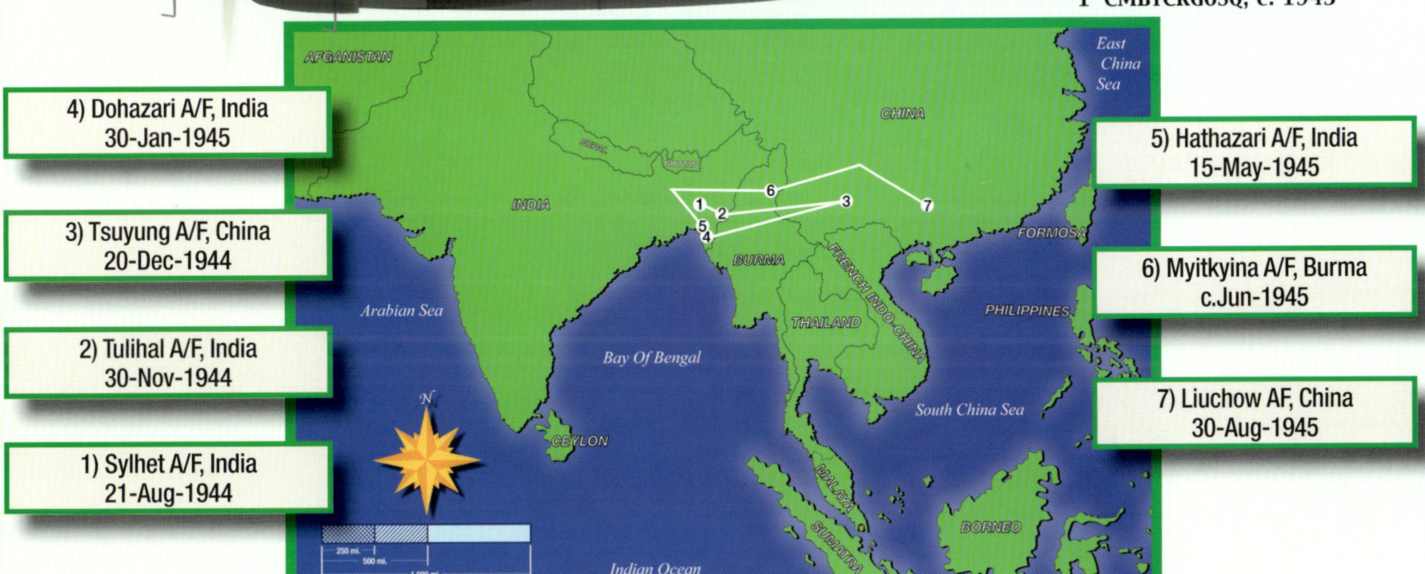

• Assigned Tenth AAF, Jun-1944 thru V-J Day •

3D Combat Cargo Group

Insignia: (unapproved)
Motto: (unknown)
Sobriquet: COM-CAR
Constituted (India):
3DCmbtCrgoGp/1 Jun 1944
Activated: 5 Jun 1944

330th TrCarrSqdn Postwar Emblem

Shortly after V-J Day, the 9th TrCarrSqdn was redesignated the 330th TrCarrSqdn, but inactivated little more than six months later (1 Oct 1945–15 Apr 1946). This unit's emblem, although short lived and never officially authorized, was deemed appropriate to include in this text.

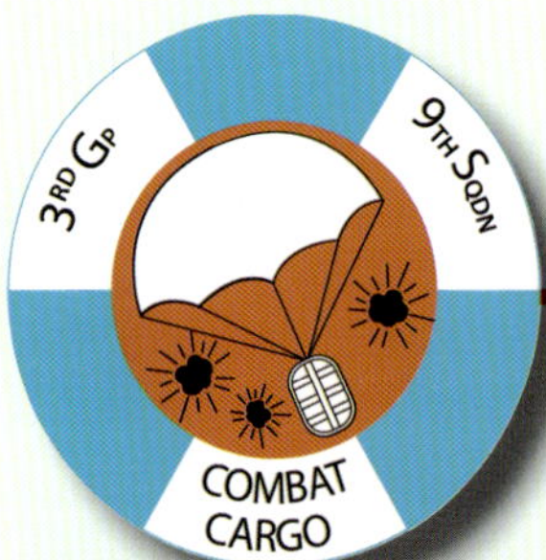

9th Combat Cargo Squadron

Insignia: (unapproved)
Sobriquet: COM-CAR IX

Constituted:
9th Combat Cargo Squadron:
1-Jan-1944
Activated: 5-Jun-1944

10th Combat Cargo Squadron

Insignia: (unapproved)
Sobriquet: COM-CAR X

Constituted:
10th Combat Cargo Squadron:
1-Jan-1944
Activated: 5-Jun-1944

11th Combat Cargo Squadron

Insignia: (unapproved)
Sobriquet:
COM-CAR XI aka Dumbo Airlines

Constituted:
11th Combat Cargo Squadron:
1-Jan-1944
Activated: 5-Jun-1944

12th Combat Cargo Squadron

Insignia: (unapproved)
Sobriquet: COM-CAR XII

Constituted:
12th Combat Cargo Squadron:
1-Jan-1944
Activated: 5-Jun-1944

Alternate Squadron Emblems

9th CmbtCrgoSqdn

12th CmbtCrgoSqdn

Squadron tactical markings were applied to the upper fin area in the form of a Roman numeral that reflected the respective Arabic squadron numbers. These devices were painted with QM 48 Identification Yellow or equivalent.

Although the proper AAF abbreviation for Combat Cargo is CmbtCrgo, the 3d CmbtCrgoGp opted to adopt COM Car as its own unique abbreviation as a unit tactical marking device. Thus, COM CAR was applied to the lower tail fin with ID Yellow using standard AAF block stencil lettering positioned immediately above and slightly larger than the aircraft serial number.

As to the serial number, the last three digits of each respective number were used as individual aircraft call signs. The first numbers of the complete serial number were often repainted black to increase in-flight legibility of the "last three" serving as each aircraft's call number.

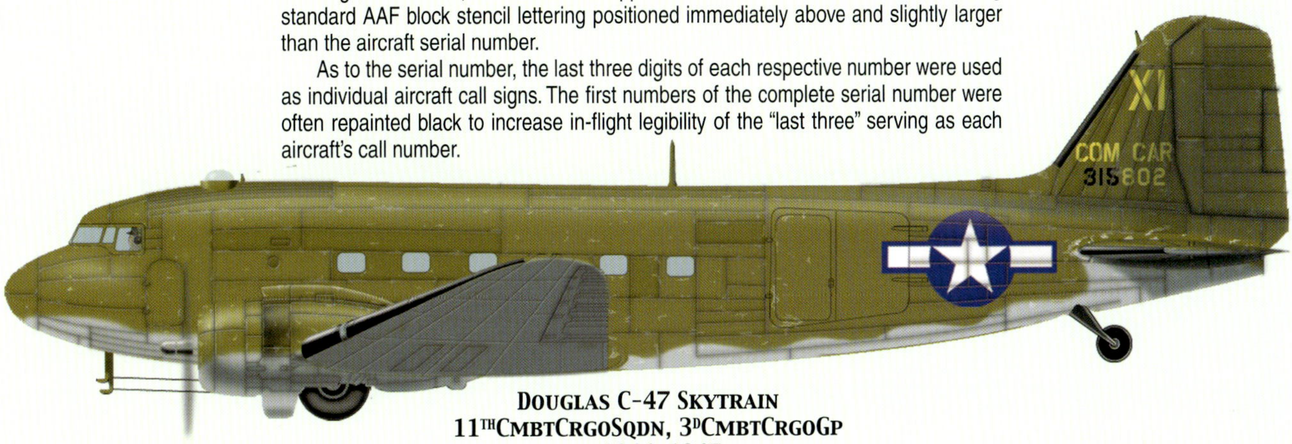

Douglas C-47 Skytrain
11thCmbtCrgoSqdn, 3dCmbtCrgoGp
c. 1944-1945

The map below shows the location of 3d CmbtCrgoGp/HQ. There were additional airfields to which the assigned squadrons of this group were stationed.

9th TCC:
Sylhet, India: 5 Jun 1944
Moran, India: 12 Jul 1944
Warazup, Burma: 27 Dec 1944
Myitkyina, Burma: 3 Jun 1945

10thCCS:
Sylhet, India: 6 June 1944
Dergon, India: 5 Aug 1944
Dinjan, India: 31 Aug 1945
Myitkyina, Burma: 30 May 1945

11th CCS:
Sylhet, India: 5 June 1944
Dinjan, India: 6 June 1944
(detachment operated from Sookerating, India, 16 June 14 1945)
Yunnani, China: 14 May 1945
Luliang, China: 20 June 1945

12th CCS:
Sylhet, India: 5 June 1944
Fenny, India: 6 June 1944
Moran, India: 1 July 1944
Tulihal, India: 1 April 1945
Ledo, India: 12 May 1945
Myitkyina, Burma: 5 June 1945

• ASSIGNED AAF/CBI, NOV-1944 THRU V-J DAY •

INDIA-CHINA DIV/ATC
15-JUN-1945

CMBTCRGO TASK FORCE
c.29-NOV-1944

4TH COMBAT CARGO GROUP

INSIGNIA: (UNKNOWN)
MOTTO: (UNKNOWN)
SOBRIQUET: (UNKNOWN)
CONSTITUTED:
4THCMBTCRGOGP/9 JUN 1944
ACTIVATED: 13 JUN 1944

13TH COMBAT CARGO SQUADRON

INSIGNIA: (UNAPPROVED)

CONSTITUTED:
13TH COMBAT CARGO SQUADRON:
9-JUN-1944
ACTIVATED: 13-JUN-1944

14TH COMBAT CARGO SQUADRON

INSIGNIA: APPROVED/ 25-NOV-1944

CONSTITUTED:
14TH COMBAT CARGO SQUADRON:
9-JUN-1944
ACTIVATED: 13-JUN-1944

15TH COMBAT CARGO SQUADRON

INSIGNIA: (UNAPPROVED)
SOBRIQUET: SMILEY'S AIRLINES

CONSTITUTED:
15TH COMBAT CARGO SQUADRON:
9-JUN-1944
ACTIVATED: 13-JUN-1944

16TH COMBAT CARGO SQUADRON

INSIGNIA: APPROVED/ 23-AUG-1944

CONSTITUTED:
16TH COMBAT CARGO SQUADRON:
9-JUN-1944
ACTIVATED: 13-JUN-1944

Other than individual aircraft names painted on the nose area of a number of 4th CmbtCrgoGp C-46 Commandos, there were no group tactical markings. This unit did not even adopt the practice of duplicating the last three digits of the serial number on the tail fin as a call sign, a practice common with other Combat Cargo Groups serving in the CB; factory applied serial numbers and tail sections remained unaltered in the group until war's end.

The sole distinctive squadron marking, albeit unofficial, was introduced by the 15th CmbtCrgoSqdn, consisting of the squadron's adopted nickname, Smiley's Airlines, being applied with Identification Yellow as a single line of text above the cabin windows. Judging from what few wartime photographs of this squadron were found, it appears several sans serif type fonts were used for these applications. By early 1945, virtually all aircraft assigned to the 15th CmbtCrgoSqdn are said to have received this squadron tag line.

CURTISS C-46 COMMANDO
15TH CMBTCRGOSQDN, 4TH CMBTCRGOGP
C. LATE 1944-1945

• Attached to Tenth AF from Twelfth AF, c.1-April thru 15-June, 1944 •

64TH Troop Carrier Group

Insignia: Approved/16-Jun-1942
Motto: Flying Support
Sobriquet: (unknown)
Constituted:
64THTrspGp/20-Nov-1940
Activated: 4-Dec-1940
Redesignated:
64THTrCarrGp/Jul-1942

Strangers in a Strange Land

The combined air echelon of the 64th TCG and 4th TCS/62d TCG was pulled out of the MTO to support operations in the CBI. For their contribution to Burmese operations (including support of Merrill's Marauders in Burma), the Tenth AF confirmed the following awards: 197 Distinguished Flying Crosses to the 64th TCG and all five Troop Carrier Squadrons (including 3 Oak Leaf Clusters), 294 Air Medals (plus 90 Clusters), five Purple Hearts, and six Distinguished Unit Citations.

SQUADRON INSIGNIA
(UNKNOWN)

16TH Troop Carrier Squadron

Insignia: (unknown)

Constituted:
16TH Transport Squadron:
20-Nov-1940
Activated: 11-Dec-1940
Redesignated:
16TH Troop Carrier Squadron
4-Jul-1942

17TH Troop Carrier Squadron

Insignia: (unapproved)

Constituted:
17TH Transport Squadron:
20-Nov-1940
Activated: 11-Dec-1940
Redesignated:
17TH Troop Carrier Squadron
4-Jul-1942

18TH Troop Carrier Squadron

Insignia: (unapproved)

Constituted:
18TH Transport Squadron:
20-Nov-1940
Activated: 11-Dec-1940
Redesignated:
18TH Troop Carrier Squadron
4-Jul-1942

35TH Troop Carrier Squadron

Insignia: (unknown)

Constituted:
35TH Transport Squadron:
20-Nov-1940
Activated: 11-Dec-1940
Redesignated:
35TH Troop Carrier Squadron
4-Jul-1942

SQUADRON INSIGNIA
(UNKNOWN)

Douglas C-47 Skytrain
4th TrCarrSqdn, 62d TrCarrGp
c. Apr through Jun-1944

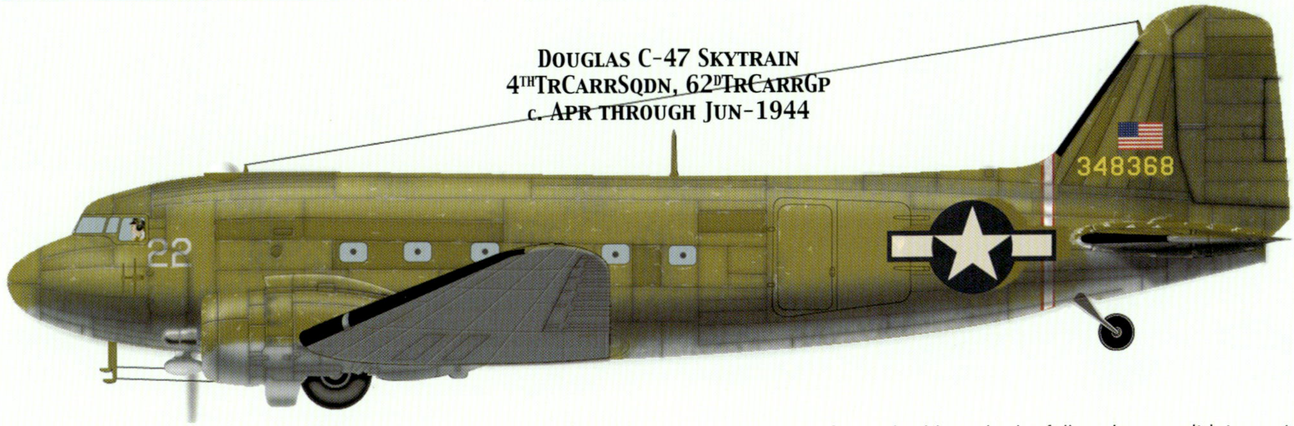

When orders were initially issued for the air echelon of the 4th TrCarrSqdn and all four squadrons of the 64th TrCarrGp to prepare for immediate temporary duty with the Tenth Air Force, everyone involved at first thought it was simply an April Fools joke. They quickly discovered the orders were anything but humorous, and within days all air crews, along with their aircraft, found themselves en route from their bases on Sicily to eastern India.

Japanese forces had launched a full scale assault into eastern India and the key city Imphal. Additional air transport was desperately needed to aid in the support and resupply of Allied ground forces confronting this massive offensive. Upon arrival, all squadrons were immediately deployed, with their respective aircraft bearing whatever markings they had when they departed from Sicily. While C-47s assigned to the 64th TrCarrGp were known to display assigned squadron numbers, the 4th TrCarrSqdn adopted no known individual tactical markings.

62d Troop Carrier Group

4th Troop Carrier Squadron

Insignia: Approved/ 17-Sep-1942

Sobriquet: Flying Jackasses

Constituted:
4th Transport Squadron (Prov): 1-Mar-1935
Redesignated:
4th Transport Squadron: 25-Jun-1935
Activated: 8-Jul-1935
Redesignated:
4th Troop Carrier Squadron: 4-Jul-1942

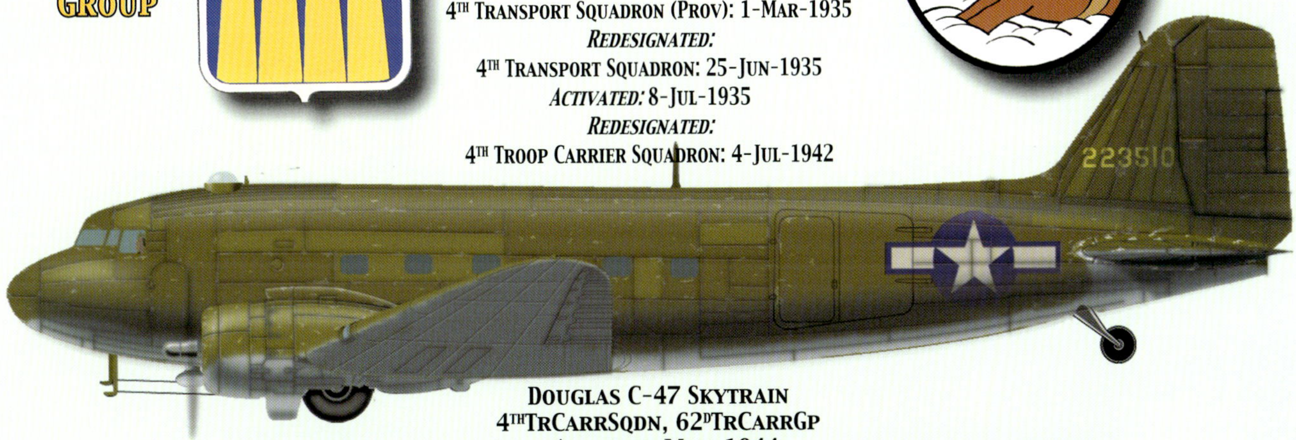

Douglas C-47 Skytrain
4th TrCarrSqdn, 62d TrCarrGp
c. Apr thru May-1944

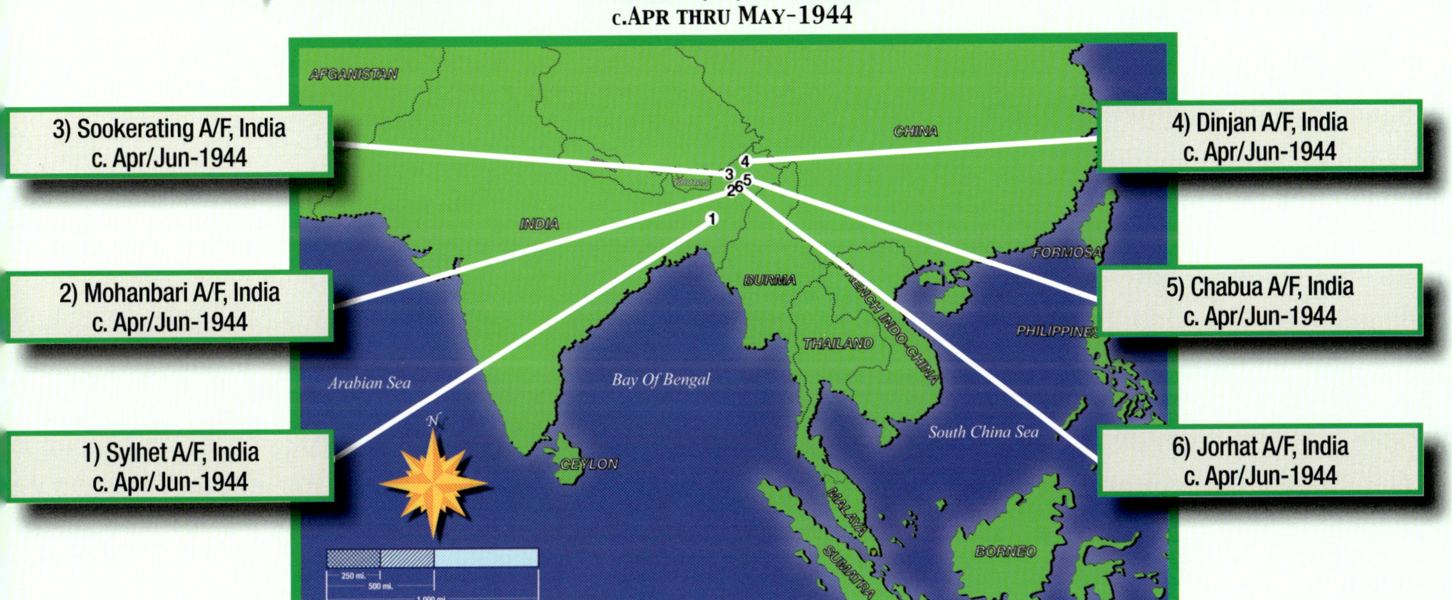

• ASSIGNED TO TENTH AF, FEBRUARY 1944 THRU V-J DAY •

443D TROOP CARRIER GROUP

INSIGNIA: (UNAPPROVED)

MOTTO: (UNKNOWN)

SOBRIQUET: (UNKNOWN)

CONSTITUTED:

1ST TROOP CARRIER GROUP/ 25-MAY-1943

ACTIVATED: 1-OCT-1943

• Modified 1st Tr CarrSqdn design •
The image above is a layered leather 1st TCS patch of WWII. The added "BMA" letters stand for "Burma-Myitkyina Airlines"; it was an optional addition to some emblem applications following the squadron's resupply and airborne operations in the Myitkyina Campaign of May 1944.

1ST TROOP CARRIER SQUADRON

INSIGNIA: (UNAPPROVED)

SOBRIQUET: TIGER FLEET

CONSTITUTED:
1ST TRANSPORT SQUADRON (PROV)
1-MAR-1935
ACTIVATED: 15-JUL-1935
REDESIGNATED:
1ST TRANSPORT SQUADRON
25-JUN-1935
1ST TROOP CARRIER SQUADRON
4-JUL-1942

1-25

2D TROOP CARRIER SQUADRON

INSIGNIA: APPROVED/ 5-MAY-1942

CONSTITUTED:
2D TRANSPORT SQUADRON (PROV)
1-MAR-1935
ACTIVATED: 15-JUL-1935
REDESIGNATED:
2D TRANSPORT SQUADRON
28-JUN-1935
2D TROOP CARRIER SQUADRON
4-JUL-1942

NO COLOR ASSIGNED 26-50

27TH TROOP CARRIER SQUADRON

INSIGNIA: APPROVED/ 25-FEB-1943

CONSTITUTED:
27TH TRANSPORT SQUADRON
19-JAN-1942
ACTIVATED: 1-FEB-1942
REDESIGNATED:
27TH TROOP CARRIER SQUADRON
4-JUL-1942

NO COLOR ASSIGNED A+ SQUADRON ASSIGNED INDIVIDUAL AIRCRAFT LETTER OR NUMBER CODE

315TH TROOP CARRIER SQUADRON

INSIGNIA: (UNAPPROVED)

CONSTITUTED:
315TH TROOP CARRIER SQUADRON
8-DEC-1943
ACTIVATED: 1-JAN-1944

NO COLOR ASSIGNED 51-75

Alternate Late War Squadron Emblems

2D TrCarrSqdn

27TH TrCarrSqdn

The two unit emblem designs seen above were unapproved alternate emblems adopted by each squadron late in their CBI deployment. While both of these squadrons had insignia approved by the War Department's Heraldry Board, each nevertheless preferred to replace their official designs with alternate images, a practice that created a major headache for future USAAF unit researchers.

322D TrCarrSqdn

Assigned first to the Fourteenth AF in September 1944 and later the Tenth AF (August 1945), the 322dTCS was attached to the 443dTCG shortly after the surrender of Japan and earned a Distinguished Unit Citation for operations conducted 5–30 September 1945.

Douglas C-47 Skytrain
27TH TrCarrSqdn, 443D TrCarrGp
6-Mar-1944 thru V-J Day

Curtiss C-46 Commando
1TH TrCarrSqdn, 443D TrCarrGp
c. Spring 1945 thru V-J Day

All four squadrons assigned to the 443d TrCarrGp began operations with the C-47 Skytrain, employing the squadron marking codes as depicted on the facing page. While three of the squadrons utilized a two-digit numerical system, the 27th incorporated this same system in addition to a letter-number combination (see illustration above and photo at left). In all cases, these codes were applied in white to the upper rudder surface area. The 27th TCS was known to have duplicated the second letter/number aft the side cockpit windows.

In early 1945, the 1st, 2nd, and 315th squadrons began transitioning to the C-46 Commando, leaving the 27th the sole unit in the 443d TCGp still operating the C-47. Only the 1st TCS is known to have adopted any sort of tactical marking, consisting of applying the squadron nickname Tiger Fleet to the upper mid-cabin area in white. White cowling rings including horizontal triangular flashing were also applied to 27th TCS C-46s. It is uncertain whether any of the C-46 squadrons adopted the respective tail markings used earlier on their C-47s.

* 3 & 5) Dinjan A/F, India
9-Jul-1944 / 11-May-1945

2) Sookerating A/F, India
9-Jun-1944

1) Sylhet A/F, India
15-Feb-1944

4) Ledo A/F, India
8-Oct-1944

6) Chihkiang A/F, China
28-Aug-1945

Note: Several squadrons were stationed temporarily at stations not indicated on the map.

U.S.A.A.F. BOMBARDMENT UNITS

CHINA-BURMA-INDIA THEATER OF OPERATIONS

Tactical Markings

Bombing efforts early in the CBI Theater were slow getting started for a wide range of reasons; those sorties that were mounted were mostly tactical in nature, involving relatively small numbers of aircraft. During this early period there was little need for distinctive unit markings. A dozen or so medium or heavy bombers all from the same group had little need for high visibility tail markings on a mission. Most groups found two or three digit numbers affixed to outboard tail surfaces were fully effective for their mission needs.

This condition was to change, as the AAF bombing campaigns quickly expanded in number and objectives. While the emphasis of the medium bombers remained primarily tactical in nature, mission objectives of the rapidly growing Heavy and Very Heavy bomb units assigned to the CBI became ever more strategic. Larger formations of bombers from different groups required a quick, easy method of group/squadron recognition to maintain effective, coordinated mission results.

These were similar problems facing AAF units in the European Theater, and similar solutions were applied in both cases. Although the bombardment units in the CBI started using high visibility markings similar to the type used in the ETO, the Eighth AF were second to none in the use of color and intricacy, and expanded to included tail, horizontal stabilizer, and wing surfaces. These additional applications of tactical markings within the Eighth directly reflected the size and complexity of strategic bombardment operations taking place in Europe. The similar type of bombing operations carried out against Japan were numerically much smaller than those conducted against Germany. Consequently, they did not require as ornate and as complex a tactical marking system as that employed by the AAF in the Pacific campaign.

Emblems

As with AAF units in all other theaters during the war, CBI bomber crews adopted their fair share of group and squadron emblems. Some of these incorporated images reflecting their particular area of operations: China-based squadron designs featured dragons, while cobras and tigers were depicted in some India-based unit insignia.

Numerous emblems adopted by some of the more newly constituted units were never approved for display and are therefore excluded from official US Air Force histories.

Some groups/squadrons made extensive use of their emblems on their respective aircraft, with early applications being applied by hand and later examples dry transfer decals.

• Assigned Twentieth AF: December 1944 thru V-J Day •

313TH BOMB WG
DECEMBER-1944

XXI BOMBER COMD
DECEMBER-1944

6TH BOMBARDMENT GROUP (VH)

INSIGNIA: APPROVED/ 22-JAN-1924

MOTTO: READY TO DEFEND

SOBRIQUET: (UNKNOWN)

ORGANIZED: 3D OBS GP/ 30-SEP-1919

CONSTITUTED & CONSOLIDATED:
6TH BOMB GP (VH)/ 28-MAR-1944

ACTIVATED: 19-APR-1944

Alternate 6th Bombardment Group Design
This image was a simplified version of the groups official emblem and incorporated elements to the 2nd pattern tactical tail markings displayed by the 6thBG later in the war.

24TH BOMBARDMENT SQUADRON (VH)

INSIGNIA: APPROVED/ 24-NOV-1944

CONSTITUTED:
24TH BOMBARDMENT SQUADRON (VH):
28-MAR-1944
ACTIVATED: 1-APR-1944

39TH BOMBARDMENT SQUADRON (VH)

INSIGNIA: (UNAPPROVED)

CONSTITUTED:
39TH BOMBARDMENT SQUADRON (VH):
28-MAR-1944
ACTIVATED: 1-APR-1944

40TH BOMBARDMENT SQUADRON (VH)

INSIGNIA: (UNAPPROVED)

CONSTITUTED:
40TH BOMBARDMENT SQUADRON (VH):
28-MAR-1944
ACTIVATED: 1-APR-1944

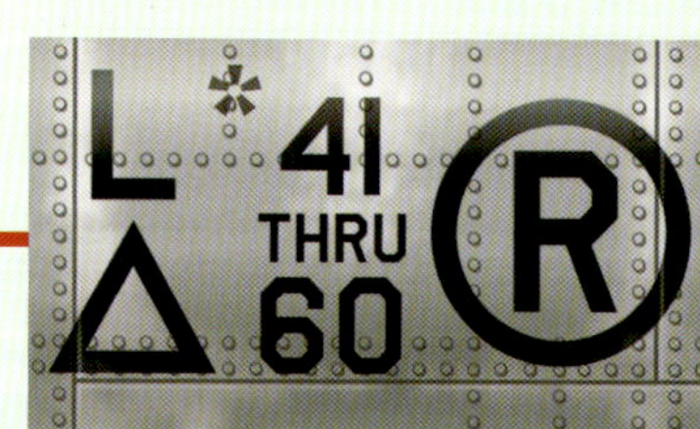

* Assigned number blocks changed with the introduction of new tactical markings c. April 1945. Revised numbers are believed to have been: 24th BS, 1-25; 39th BS, 25-50; and 40th BS, 50-70

6th BombGp/B-29s
Second Pattern Tactical Markings: c.December thru April 1945

Shortly after taking up station on the island of Tinian, the 6th BG adopted the tactical markings depicted (right). All markings were applied vertically on the tail fin, with the top upper case letter "L" denoting the 6th BombGp, the equilateral triangle representing the 313th BombWg, and the bottom Arabic number being the assigned aircraft-in-squadron designation. Factory applied serial numbers were retained with this early tactical tail marking system.

A few ships bearing these first pattern tactical markings displayed red engine cowlings, but it is unknown just how widespread the practice was.

6th BombGp/B-29s
Second Pattern Tactical Markings: c.April 1945 thru V-J Day

In April 1945, a new group marking was adopted within the 6th BombGp consisting of a large uppercase "R" centered in a wide circular outline. Both devices were directed to be affixed in black to the tail surface of all the group's B-29s; thus, the Circle-R became the new tactical marking for the unit, with assigned black aircraft numbers relocated to the rear portion of the fuselage and a smaller version duplicated on the forward nose area. In some cases the last four digits of the serial number were reapplied to the lower fin area, but this practice appears to have been limited within the group.

By war's end, virtually all B-29s in the 6th BombGp were adorned with red tail tips and matching engine cowlings. Lead ships within the group were recognized with the addition of two wide red vertical stripes encircling the forward empennage area.

In April 1945, the 313th BombWg's order to replace all individual nose art (especially the nude women) with a modified version of the 6th BombGp emblem became effective. Under the new guidelines, individual aircraft names were permitted as long as vulgarity and profanity were not used. Several variations of the group's pirate image were adopted for this use. The most popular version incorporated a trailing flames pattern wherein the aircraft name was in the white area of the modified design. By war's end, virtually all B-29s operating with the 6th BombGp bore these tactical unit markings.

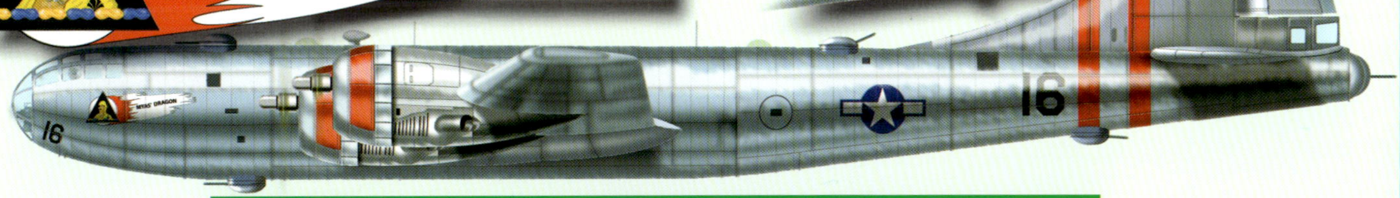

• Assigned Tenth AF: March-1942 thru V-J Day •

7th Bombardment Group (H)

Insignia: Approved: 30-Jan-1933
Motto: Death From Above
Sobriquet: (unknown)
Organized: 1st Army Obs Gp/1-Oct-1919
Redesignated: 7th Gp (Obs)/ Mar-1921
7th Bomb Gp/ 1923
7th Bomb Gp (H)/ 1939
Activated: 1-Jun-1928

11th BmbSqdn • 22D BombSqdn
Both of these squadrons were originall assigned to the 7th BG early in the war, bu were transferred to the 341st BG in Septembe 1942.

The eagle emblem of the 22dBS (above was originally adopted by this unit while servin in India, but was ultimately rejected for officia use, resulting in an alternate desig subsequently submitted and formerly approve by the Heraldic Section in March 1945.

9th Bombardment Squadron (H)

Insignia: Approved/26-Jul-1932
(From WWI Emblem)
Sobriquet: The Flying Cobras

Organized:
9th Aero Sqdn/14-Jun-17
Redesignated:
9th Sqdn/14-Mar-1921
9th Obs Sqdn/25-Jan-1923
9th Bomb Sqdn/24-Mar-1923
9th Bomb Sqdn (H)/6-Dec-1939
Activated: 1-Apr-1931

No color assigned — Aircraft 20-39 Number-In-Squadron

436th Bombardment Squadron (H)

Insignia: Approved/2-Feb-1924
(From WWI Emblem)
Sobriquet: The Outlaws

Organized:
9th Aero Sqdn/14-Jun-17
Redesignated:
9th Sqdn/14-Mar-1921
9th Obs Sqdn/25-Jan-1923
9th Bomb Sqdn/24-Mar-1923
9th Bomb Sqdn (H)/6-Dec-1939
Activated: 1-Apr-1931

No color assigned — Aircraft 60-79 Number-In-Squadron

492d Bombardment Squadron (H)

Insignia: (unapproved)
Sobriquet:
Eager Beaver Bombing Co.

Organized:
80th Aero Sqdn/15-Aug-1917
Redesignated:
492d Aero Sqdn/1-Feb-1918
492d Bomb Sqdn (H)/19-Sep-1942
Reactivated: 25-Oct-1942

No color assigned — Aircraft 80-99 Number-In-Squadron

493d Bombardment Squadron (H)

Insignia: (unapproved)
Sobriquet: (unknown)

Constituted:
493d Bomb Sqdn (H)/19-Sep-1942
Activated: 25-Oct-1942

No color assigned — Aircraft 40-59 Number-In-Squadron

• Squadron Emblem Variations •

9th BombSqdn(H)

Each of these four designs represented their respective units sometime during WWII. The exact chronology of use has been obscured with the passage of time due to the unofficial status of all the emblems involved, but there is enough surviving physical evidence to verify the existence and use of these insignia in a variety of forms during the war.

492d BombSqdn(H)

7th BombGp/B-24s
First Tactical Markings: c. 1942–1943

The original tactical markings employed on B-24s of the 7th BG consisted of the application of a squadron's assigned numerical designation in black to the outboard fin surfaces. The factory applied serial numbers appear to have been painted over in most wartime photographs.

9th BombSqdn
Early Markings

7th BombGp/B-24s
Final Tactical Markings: c. 1944 thru V-J Day

9th BombSqdn

436th BombSqdn

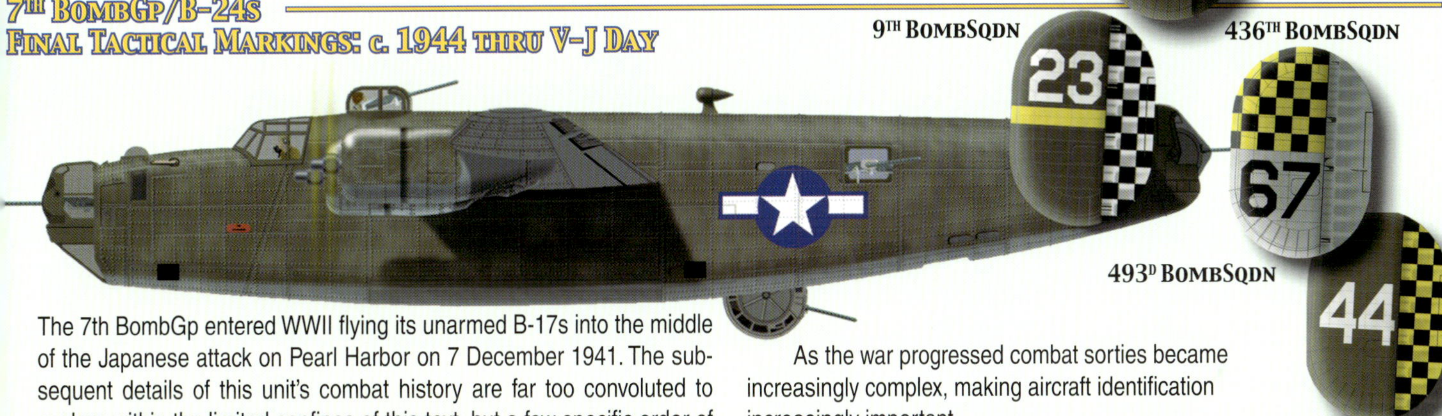

493d BombSqdn

The 7th BombGp entered WWII flying its unarmed B-17s into the middle of the Japanese attack on Pearl Harbor on 7 December 1941. The subsequent details of this unit's combat history are far too convoluted to explore within the limited confines of this text, but a few specific order of battle details are necessary: the 7th BG was originally comprised of the 9th, 11th, 22d, and 436th Bombardment Squadrons. The 11th and 22d BombSqdns were transferred to the 341st BombGp and replaced by two newly formed units—the 492d and 493d Bombardment Squadrons—with the entire group fully converted to the B-24 Liberator. Early combat operations did not require elaborate tactical markings and markings were confined to number-in-squadron tail markings until 1944.

As the war progressed combat sorties became increasingly complex, making aircraft identification increasingly important.

By war's end, virtually all B-24s assigned to the 7th BG bore the squadron tail markings depicted above—with one notable exception. For some reason no tactical markings for the 492d Bombardment Squadron have turned up. Although a two digit numerical series was authorized for use by the 492d squadron, no empirical evidence has surfaced that validates the applied use of these devices, nor any other tactical tail markings, such as those adopted by the other three squadrons in the group.

4 & 6) Pandaveswar A/F, India
12-Dec-1942 / 5-Oct-1944

2) Dum-Dum A/F, India
30-May-1942

1 & 3) Karachi A/F, India
12-Mar-1942 / 9-Sep-1942

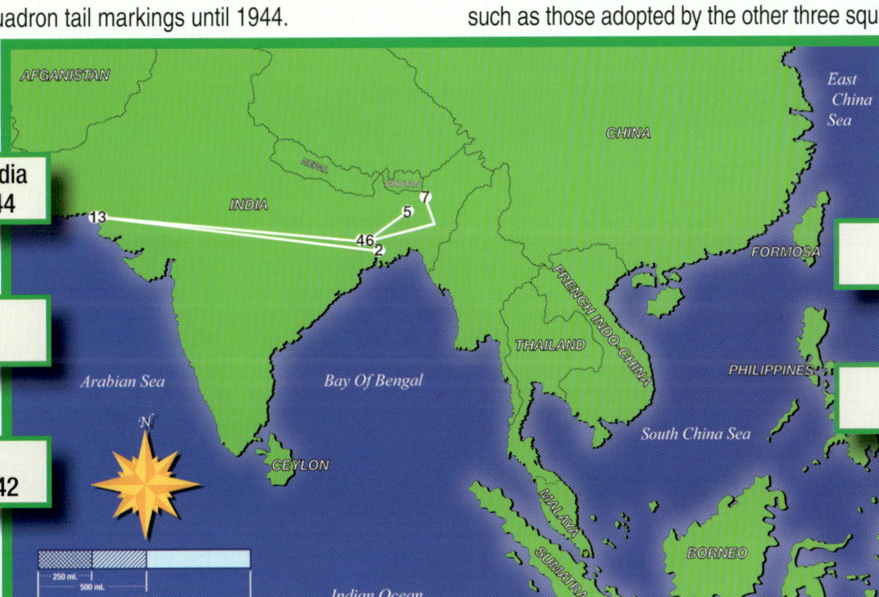

5) Kurmitola A/F, India
17-Jan-1944

7) Tezpur A/F, India
7-Jun-1945

Note: The airfields on the map indicate the duty stations of Headquarters, 7th Bomb Group. The 9th, 436th, and 492d Bomb Sqdns were stationed temporarily at additional airfields far too numerous to include.

• Assigned Twentieth AF: December 1944 thru V-J Day •

313TH Bomb Wg
December-1944

XXI Bomber Comd
December-1944

9TH Bombardment Group (VH)

Insignia: Approved/ 20-Mar-1924
Motto: Always Ready
Sobriquet: (unknown)
Authorized: 9TH Gp (Obs)/19-Jul-1922
Organized: 1-Aug-1922
Redesignated:
9TH Bomb Group/ 1935
9TH Bomb Gp (M)/ 1939
9TH Bomb Gp (H)/ 1940
9TH Bomb Gp (VH)/ Mar 1944

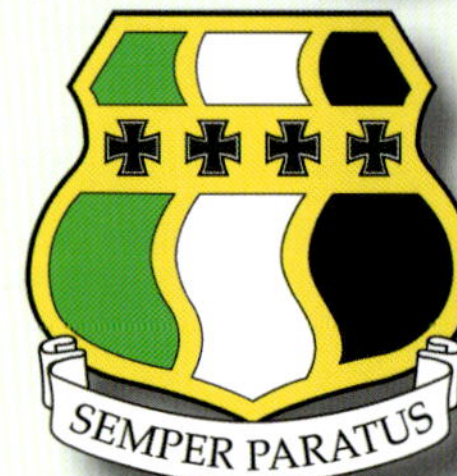

Modified 9th Bombardment Group Emblem

This simplified variation of the approved unit emblem was used in preference to the more complex authorized design (left) and even appeared on the cover of *War Journal*, the official 1945 published historical record of the 9th BG's CBI combat operations.

1ST Bombardment Squadron (VH)

Insignia: Approved/ 14-Jul-1931

Organized:
1ST Provisional Aero Squadron/ 5-Mar-1913
Redesignated:
1ST Aero Squadron/ 8-Dec-1913
1ST Obs Squadron/ 25-Jan-1923
1ST Bombardment Squadron/ 1-Mar-1935
1ST Bombardment Squadron (M)/ 6-Dec-1939
1ST Bombardment Squadron (H)/ 20-Nov-1940
1ST Bombardment Squadron (VH)/ 28-Mar-1944

5TH Bombardment Squadron (VH)

Insignia: Approved/ 27-May-1924

Organized: 5TH Aero Squadron/ 5-May-1917
Redesignated:
Squadron A-Souther Field, GA/ 15-Jul-1918
5TH Aero Squadron/ 24-Oct-1919
5TH Squadron/ 14-Mar-1921
5TH Observation Squadron/ 25-Jan-1923
5TH Bombardment Squadron/ 1-Mar-1935
5TH Bombardment Squadron (M)/ 6-Dec-1939
5TH Bombardment Squadron (H)/ 20-Nov-1940
5TH Bombardment Squadron (VH)/ 28-Mar-1944

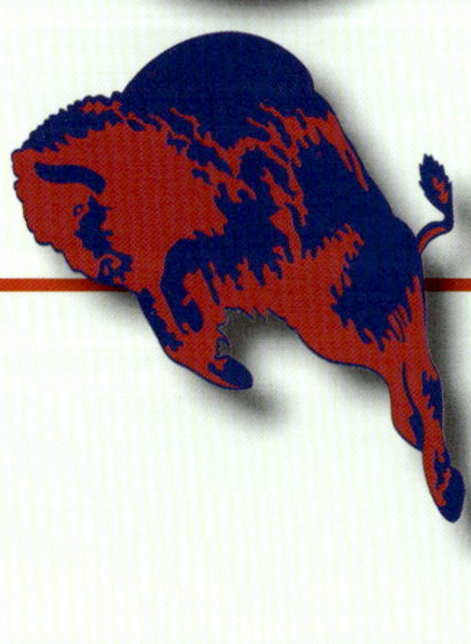

99TH Bombardment Squadron (VH)

Insignia: Approved/ 4-Mar-1924

Organized: 99TH Aero Squadron/ 21-Aug-1917
Redesignated:
99TH Squadron/ 14-Mar-1921
99TH Observation Squadron/ 25-Jan-1923
99TH Bombardment Squadron/ 1-Mar-1935
99TH Bombardment Squadron (M)/ 6-Dec-1939
99TH Bombardment Squadron (H)/ 20-Nov-1940
99TH Bombardment Squadron (VH)/ 28-Mar-1944

Evolution Of A Squadron Emblem

The color buffalo artwork (left) was the first insignia of the 99th Aero Squadron and dates to 4 May 1918, immediately prior to the squadron going to war in France with the US Fifth Corps Observation Group. Following WWI, this same image was submitted and subsequently approved by the secretary of war on 4 March 1924.

Long before this insignia was officially recognized there were some that apparently did not take to the "abstract" design of the original emblem, as evidenced by the accompanying photo of one of the squadron's WWI French built Salmson SA2. A request to officially revise the original buffalo image was submitted on 15 October 1943, but the request was denied. In spite of this, the design (facing page) has become the "official—unapproved" WWII emblem for the 99th BG.

9th BombGp/B-29s First Pattern Tactical Markings: c. January 1945

Original squadron/group tactical markings were consistent with 313th BW specifications (see the images at right). In April 1945, new 313th BW tactical markings were ordered. As seen below, the new group Circle-X dominated the entire tail section. In most cases the original serial numbers were removed with this new application, but in some cases these numbers were simply over painted. Two digit number-in-squadron designators were relocated to the rear fuselage, with a smaller version duplicated on the forward nose area. A new addition to the group's marking scheme was the use of ANA Insignia White as the unit's color designator, which was applied to engine cowlings and tail tips. 313th BW Command Stripes (below) were also adopted at this time.

9th BombGp/B-29s Second Pattern Tactical Markings: c. May 1945 through V-J Day

• Assigned Ninth AF: Jul-1942 • Twelfth AF: Aug-1943 • Tenth AF: Mar-1944 thru V-J Day •

57th Bomb Wing

Northwest African Tactical Air Force

IX Bomber Command

*12th Bombardment Group (M)

Insignia: Approved/ 3-Feb-1942

Motto: The Spirt Conquers All

Sobriquet: The Earthquakers

Constituted: 12th Bomb Gp (L)/20-Oct-1940

Redesignated: 12th Bomb Gp (M)/ Dec-1941

Activated: 15-Jan-1941

This Disney design was developed for the 82d BombSqdn(L) shortly after the unit was activated as a dive bombing squadron at McChord A/F in Washington state. The Bull Dog insignia (below) was the replacement emblem developed shortly after the 82d was subsequently redesignated a Medium Bombardment unit.

81st Bombardment Squadron (M)

Insignia: Approved/ 6-Jan-1942
Sobriquet: Battering Rams
aka The Billy Goats

Constituted:
81st Bomb Sqdn (L)/ 20-Nov-1940
Redesignated:
81st Bomb Sqdn (M)/ 30-Dec-1941
Activated: 15-Jan-1941

No Color Assigned — Aircraft 1-25 Number-In-Squadron

82d Bombardment Squadron (M)

Insignia: Approved/ 24-Dec-1941
Sobriquet: Bull Dogs

Constituted:
82d Bomb Sqdn (L)/ 20-Nov-1940
Redesignated:
82d Bomb Sqdn (M)/ 30-Dec-1941
Activated: 15-Jan-1941

No Color Assigned — Aircraft 26-51 Number-In-Squadron

83d Bombardment Squadron (M)

Insignia: Approved/ 8-Aug-1944
Sobriquet: Black Angels

Constituted:
83d Bomb Sqdn (L)/ 20-Nov-1940
Redesignated:
83d Bomb Sqdn (M)/ 30-Dec-1941
Activated: 15-Jan-1941

No Color Assigned — Aircraft 52-75 Number-In-Squadron

434th Bombardment Squadron (M)

Insignia: Approved/ 18-Feb-1942
Sobriquet: Four & Three-Quarters
aka The Cyclones

Constituted:
19th Rcn Sqdn (L)/ 20-Nov-1940
Redesignated:
94th Bomb Sqdn (L)/ 14-Aug-1941
94th Rcn Sqdn (M)/ 30-Dec-1940
434th Bomb Sqdn (M)/ 22-Apr-1942
Activated: 15-Jan-1941

No Color Assigned — Aircraft 76-99 Number-In-Squadron

* Served earlier in combat in the MTO: refer to *Battle Colors/Vol.IV*

• No Rest For The Weary •

After approximately eighteen months of continuous combat sorties in the EAME Theater, instead of a breather, the 12th Bombardment Group was transferred from Italy to India for additional operations in the CBI.

The 12th BombGp was transferred en total, including flight and ground crews and their assigned inventory of B-25J and H series Mitchell medium bombers. These aircraft came with existing number-in-squadron code designators that remained unchanged with the group's reassignment to the CBI.

These markings were simple and straightforward, with no known squadron color designations involved. Each individual aircraft code was applied with white paint to the outboard surfaces of the vertical tails. Although aircraft serial numbers were retained, it appears these devices were reapplied after reaching India using black paint, replacing the original factory applied Insignia Yellow digits.

As in the EAME, there is no evidence the 12th BombGp used any type of command ship designators on its aircraft in the CBI.

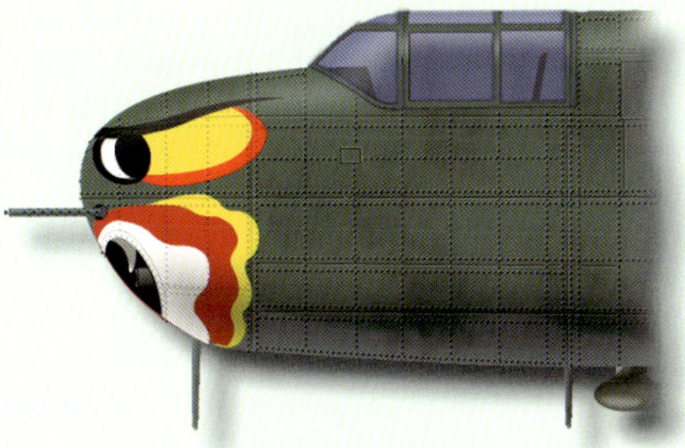

• Facing The Facts •

In researching wartime photographic prints of the 12th BombGp, a number of images will be encountered depicting the group's B-25s adorned with Demon faces affixed to the frontal nose area. While many of this unit's B-25s were in fact painted in this manner, these Demon faces were never adopted as an official group or squadron tactical marking device, as was the case with some other units (e.g., 38thBombGp(M) of the Fifth AF—refer to *Battle Colors/Vol. V*). These painted demon noses may have at one time been intended to be adopted as a tactical marking for the 12th BombGp, but if such was the case, it never came to pass.

81TH BOMBSQDN

1) Tezgan A/F, India
c. 21-Mar-1944

2 & 4) Pandaveswar A/F, India
13-Jun-1944 / 8-Jun-1945

3) Fenny A/F, India
16-Jul-1944

Note: Refer to *Battle Colors/ Vol.IV* for station assignments with the Ninth and Twelfth AF.

• ASSIGNED TWENTIETH AF: C.MARCH/APRIL 1945 THRU V-J DAY •

315TH BOMBARDMENT WING

XXI BOMBER COMMAND

16TH BOMBARDMENT GROUP (VH)

INSIGNIA: (UNKNOWN)
MOTTO: (UNKNOWN)
CONSTITUTED:
16TH BOMB GP (VH)/28-MAR-1944
ACTIVATED: 1-APR-1944

15TH BOMBARDMENT SQUADRON (VH)

INSIGNIA: APPROVED/ 13-APR-1945

CONSTITUTED:
15TH BOMB SQDN (VH)/28-MAR-1944
ACTIVATED: 1-APR-1944

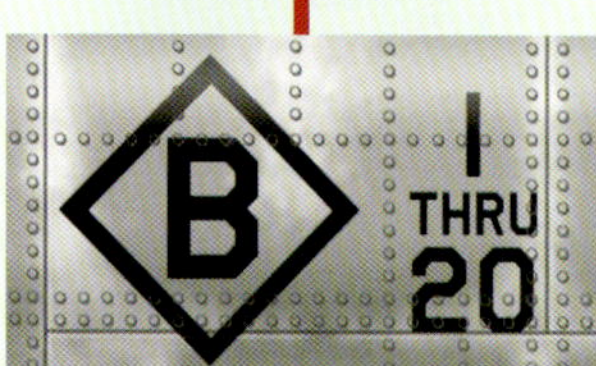

16TH BOMBARDMENT SQUADRON (VH)

INSIGNIA: APPROVED/ 3-AUG-1945

CONSTITUTED:
16TH BOMB SQDN (VH)/ 28-MAR-1944
ACTIVATED: 1-APR-1944

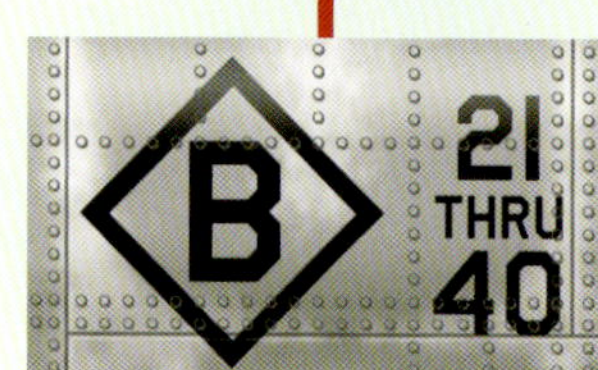

17TH BOMBARDMENT SQUADRON (VH)

INSIGNIA: APPROVED/ 30-JUN-1945

CONSTITUTED:
17TH BOMB SQDN (VH)/ 28-MAR-1944
ACTIVATED: 1-APR-1944

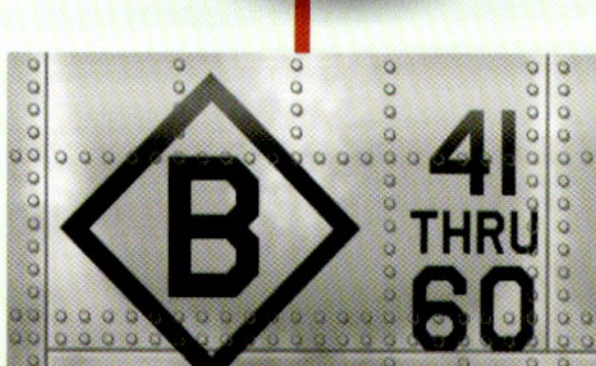

21ST BOMBARDMENT SQUADRON (VH)

INSIGNIA: (UNKNOWN)

CONSTITUTED:
21ST BOMB SQDN (VH)/ 28-MAR-1944
ACTIVATED: 1-APR-1944

INACTIVATED: 10-MAY-1944
REACTIVATED: 1-JUN-1944

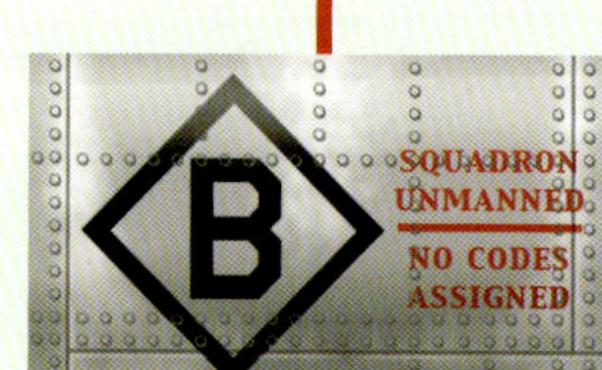

16TH BombGp/B-29s
Tactical Markings: c. March 1945 through V-J Day

As was the case with all 315th Bombardment Wing tactical markings, those assigned to the 16th BombSqdn were simple and colorless, with the Triangle B configuration dominating the entire vertical fin and rudder tail assembly. Consistent with 315th BombWg policy, these devices were applied in black to both sides of the tail assembly, with the original aircraft serial numbers either entirely or at least partially removed.

Individual aircraft were identified with assigned one- or two-digit number-in-squadron codes applied in black immediately aft the national emblem on both sides of the rear fuselage.

All B-29s assigned to the 16th BombGp were B series, recognizable by their lack of gun turrets, with the exception of the rear tail gun position. The AN/APQ-7 Eagle Radar and AN/APG-15 rear turret aiming radar gave the B series a distinctive profile.

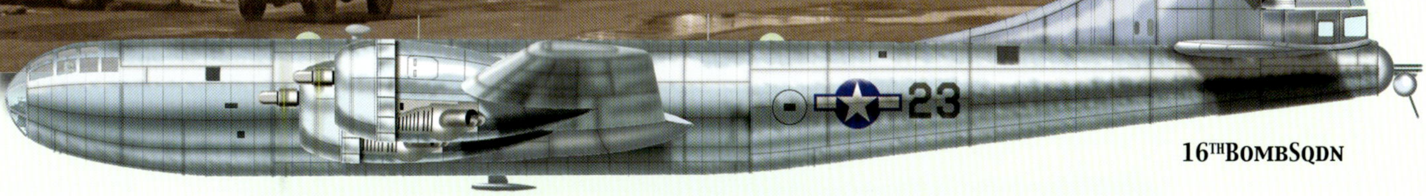

16TH BombSqdn

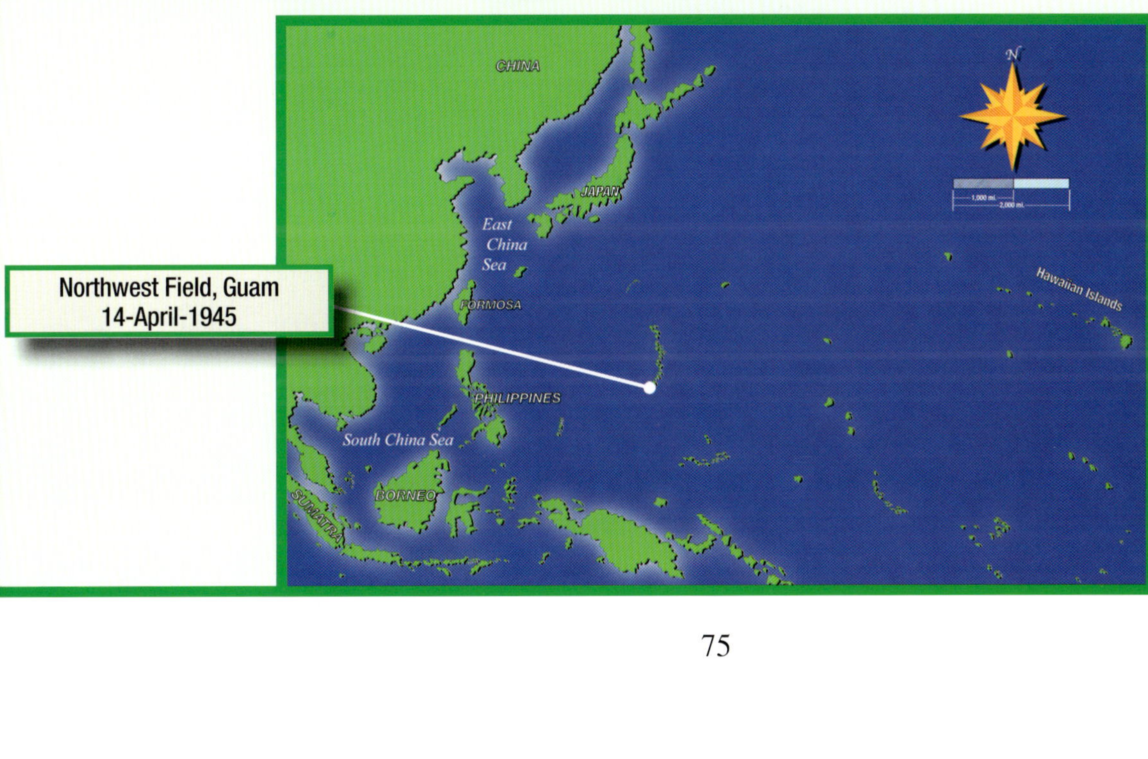

• Assigned Twentieth AF: c.March/April-1944 thru V-J Day •

314th BombWg
April-1944

XXI Bomber Comd
April-1944

19th Bombardment Group (VH)

Insignia: Approved/ 19-Oct-1936
Motto: On Wings We Conquer
Authorized: 19th Obs Gp/ 18-Oct-1927
Redesignated: 19th Bomb Gp/1929
19th Bomb Gp (H)/ 1939
19th Bomb Gp (VH)/ Apr-1944
Activated: 24-Jun-1942/ 1-Apr-1944

• Alternate 28th Bomb Sqdn Emblem
This variation artwork was often used as substitute image in preference to the original approved WWI design.

28th Bombardment Squadron (VH)

Insignia: Approved/ 14-Feb-1924
From WWI Emblem

Organized:
28th Aero Sqdn/ 22-Jun-1917
Reconstituted:
28th Sqdn/ 9-Jun-1922
Redesignated:
28th Bomb Sqdn/ 25-Jan-1923
28th Bomb Sqdn (M)/ 6-Dec-1939
28th Bomb Sqdn (H)/ 16-Nov-1941
28th Bomb Sqdn (VH)/ 28-Mar-1944

30th Bombardment Squadron (VH)

Insignia: Approved/ 9-Jan-1933

Organized:
30th Aero Sqdn/ 13-Jun-1917
Reconstituted:
30th Bomb Sqdn/ 24-Mar-1923
Redesignated:
30th Bomb Sqdn/ 25-Jan-1923
30th Bomb Sqdn (H)/ 6-Dec-1939
30th Bomb Sqdn (VH)/ 1-Apr-1944

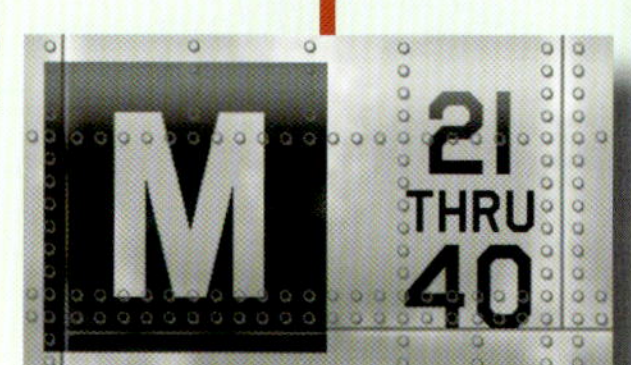

93d Bombardment Squadron (VH)

Insignia: *Approved*/ 22-Apr-1942
From WWI Emblem

Organized:
93d Aero Sqdn/ 21-Aug-1917
Reconstituted:
93d Bomb Sqdn/ 1-Mar-1935
Redesignated:
93d Bomb Sqdn (H)/ 20-Oct-1939
93d Bomb Sqdn (VH)/ 1-Apr-1944

19th BombGp/B-29s
Tactical Markings: c.April 1945 through V-J Day

Group markings consisted mainly of a large black square encompassing the lower tail fin and rudder surface areas. The group designator—an upper case letter "M"—was centered and masked out on this square, letting the metal surface show through as the letter image. Fin serial numbers were either removed prior to application of this device or simply over painted. The small upper case letter "A"s (see top two photos) were the tactical markings of the 497th BombGp, the unit from which these aircraft were transferred.

Numerical codes were assigned to each squadron and were applied in black to the rear fuselage, aft the national emblem.

A duplicate letter "M" and the aircraft serial number were also applied in black to the center outfacing surfaces of the number one and four engine cowlings. By war's end, the color ANA 506 Orange Yellow would be adopted as a letter/numeral fill color for all 314th BombWg groups.

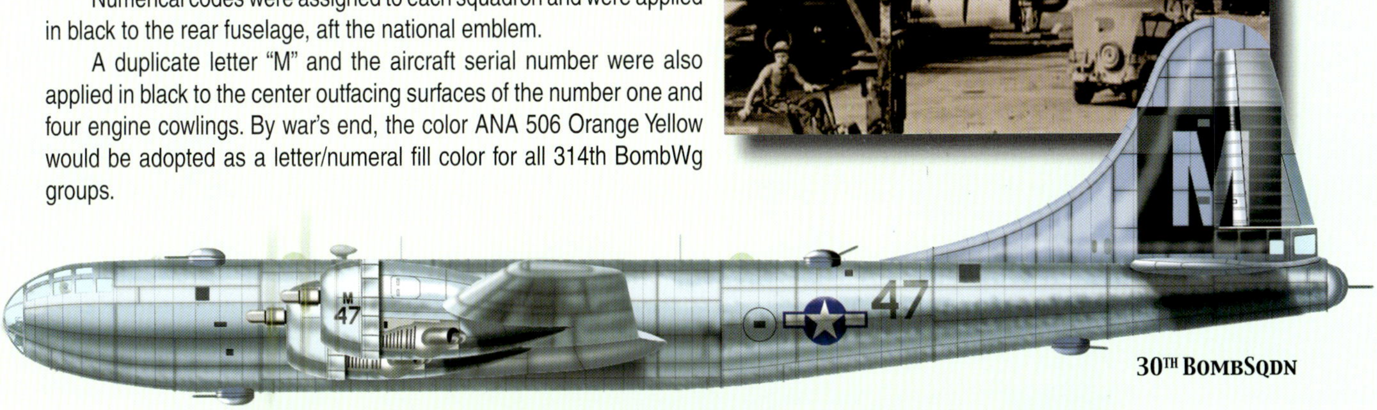

30th BombSqdn

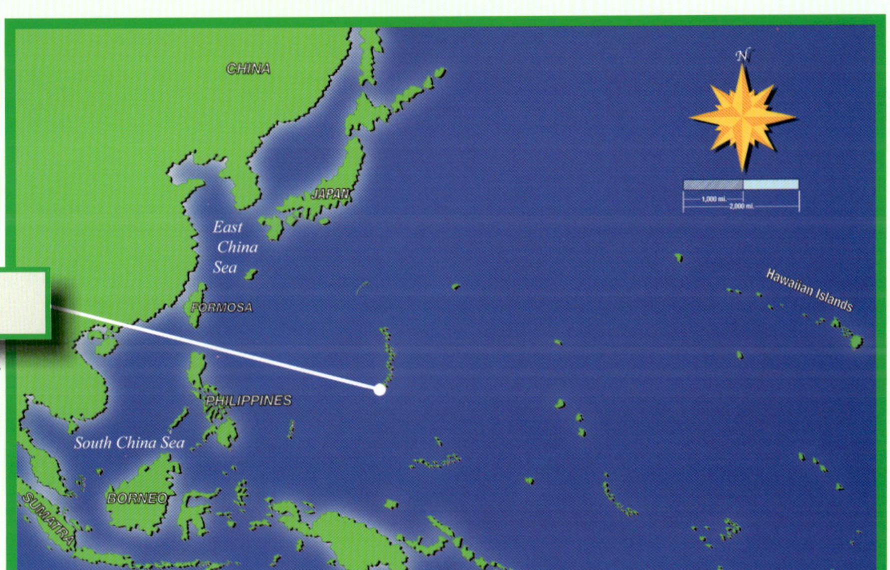

North Field, Guam
16-Jan-1945

Note: Refer to *Battle Colors/ Vol. V* for earlier southwest Pacific area station assignments of the 19thBG with the USAAC and Fifth AF.

• ASSIGNED TWENTIETH AF: JANUARY 1945 THRU V-J DAY •

314TH BOMB WG
DECEMBER-1944

XXI BOMBER COMD
DECEMBER-1944

29TH BOMBARDMENT GROUP (VH)

INSIGNIA: APPROVED/ 14-OCT-1940
MOTTO: POWER FOR PEACE
CONSTITUTED:
29TH BOMB GP (H)/22-DEC-1939
ACTIVATED: 1-FEB-1940
REDESIGNATED:
29TH BOMB GP (VH)/ 1944
ACTIVATED: 1-APR-1944

• 314th Bombardment Wing •
This emblem (approved 20-Jan-1945 and a simplified version consisting o a world globe began appearing or both sides of the group's aircraft ir May 1945. These insignia were positioned just aft the greenhouse.

6TH BOMBARDMENT SQUADRON (VH)

INSIGNIA: APPROVED/ 6-APR-1942
CONSTITUTED:
6TH BOMBARDMENT SQUADRON (H)/ 22-DEC-1939
REDESIGNATED:
6TH BOMBARDMENT SQUADRON (VH)/ 1-APR-1944
ACTIVATED:
1-FEB-1940 / 1-APR-1944

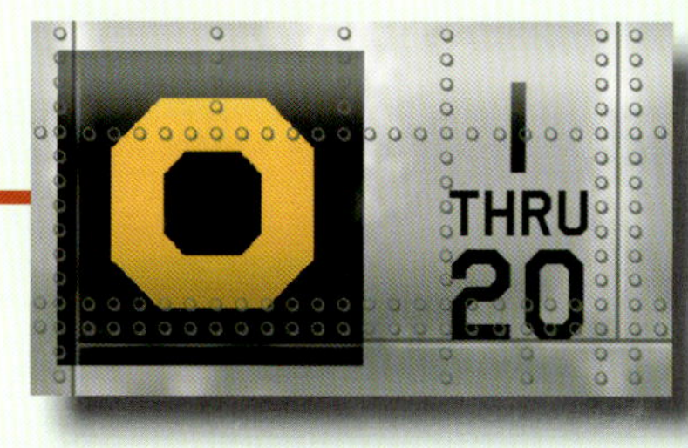

43D BOMBARDMENT SQUADRON (VH)

INSIGNIA: APPROVED/ 6-APR-1942
CONSTITUTED:
29TH BOMBARDMENT SQUADRON (H)/ 22-DEC-1939
REDESIGNATED:
43D BOMBARDMENT SQUADRON (VH)/ 1-APR-1944
ACTIVATED:
1-FEB-1940 / 1-APR-1944

52D BOMBARDMENT SQUADRON (VH)

INSIGNIA: APPROVED/ 18-APR-1942
CONSTITUTED:
52D BOMBARDMENT SQUADRON (H)/ 22-DEC-1939
REDESIGNATED:
52D BOMBARDMENT SQUADRON (VH)/ 1-APR-1944
ACTIVATED:
1-FEB-1940 / 1-APR-1944

29th BombGp/B-29s Tactical Markings: c.Jan–Sept 1945

When first deployed to Guam, the 29th BombGp is said to have been assigned tactical markings prior to the later Square O markings. Unfortunately, no conclusive evidence has been found that confirms this claim.

Originally, the Square O was applied in a manner consistent with all 314th BombWg bomb groups, i.e., a large black square painted on the fin/rudder surface with the aircraft surface finish serving as the letter color. These devices were normally applied directly over the existing aircraft serial numbers, leaving some of the serial digits visible.

Each aircraft was assigned a number-in-squadron code applied in black to the rear fuselage. The codes, along with the group's "O" designator, were additionally affixed to the outboard surfaces of the No. 1 and No. 4 engine cowlings.

Later, the O portion of the tail marking began to be painted a solid ANA 506 Orange Yellow, while a duplicate aircraft code number flanked with an uppercase "O" on each side—all in color and outlined in black—was affixed to the front lower nose area immediately below the ship's greenhouse.

Lead ships in the group were identified by wide vertical black and Yellow (or Orange-Yellow) color bands applied to the rear fuselage and tail fin. A large uppercase "O" followed by the lead ship's code number was duplicated in black on the upper surfaces of both wings. These markings were accompanied with lead ship color bands applied chord-wise to the wing's surfaces. These bands were considerably narrower than devices applied to the rear fuselage and consisted of two thin parallel black color bands bordering a somewhat wider Yellow/Orange-Yellow band on the outboard side of No. 1 and No. 4 engines.

It is not known whether these markings were duplicated on the under wing surface areas.

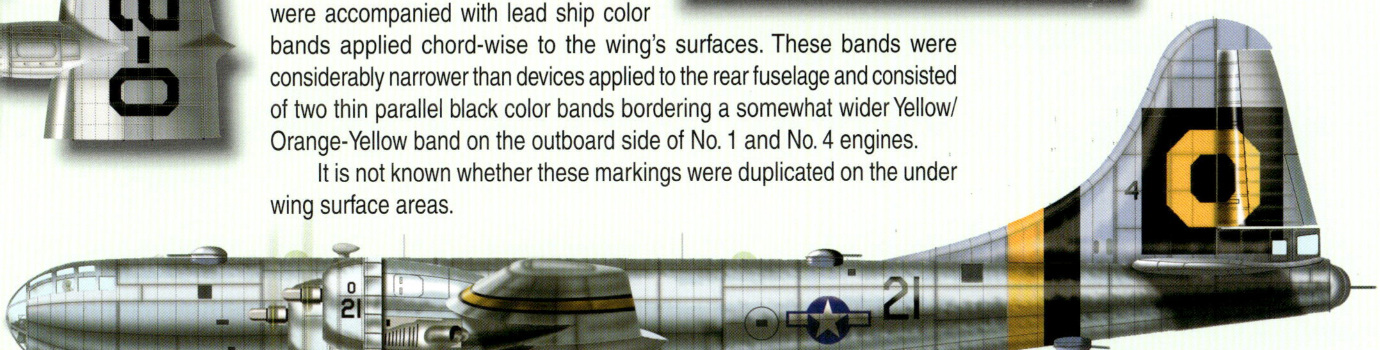

6th BombSqdn

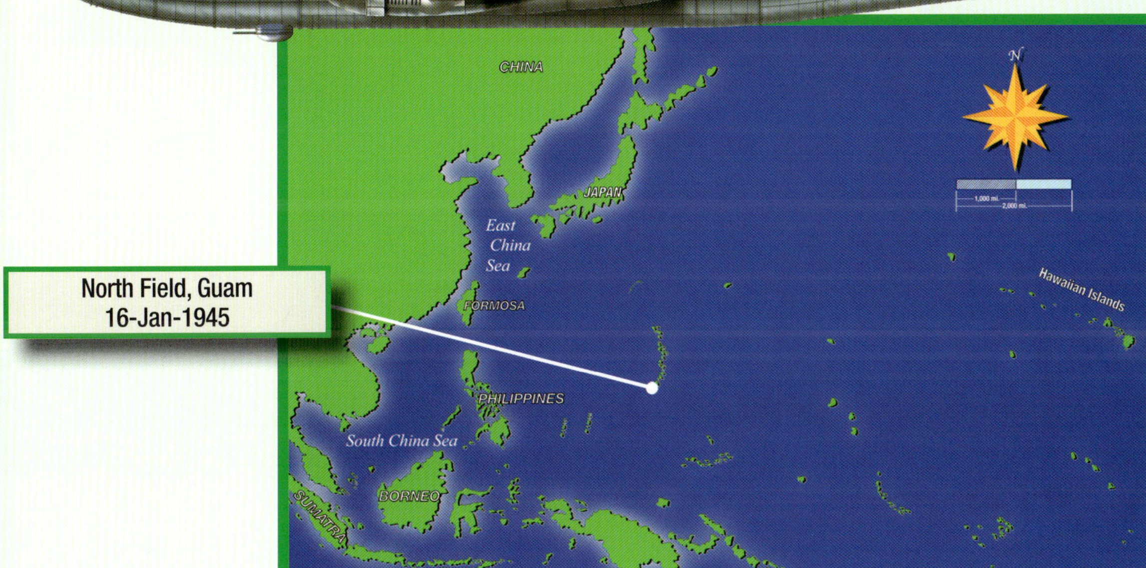

• Assigned Twentieth AF: February 1945 thru V-J Day •

314th Bomb Wg
February-1945

XXI Bomber Comd
February-1945

• 314th Bombardment Wing •
This emblem (approved 20-Jan-1945) an
a simplified version consisting of a worl
globe began appearing on both sides c
the group's aircraft in May 1945. Thes
insignia were often positioned just aft th
greenhouse on replacement aircraft in th
314th BombWg as an alternate to the olde
"City Of . . ." nose markings.

39th Bombardment Group (VH)

Insignia: (proposed)
Motto: Always Triumphant
Constituted:
39th Bomb Gp (H)/20-Nov-1940
Activated: 15-Jan-1941
Redesignated:
39th Bomb Gp (VH)/ 1944
Activated: 1-Apr-1944

60th Bombardment Squadron (VH)

Insignia: (unknown)
Constituted:
60th Bombardment Squadron (H)/ 20-Nov-1940
Redesignated:
60th Bombardment Squadron (VH)/ 1-Apr-1944
Activated:
15-Jan-1941 / 1-Apr-1944

61st Bombardment Squadron (VH)

Insignia: Approved/ 15-May-1942
Constituted:
61st Bombardment Squadron (H)/ 20-Nov-1940
Redesignated:
61st Bombardment Squadron (VH)/ 1-Apr-1944
Activated:
15-Jan-1941 / 1-Apr-1944

62d Bombardment Squadron (VH)

Insignia: (unknown)
Constituted:
62d Bombardment Squadron (H)/ 20-Nov-1940
Redesignated:
62d Bombardment Squadron (VH)/ 1-Apr-1944
Activated:
15-Jan-1941 / 1-Apr-1944

39th BombGp/B-29s
Tactical Markings: c. February 1945 through V-J Day

The 39th Bombardment Group was identified by a large square "P" applied with Black to the tail section of its B-29s. Accompanying this marker were subordinate markings, including individual aircraft-in-squadron code numbers applied in Black to the rear area of the fuselage, aft the national emblem. Additionally, a smaller version of the group's "P" accompanied by respective aircraft codes was affixed to the outboard facing sides of the No.1 and No.4 engine cowlings, again with Black paint.

Another visual characteristic of 39th Bombardment Group and 314th Bombardment Wing aircraft was the presence of the "City Of . . ." US War Bonds Drive emblem adorning both sides of the ship's forward nose area.

As with all 314th BombWg B-29s, lead ships in the 39th BombGp displayed stripes on the tail section and outer wings by war's end.

61st BombSqdn

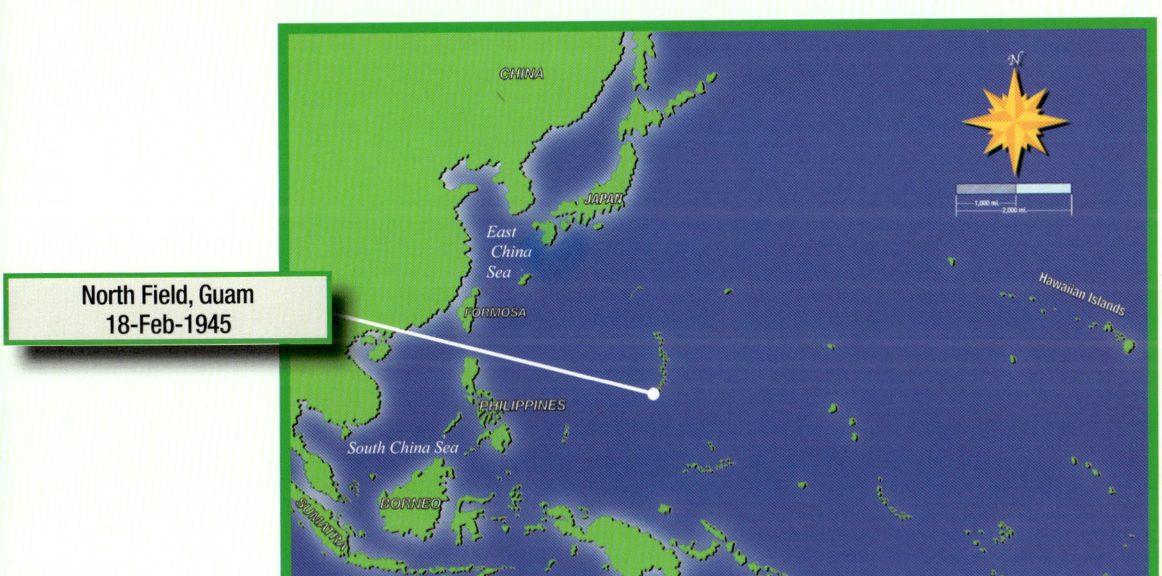

• Assigned Twentieth AF: June 1944 thru V-J Day •

58th Bombardment Wing — XXI Bomber Command — XX Bomber Command

40th Bombardment Group (VH)

Insignia: Approved/ 28-Mar-1942

Motto: (None)

Sobriquet: Kasu Tsuchi

Constituted:

40th Bomb Gp (M)/22-Nov-1940

Activated: 1-Apr-1941

Redesignated:

40th Bomb Gp (H)/ May-1942

40th Bomb Gp (VH)/ Nov-1943

• Early Group Emblem •

Designed by Disney Studios, this image represented the 40th BombGp when the unit was protecting the airways and shipping lanes between Puerto Rico and the Panama Canal.

25th Bombardment Squadron (VH)

Insignia: Approved/ 15-Feb-1924

From WWI Emblem

Organized:

20th Aero Sqdn/13-Jun-1917

Redesignated:

25th Aero Sqdn/22-Jun-1917

25th Sqdn/30-Aug-1921

25th Bomb Sqdn/25-Jan-1923

25th Bomb Sqdn (M)/ 6-Dec-1939

25th Bomb Sqdn (H)/ 20-Nov-1940

28th Bomb Sqdn (VH)/20-Nov-1943

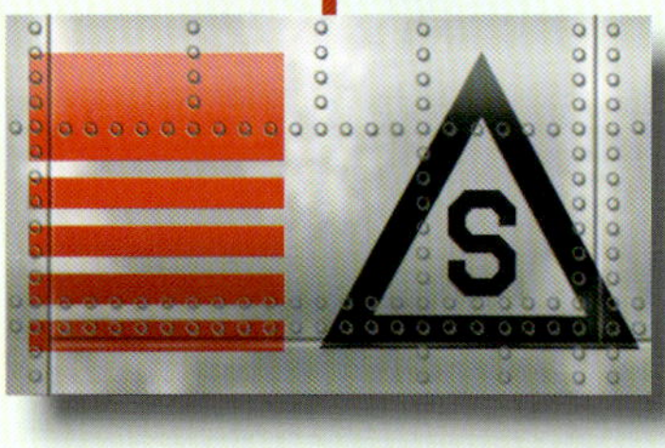

Early Numbering: 1–12

Later numbering system was sporadic and varied considerably

44th Bombardment Squadron (VH)

Insignia: Approved/ 7-Feb-1942

Constituted:

44th Bomb Sqdn (M)/22-Nov-1940

Activated: 1-Apr-1941

Redesignated:

44th Bomb Sqdn (H)/ 7-May-1942

44th Bomb Sqdn (VH)/ 20-Nov-1943

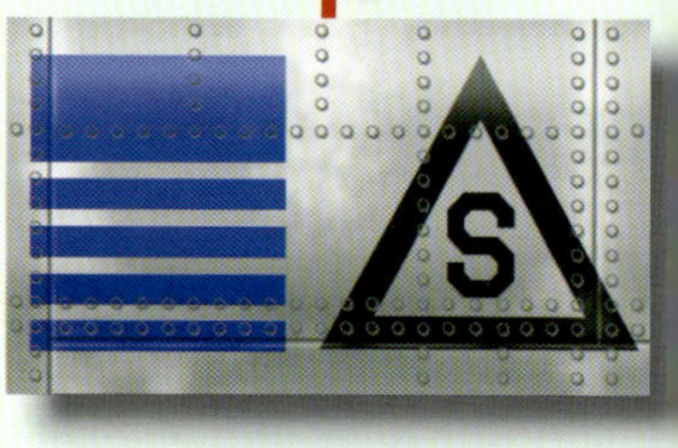

Early Numbering: 14–26

Later numbering system was sporadic and varied considerably

45th Bombardment Squadron (VH)

Insignia: Approved/ 6-Mar-1942

Constituted:

45th Bomb Sqdn (M)/ 22-Nov-1940

Activated: 1-Apr-1941

Redesignated:

45th Bomb Sqdn (H)/ 7-May-1942

45th Bomb Sqdn (VH)/ 20-Nov-1943

Early Numbering: 27–38

Later numbering system was sporadic and varied considerably.

*395th Bombardment Squadron (VH)

Insignia: (Unapproved)

Constituted:

5th Rcn Sqdn (M)/ 22-Nov-1940

Activated: 1-Apr-1941

Redesignated:

395th Bomb Sqdn (M)/ 22-Nov-1942

395th Bomb Sqdn (H)/ 7-May-1942

395th Bomb Sqdn (VH)/ 20-Nov-1943

Disbanded: 20-Oct-1944

40TH BombGp/B-29s
First Pattern Tactical Markings: c. May 1944

Shortly after arriving in India, the 40th BG adopted a system of tactical markings consisting of painting the vertical tail tip in assigned squadron colors. Immediately below the tip were four thin horizontal bars of matching color; these devices were applied to fin and rudder surfaces. A large single Black letter was affixed to the lower fin area, just below the aircraft serial numbers, and served as aircraft recognition codes. No other tactical devices were employed by the group at this time.

5TH RcnSqdn
(later-395TH BS)

The emblem at left was designed by Disney artist Hank Porter early in the squadron's history when it was designated the 5th Reconnaissance Squadron, patrolling in the Caribbean area early in the war.

40TH BombGp/B-29s
Second Pattern Tactical Markings: c. May 1945 thru V-J Day

44TH BombSqdn(VH)/
40th BombGp/XXI BmrCmd

• Unofficial Late War Kasu-tsuchi Group Emblem •

In a formal letter to HQ/58th BW from HQ/40th BG dated 2 August 1945, the 40th requested permission to adopt an unofficial secondary insignia for the group based upon the legendary Japanese fire god Kagu-tshchi (or Kagutsuchi). The reasons cited for the request were increased public relations, enhanced esprit de corps among the 49th BG, and good PSYOPS warfare against the Japanese homeland. The rest is history. An inter-group contest was held to come up with a new insignia, with the winning design ending up adorning the port side nose of a large number of the group's B-29s. Just how well the PSYOPS part of this campaign worked is really unknown; the morale effect on the men of the 40th proved to be precisely what had been hoped for.

With a station transfer from India to Tinian Island came new unit markings for the 58th BombWg consisting of a heavily outlined equilateral triangle containing an AAF style upper case stencil letter that identified the group assignment. In the case of the 40th BombGp this was the letter "S"; after removal of the aircraft tail serial number, this device was affixed using Black paint. While the triangle was applied to tail and rudder surfaces, the group letter designator was confined to the fin area proper. Squadron colors were retained on the tip of the vertical stabilizer, but the horizontal bands were dropped.

The former aircraft tail identification letter was replaced with Arabic numerals—twenty per squadron—applied in Black to the forward nose area, rear fuselage (just aft the national emblem), and the outboard facing cowling surfaces of No.1 and No.4 engines. Individual nose art within the group was common, but restricted to the starboard nose.

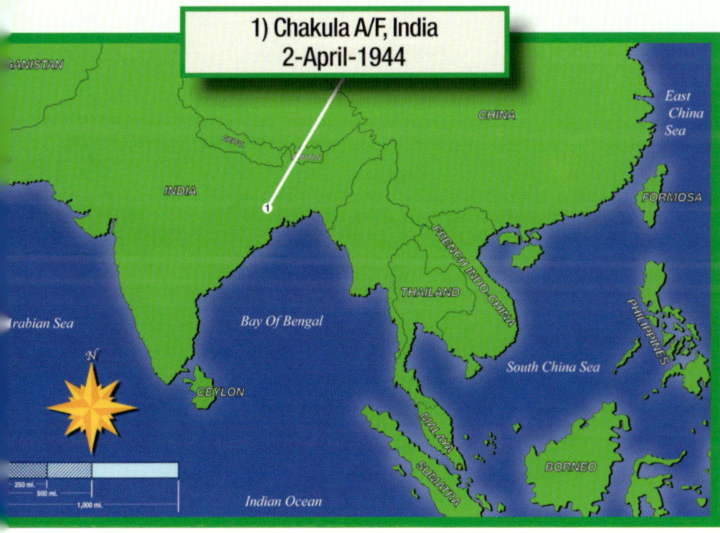

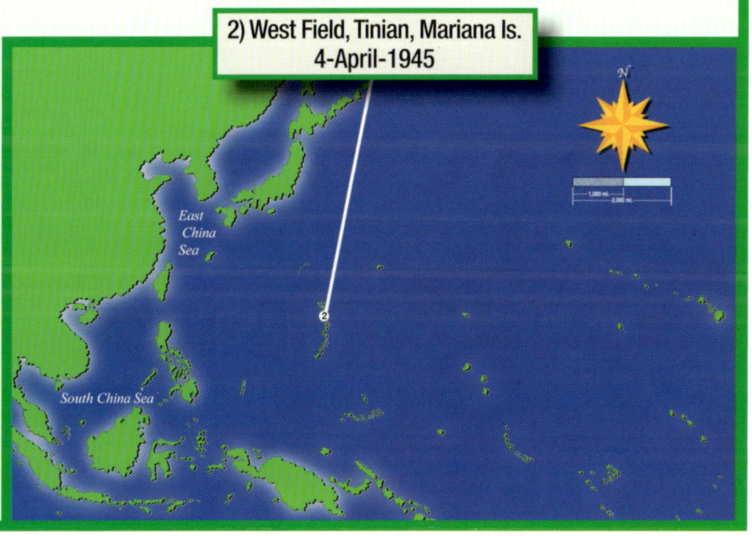

• ASSIGNED FOURTEENTH AF: MARCH 1943 THRU V-J DAY •

68TH COMP WG
c. FEB-1943

308TH BOMBARDMENT GROUP (H)

INSIGNIA: (UNAPPROVED)
MOTTO:
WHEN STRUCK DOWN I RISE AGAIN
CONSTITUTED:
308TH BOMB GP (H)/28-JAN-1942
ACTIVATED: 15-APR-1942

308thBombGp emblem symbolism is described in a formal design approval request application forwarded to the US War Department / Heraldry Section dated 8-Dec-1944. No decision recorded:

"The bombardment functions of the organization are allegorically implied by the ability of the organization to grow, in spite of possible losses of some of its branches, and by the mythical head of the Gorgon Medusa, supposedly capable of overcoming all opposition.

"The oak tree denotes the strength of the organization and the numerical designation is indicated by the three branches, the zero formed by the shield and the eight leaves on each branch (308).

"The motto 'Percussus Resurgo' ('When Struck Down I Rise Again') is suggested as being appropriate to the symbolism of the shield and to characteristics of the personnel."

*373D BOMBARDMENT SQUADRON (H)

INSIGNIA: (UNAPPROVED)

CONSTITUTED: 28-JAN-1942
ACTIVATED: 15-APR-1942

374TH BOMBARDMENT SQUADRON (H)

INSIGNIA: (UNAPPROVED)
(DISPLAYED BUT NOT APPROVED UNTIL 23-JUL-1952)

CONSTITUTED: 28-JAN-1942
ACTIVATED: 15-APR-1942

375TH BOMBARDMENT SQUADRON (H)

INSIGNIA: APPROVED/11-JAN-1943

CONSTITUTED: 28-JAN-1942
ACTIVATED: 15-APR-1942

425TH BOMBARDMENT SQUADRON (H)

INSIGNIA: APPROVED/25-AUG-1943

CONSTITUTED:
36THRCNSQDN(H)/ 28-JAN-1942
ACTIVATED: 15-APR-1942
REDESIGNATED:
425THBOMBSQDN(H)/ 22-APR-1942

* The 373DBombSqdn(H) was transferred to the 494THBombGp(H), Seventh AF on 21-Jul-1945.

Early in the unit's deployment to China, the 308th BombGp adopted a simple numerical code for individual aircraft identification. These three digit codes were in the 451–550 range and were applied to the outboard tail fin surfaces in white, positioned either immediately above or below the factory applied serial numbers. Use of these numerical codes continued for a time after the 308th BombGp adopted squadron tail markings beginning in early 1944, but their use was eventually phased out. Shark faces on the group's B-24s began appearing in late 1944; although not standardized in configuration, these devices found wide acceptance within the group's squadrons.

374TH BOMBSQDN

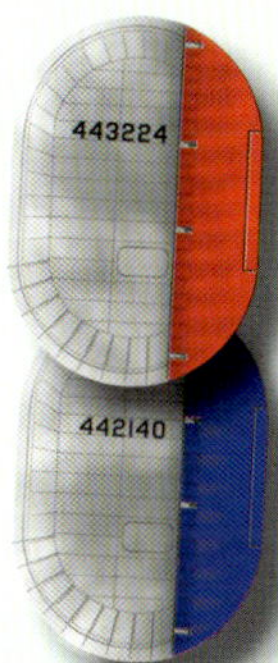

373D BOMBSQDN

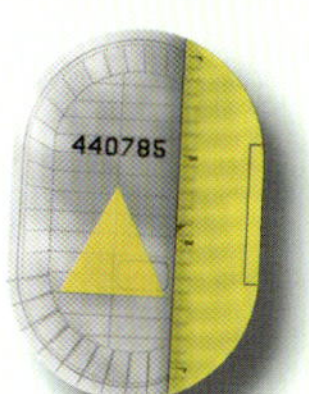

374TH BOMBSQDN

375TH BOMBSQDN

When tactical tail markings were first adopted, the 373d BombSqdn painted outboard facing surfaces of their tail rudders in a solid red or blue. Overall red eventually became the standard color representing the squadron. Yellow was the color adopted by the 374th BombSqdn; in addition to applying this color to their aircraft rudders, an equilateral triangle device was additionally applied with yellow to the lower portion of the vertical fin.

The 375th BombSqdn elected to divide their ships' outboard facing rudder surfaces vertically into three equal sections. The two outside sections were painted Insignia Blue, with the center section painted Insignia White. For a time the 375th additionally adopted the use of a large, single letter painted black and positioned just below the factory applied serial number. Exactly when this practice was implemented or for how long is unknown.

In the 425th BombSqdn, the inboard and outboard surfaces of the ships' rudders were painted in an alternating pattern consisting of eight diagonal yellow stripes of equal width and spacing. The factory applied OD paint finish underneath the yellow stripes remained and served as the second color of this pattern. In mid-1944, the original squadron tactical tail marking pattern was modified for application on newer replacement ships arriving with unpainted metal finishes. The diagonal stripes were reduced to four yellow stripes, with five alternating black stripes added to replace those areas originally showing OD.

The practice of applying the squadron's tactical markings to inboard and outboard rudder surfaces was also modified, with the newer pattern only applied to the outboard rudder surfaces, the inboard sides remaining totally unmarked.

425TH BOMBSQDN

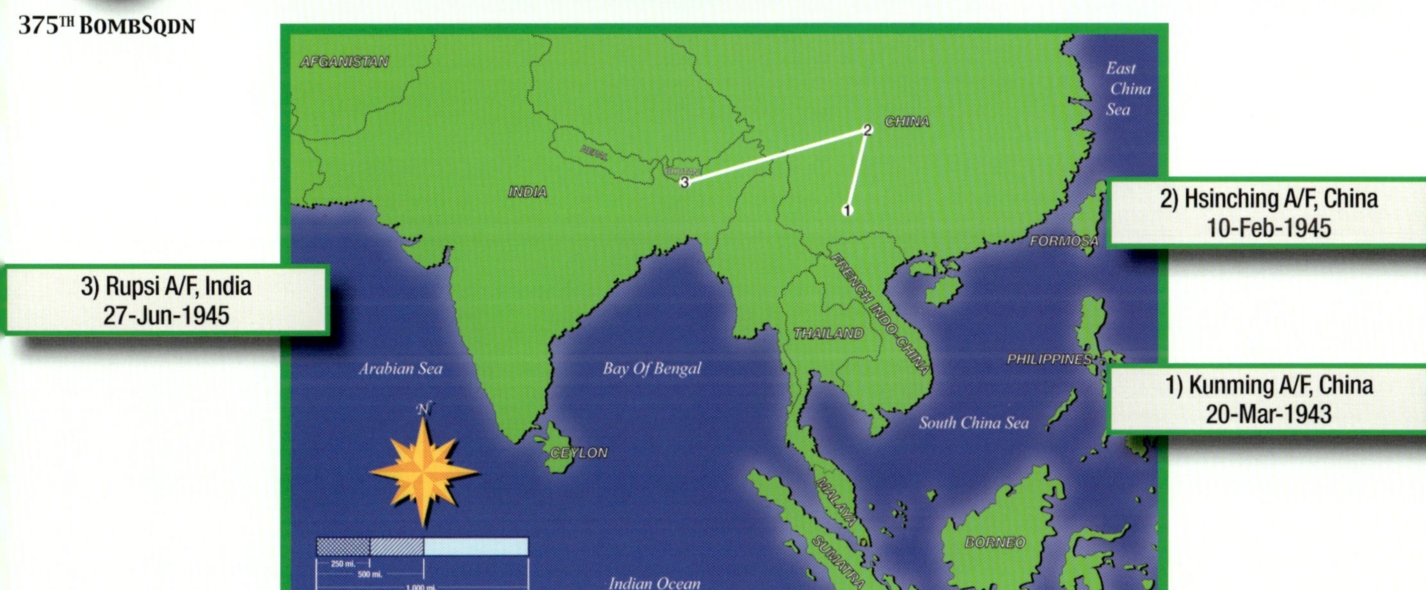

• Assigned Twentieth AF: c. February-1945 thru V-J Day •

314th Bomb Wg
Feb-1945

XXI Bomber Comd

330th Bombardment Group (VH)

Insignia: (unapproved)
Motto: 'For Freedom/For The Liberty'
Sobriquet: (unknown)
Constituted:
330th Bomb Gp(H)/ 1-Jul-1942
Activated: 1-Jul-1942
Redesignated:
330th Bomb Gp (VH)/ 1-Apr-1944

• 330thBombGp Variations •
Several typical examples of the problems encountered with unapproved unit emblems. The insignia depicted here and opposite were common interpretations of the same basic design often seen during WWII.

457th Bombardment Squadron (VH)

Insignia: (unapproved)

Constituted:
457th Bomb Sqdn (H)/ 1-Jul-1942
Activated: 6-Jul-1942
Redesignated:
457th Bomb Sqdn (VH)/ 1-Apr-1944

K 1 THRU 20

458th Bombardment Squadron (VH)

Insignia: Approved/ 27-Jun-1945

Constituted:
458th Bomb Sqdn (H)/ 1-Jul-1942
Activated: 6-Jul-1942
Redesignated:
458th Bomb Sqdn (VH)/ 1-Apr-1944

K 21 THRU 40

K 41 THRU 60

459th Bombardment Squadron (VH)

Insignia: *Approved*/ 6-Apr-1945

Constituted:
459th Bomb Sqdn (H)/ 1-Jul-1942
Activated: 6-Jul-1942
Redesignated:
459th Bomb Sqdn (VH)/ 1-Apr-1944

330th BombGp/B-29s
ACTICAL MARKINGS: c. FEBRUARY 1945 THROUGH V-J DAY

This was a commonly used, simplified version of the two more complex examples of the 330th BombGp emblem (see facing page). As was the case with most USAAF combat units, artistic skills within the group varied considerably, culminating in equally varied end results.

everal locations: the rear fuselage area and the bottom forward ose flanked by the group letter "K." The outside surfaces of No.1 nd No.4 engine cowlings, originally in black characters, were ventually replaced with ANA 506 Orange Yellow letter and umeral(s) set in a Black rectangle. Lead ships had the group tter, assigned number, and leader stripes applied to both wing urfaces.

As with all 314th BombWg serving Heavies, a good number of the 330th BombGp's B-29s displayed the characteristic "City Of . . ." nose graphics. Whether by design or happenstance, the vast majority of surviving wartime photographs of this group's aircraft clearly show this iconic device affixed to the starboard side of its assigned aircraft. This placement was in direct contrast to the placement selected by other groups, such as the 19th BombGp, which applied this same device on the port side nose area of its assigned aircraft.

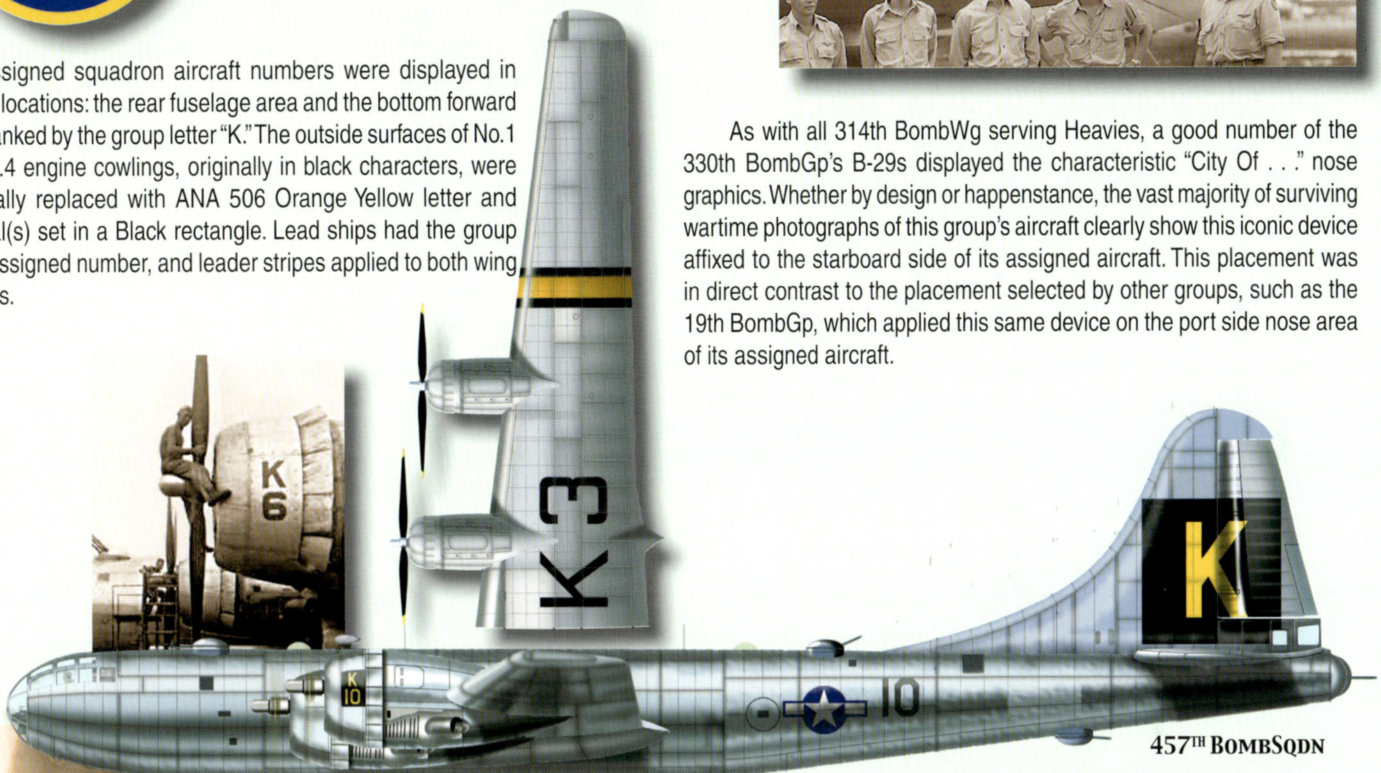

457th BombSqdn

By the end of the war all B-29s serving under the overall command of the 314th BombWg were very much standardized, inasmuch as all tactical markings were concerned. This held true in every category, from size of letters and/or numeral(s) used to precisely where these devices were to be affixed to the aircraft frame, including what specific color(s) were to be used.

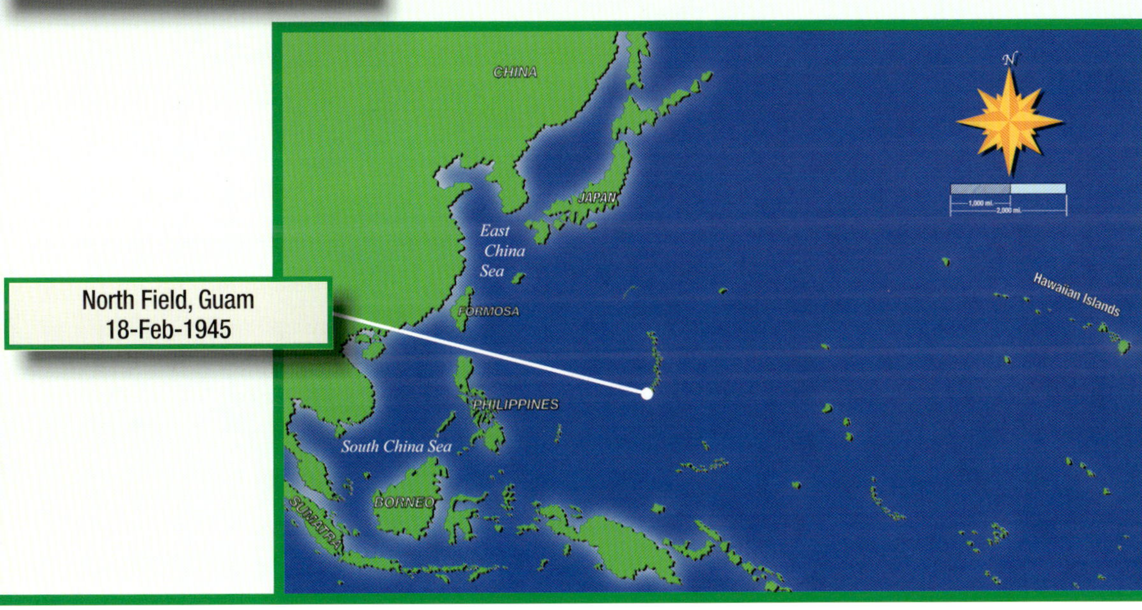

• Assigned Twentieth AF: c. April-1945 thru V-J Day •

315th Bomb Wg
April-1945

XXI Bomber Comd
April-1945

331th Bombardment Group (VH)

Insignia: Approved/ 22-Dec-1942
Motto: With Undaunted Heart
Constituted:
331st Bomb Gp (H)/ 1-Jul-1942
Activated: 6-Jul-1942
Redesignated:
331st Bomb Gp (VH)/ c.Jun-1944
Activated: 12-Jul-1944

355th Bombardment Squadron (VH)

Insignia: Approved/ 16-Aug-1943

Constituted:
355th Bombardment Squadron (H)/ 28-Jan-1942
Activated: 1-Jun-1942
Redesignated:
355th Bombardment Squadron (VH)/ 27-Jun-1944
Activated: 7-Jul-1944

356th Bombardment Squadron (VH)

Insignia: Approved/ 21-Mar-1945

Constituted:
356th Bombardment Squadron (H)/ 28-Jan-1942
Activated: 1-Jun-1942
Redesignated:
356th Bombardment Squadron (VH)/ 27-Jun-1944
Activated: 7-Jul-1944

357th Bombardment Squadron (VH)

Insignia: Approved/ 21-Mar-1945

Constituted:
357th Bombardment Squadron (H)/ 28-Jan-1942
Activated: 1-Jun-1942
Redesignated:
357th Bombardment Squadron (VH)/ 27-Jun-1944
Activated: 7-Jul-1944

• Orphan Emblems •

At one time both of these designs represented the same unit, the 356th BombSqdn. It is believed the top image can be credited to Walter Lantz Productions, while the bottom image was designed for the squadron by O'Brien Printing Co. when the squadron was stationed at Pueblo AAB, Pueblo, Colorado.

Although neither emblem was ever officially approved for display, it is known the Tiger insignia was designed mid- to late 1942. It is believed the Wabbitt design was a follow-up emblem to the Tiger image, and was itself ultimately replaced by the approved 1945 goofy duck emblem (facing page). Of these three insignia, it is left to the individual reader to decide which would have been the "top pick" to represent this squadron during this point in history.

331st BombGp/B-29s Tactical Markings: c. May through V-J Day

The lack of photographic evidence pertaining to the 331st BombGp could be attributed in part to the group's late arrival in the war. It could also be argued the lack of visual appeal inherent with the group's tactical aircraft markings may have been another contributing factor. Unlike units such as the 314th BombWg that used high visibility tactical markings as an effective public relations tool (e.g., "City Of . . ." nose emblems), the 331st settled solely on the application in black of the group's Triangle "L" and aircraft-in-squadron code.

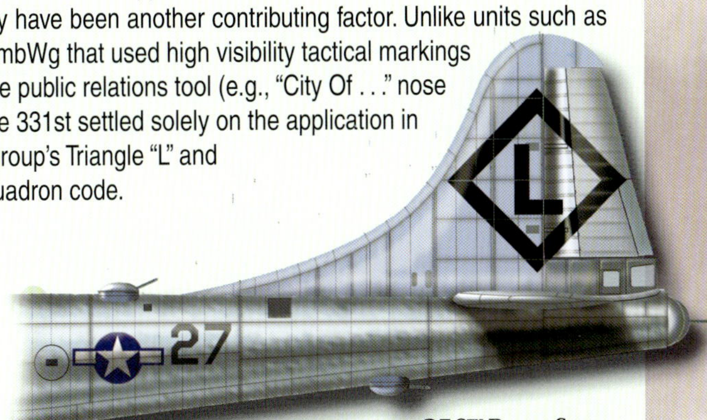

356th BombSqdn

Here (right) is the only official USAAF photo that turned up in researching this group. This shot actually features some 331st personnel passing time by watching a model airplane in flight overhead. The B-29 in the background shows the only tactical markings adopted by the group, but the aircraft was not the object of the photo—it just happened to be there. A little make-up can go a long way attracting attention.

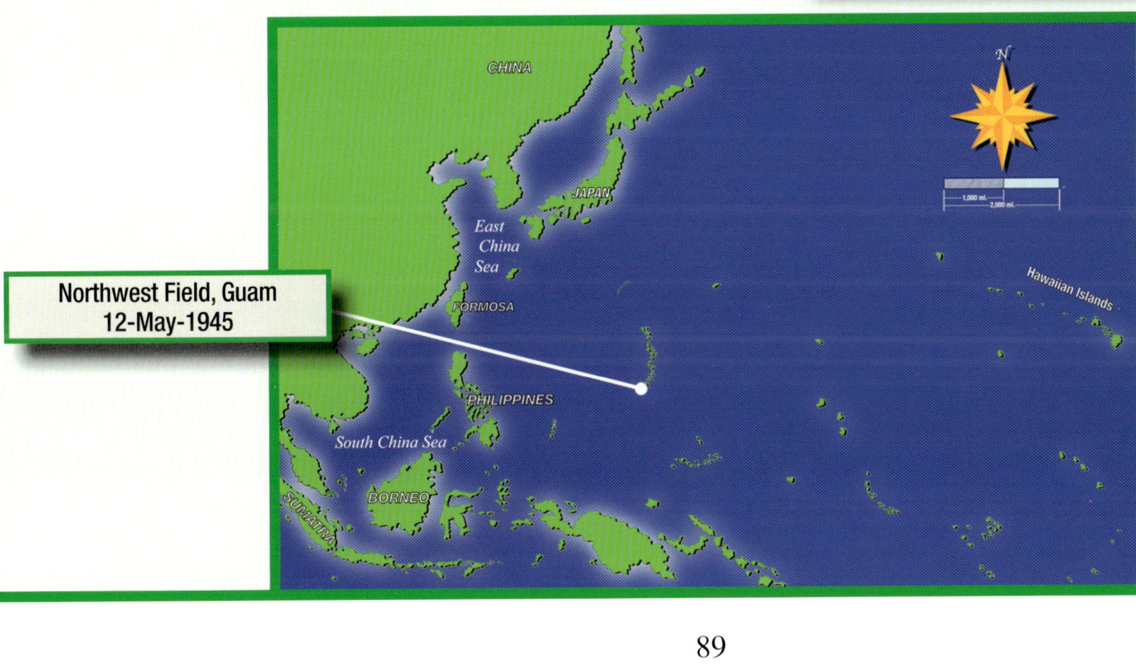

• Assigned Tenth AF: September 1942 / Fourteenth AF: January 1944 thru V-J Day •

69th Comp Wg
Jan-1944

Tenth AF
Aug-1943

341st Bombardment Group (M)

Insignia: (unapproved)
Motto: (unknown)
Sobriquet: Flying Falcons
aka China Clippers
Constituted:
341st Bomb Gp (M)/ 14-Aug-1942
Activated: 15-Apr-1942

Although the approved emblem (below) shows the proper colors to be used in this image, i also includes the use of longitudinal anc latitudinal lines in the design. Substitution o these devices, including contour land forms (as seen in the period patch above), was a common substitution on uniforms, signage and aircraft.

11th Bombardment Squadron (M)

* *Insignia:* Approved/ 2-Mar-1924
from squadrons WWI emblem
Sobriquet: Jiggs Squadron

Organized:
11thAeroSqdn/ 26-Jun-1916
Redesignated:
11th Sqdn/ 14-Mar-1921
11th BombSqdn/ 25-Jan-1923
11th BomnSqdn(H)/ 6-Dec-1939
11th BombSqdn(M)/ c.15-Sep-1942

** Jiggs, the WWI emblem created by George McManus from the syndicated cartoon strip, *Bringing Up Father* (see C.A.T.F. p.12).

22d Bombardment Squadron (M)

Insignia: Approved/ 19-Mar-1945
Sobriquet: Battlin Bulldogs

Constituted:
22d BombSqdn(H)/ 28-Jan-1942
Activated: 20-Oct-1939
Redesignated:
22d BombSqdn(M)/ c.15-Sep-1942

490th Bombardment Squadron (M)

Insignia: (unapproved)
Sobriquet: Burma Bridge Busters

Constituted:
490th BombSqdn(M)/ 14-Aug-1942
Activated: 15-Apr-1942

491st Bombardment Squadron (M)

Insignia: Approved/ 19-Oct-1944
Sobriquet: Ringer Squadron

Constituted:
79th AeroSqdn/ 15-Aug-1917
Redesignated:
491st AeroSqdn/ 1-Feb-1918
491st BombSqdn/ c.1936
491st BombSqdn(M)/ 14-Aug-1942

There is some photographic evidence (left) that the 341st BombGp briefly adopted the use of letter/number tail codes throughout its four squadrons. Conclusive documentation verifying the use and allocation of such devices has yet to surface, and today all that remains are a few photos showing an assortment of random numbers and/or letters affixed to not only the outboard vertical tails, but nose sections, as well.

This emblem represented the 491st BombSqdn until it was officially replaced by the Ringer design (opposite page). There is nothing on file indicating whether this design was ever submitted to the Heraldic Section for official approval.

A variation of the unofficial Skull & Wings emblem of the 490th BombSqdn, along with a period photo showing a common application of this design to the nose of one of the squadron's B-25s. Designed for the first commander of the 490th, this emblem saw extensive service, representing the squadron in India, Burma, and China. In spite of this, the emblem was never formerly approved for use by the US War Department Heraldic Section and there is nothing on file as to whether this design was rejected or simply never submitted through proper channels for approval.

This early unapproved King of the Air emblem was widely displayed by the 22d BombSqdn 1942–1943. Also often referred to as the Bombing Eagles, this image was officially replaced with the bulldog (facing page) after the 341st BombGp relocated to China.

The display of squadron emblems on both sides of aircraft fuselage nose surfaces was prevalent in the entire 341st BombGp, with most appearing to have been hand painted, as opposed to the use of dry transfer decals. The application of shark faces to the front of B-25Hs was also a popular, albeit unofficial marking in the group. Patterns and colors varied widely, with complete individuality the order of the day. Some of these designs included certain details, such as eyes and nostrils, but this varied from one aircraft to another even in the same squadron.

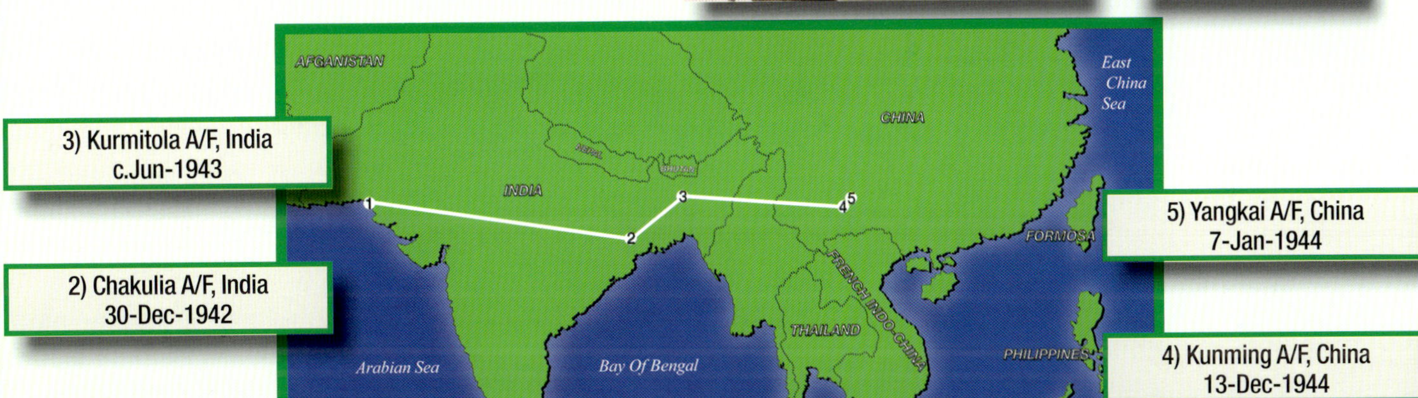

Note: Airfields on the adjacent map indicate duty stations of Headquarters, 341st BombGp(M). All squadrons serving with this group were also temporarily detached to additional CBI airfields far too numerous to include.

• Assigned Twentieth AF: April 1944 thru V-J Day •

58th Bomb Wg
c.Apr-1943

XXI Bomber Comd
c.Apr-1945

XX Bomber Comd
c.Apr-1943

444th Bombardment Group (VH)

Insignia: (Unapproved)
Motto: To Victory–To Freedom
Constituted:
444th Bomb Gp (H)/ 15-Feb-1943
Activated: 1-Mar-1943
Redesignated:
444th Bomb Gp (VH)/ c.Nov-1943

676th Bombardment Squadron (VH)

Insignia: Approved/ 27-Jun-1945
Sobriquet: The Reluctant Dragons

Constituted:
676th BombSqdn(H)/15-Feb-1943
Activated: 1-Mar-1943
Redesignated:
676th BombSqdn(VH)/ 20-Nov-1943

©Walt Disney

677th Bombardment Squadron (VH)

* *Insignia:* Approved/ 31-Oct-1946

Constituted:
677th BombSqdn(H)/ 15-Feb-1943
Activated: 1-Mar-1943
Redesignated:
677th BombSqdn(VH)/ 20-Nov-1943

678th Bombardment Squadron (VH)

Insignia: (Unapproved)

Constituted:
678th BombSqdn(H)/ 15-Feb-1943
Activated: 1-Mar-1943
Redesignated:
678th BombSqdn(VH)/ 20-Nov-1943

679th Bombardment Squadron (VH)

Insignia: (Unapproved)

Constituted:
679th BombSqdn(H)/ 15-Feb-1943
Activated: 1-Mar-1943
Redesignated:
679th BombSqdn(VH)/ 20-Nov-1943

Disbanded: 12-Oct-1944

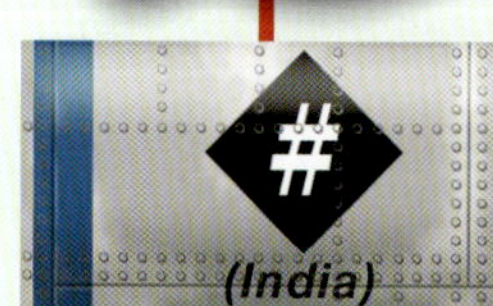

44TH BombGp/B-29s
actical Markings: c. August 1944-May 1945

The first adopted tac marking was a small Insignia Blue or black diamond painted high on the tail fin. Yellow or white two-digit call numbers were in the center of the diamond. This marking was applied as a black number on a white diamond on the few camouflaged B-29s in the group. In all cases factory serial numbers were retained.

Each squadron had a series of numbers assigned for a time (i.e., K-14, K-65, K-215, K-296, etc.) that were affixed to the nose area. The exact numerical series assigned to each squadron is unknown.

In mid-summer 1944, the group added squadron colors to engine nacelles and a 24 in. (approx.) encircling fuselage band between the wing trailing edge and the national emblem.

676TH BombSqdn

44TH BombGp/B-29s
actical Markings: c. May 1945 through V-J Day

With the 444th's move to Tinian Island came new and higher profile tail markings. The diamond and serial number were replaced with a large letter "N" enclosed by a heavy bordered triangle, both applied in black. The aircraft call numbers were relocated to the rear fuselage, aft the national emblem. These numerical devices are reputed to have been issued in the following series of blocks:

677thBS: 10–24
677thBS: 50–64
678thBS: 30–44

Painting the fuselage band and engine nacelles in squadron colors was retained. At some point the practice of painting the nose wheel covers in squadron color was adopted, but no memos or fragmentary field orders referring to this and other specifics pertaining to the group's markings have been found, making it very difficult to establish precise implementation dates, etc., for these markings.

Shortly after getting settled in at their new station, replacement B-29s began arriving with all under surfaces painted in ANA Jet for night bombing operations over Japan.

All squadrons made good use of their respective emblems even before the unit's transfer to Tinian. These were supplied as dry transfer decals and affixed to the bombers' forward nose area.

678TH BombSqdn

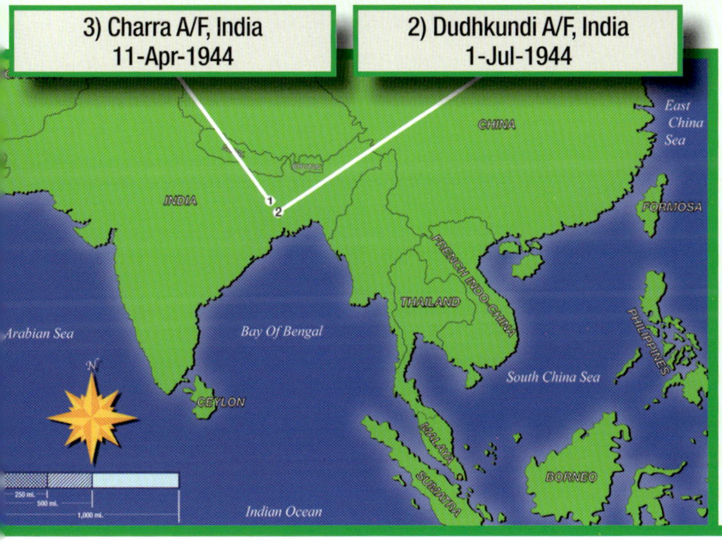

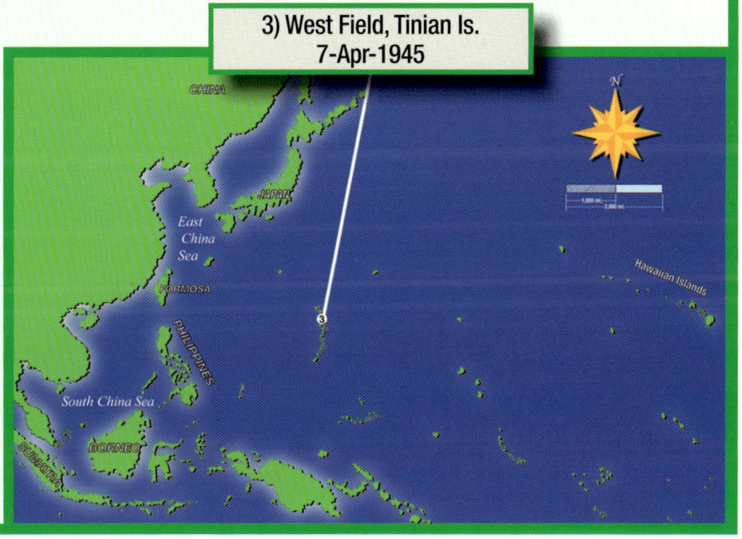

• Assigned Twentieth AF: June 1944 thru V-J Day •

58th Bomb Wg c.Apr-1944 — **XXI Bomber Comd** c.Apr-1945 — **XX Bomber Comd** c.Apr-1944

462d Bombardment Group (VH)

Insignia: (Unapproved)

Motto: With Malice Toward Some

Sobriquet: The Hellbirds

Constituted:
462d Bomb Gp (H)/ 19-May-1943

Activated: 1-Jul-1943

Redesignated:
462d Bomb Gp (VH)/ c.Nov-1943

Following the Twentieth AF revised T/O of 10 October 1944, the three remaining squadrons comprising the group (768th, 769th, and 770th BombSqdn) were instructed to paint their rudders red. The individual fin call letters and squadron numerical designators were retained, but red rudders became the new tactical color representing the 462d BombGp until the group's transfer to Tinian Island and the XXI Bomber Command.

NUMBERS
2-16

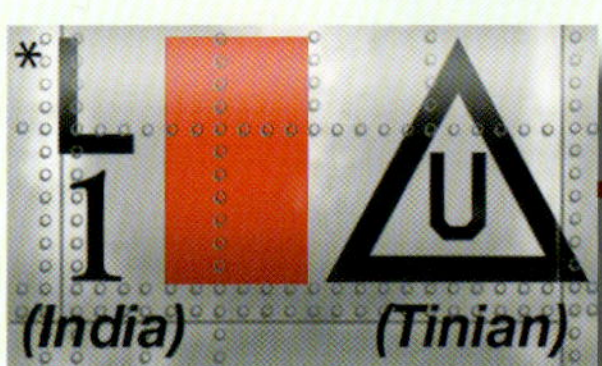

768th Bombardment Squadron (VH)

Insignia: (Unknown)

Constituted:
768th BombSqdn(H)/ 19-May-1943
Activated: 1-Jul-1943
Redesignated:
768th BombSqdn(VH)/ 20-Nov-1943

NUMBERS
20-33

769th Bombardment Squadron (VH)

Insignia: (Unknown)

Constituted:
769th BombSqdn(H)/ 19-May-1943
Activated: 1-Jul-1943
Redesignated:
769th BombSqdn(VH)/ 20-Nov-1943

NUMBERS
40-53

770th Bombardment Squadron (VH)

Insignia: (Unknown)

Constituted:
770th BombSqdn(H)/ 19-May-1943
Activated: 1-Jul-1943
Redesignated:
770th BombSqdn(VH)/ 20-Nov-1943

771st Bombardment Squadron (VH)

Insignia: (Unknown)

Constituted:
771st BombSqdn(H)/ 19-May-1943
Activated: 1-Jul-1943
Redesignated:
771st BombSqdn(VH)/ 20-Nov-1943

Disbanded: 22-Oct-1944

* While serving in the CBI, individual call letter/number combinations were assigned to each aircraft in all four squadrons. With the exception of the 771st BombSqdn (disbanded on 22 Oct 1944), the 768th, 769th and 770th BombSqdn were issued new call numbers when the 462d BombGp was relocated to Tinian Island.

62D BombGp/B-29s
actical Markings: c.June 1944-Apr 1945

When first deployed to the CBI, aircraft of the 462d BombGp were distinguished by assigned squadron colors applied to the entire rudder surface. Accompanying this tactical marking was the application of a large single black individual call letter positioned on the upper fin area directly above the factory applied serial numbers, which were fully retained during the group's tour in India. A third marking element was later added in October 1944, consisting of a single large black Arabic numeral applied to the lower fin directly below the serial number. These single digit fin numbers represented the squadron assignment of each respective aircraft; their use would continue while in the CBI:

1 = 768th BombSqdn / 2 = 769th BombSqdn
3 = 770th BombSqdn / 4 = 771st BombSqdn

There are a few photographs showing the call letter and squadron number repeated in smaller versions on the outer nacelles of the No. 1 and No. 4 engines, but the extent of this application is uncertain. When originally deployed to Piardoba, India, there were a number of fully camouflaged B-29s assigned to the group. Just how many (if any) of these camouflaged aircraft received these tactical markings is unknown.

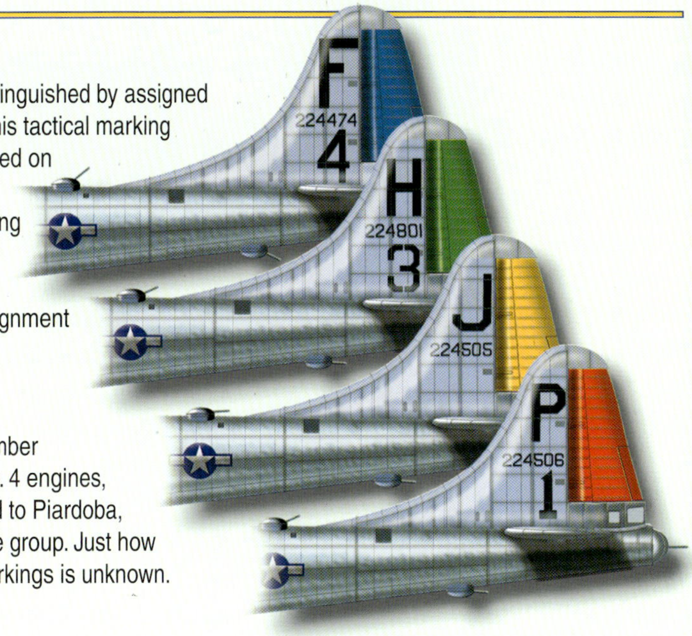

62D BombGp/B-29s
actical Markings: c.April 1945 thru V-J Day

Shortly after their relocation from India to Tinian Island, the 462d BombGp's old tactical markings were modified (right). The rudders were repainted in the earlier squadron CBI colors, but the call letter and numerical squadron identifier on the tail fin were eliminated altogether, as were the factory applied serial numbers. These earlier markings were replaced with the 58th BombWg's new, heavy Black outlined equilateral triangle device applied to fin and rudder surfaces. Centered in this symbol was an uppercase letter "U," the new designator of the 462d BombGp. Also replaced were the single letter call signs, substituted with numerical call signs applied in Black to the rear fuselage area, immediately aft the national emblem.

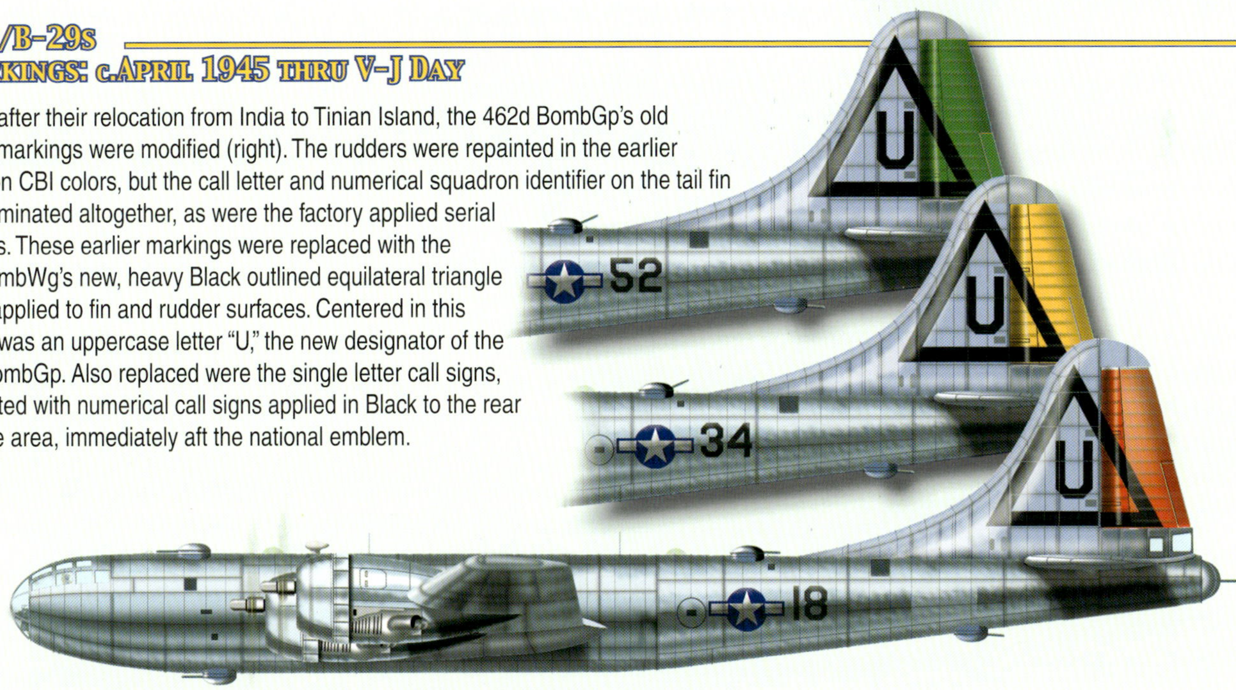

OTE: Many B-29s assigned to the 462d BombGp displayed the unit's *Hellbirds - With Malice Toward Some* emblem on the starboard nose section.

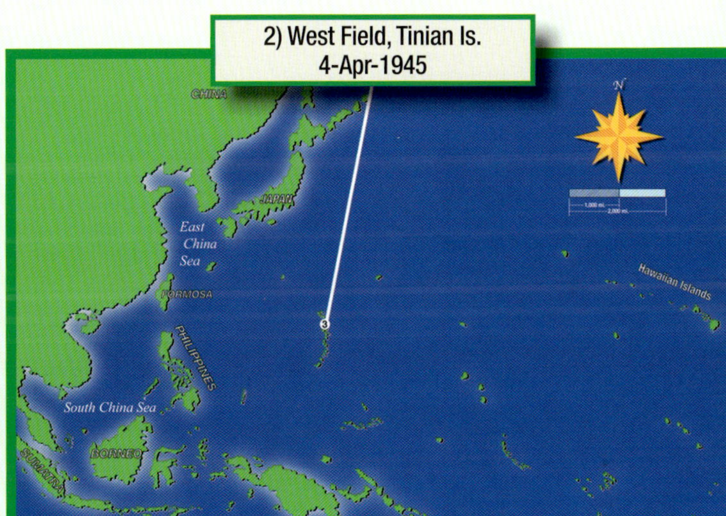

• Assigned Twentieth AF: June 1944 thru V-J Day •

58TH Bomb Wg
c.Jun-1943

XXI Bomb Comd
c.Apr-1945

XX Bomb Comd
c.Jun-1943

468TH Bombardment Group (VH)

Insignia: (Unapproved)
Motto: (Unknown)
Sobriquet:
The Billy Mitchell Group
Constituted:
468TH Bomb Gp (H)/ 19-May-1943
Activated: 1-Aug-1943
Redesignated:
468TH Bomb Gp (VH)/ c.Nov-1943

Here are the two versions of the 468th BombGp's unapproved emblem. This design was based on the flag once flown on Gen. William "Billy" Mitchell's personal boat. The flag was a gift to the 498th BombGp from Mrs. Elizabeth Mitchell, Gen. Mitchell's widow. Research failed to determine precisely why the 468th was selected for the honor of being presented the flag by Mrs. Mitchell.

NUMBERS
1-16

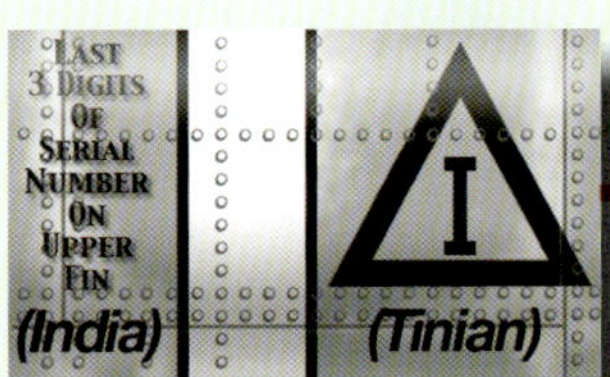

792D Bombardment Squadron (VH)

Insignia: (Unknown)

Constituted:
792DBombSqdn(H)/ 19-May-1943
Activated: 1-Aug-1943
Redesignated:
792DBombSqdn(VH)/ 20-Nov-1943

NUMBERS
21-35

793D Bombardment Squadron (VH)

Insignia: (Unknown)

Constituted:
793DBombSqdn(H)/ 19-May-1943
Activated: 1-Aug-1943
Redesignated:
793DBombSqdn(VH)/ 20-Nov-1943

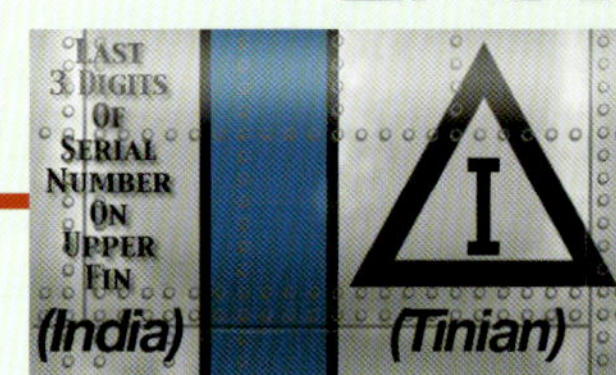

NUMBERS
41-54

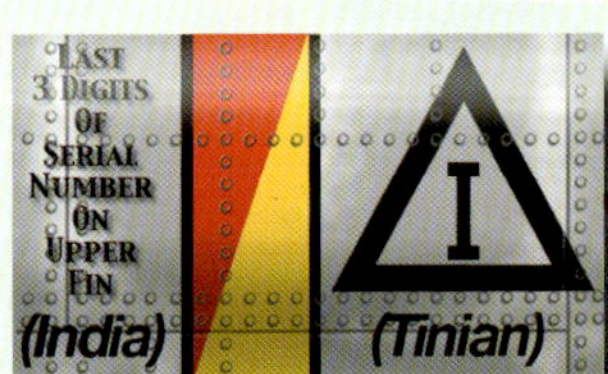

*794TH Bombardment Squadron (VH)

Insignia: (Unknown)

Constituted:
794THBombSqdn(H)/ 19-May-1943
Activated: 1-Aug-1943
Redesignated:
794THBombSqdn(VH)/ 20-Nov-1943

795TH Bombardment Squadron (VH)

Insignia: (Unknown)

Constituted:
795THBombSqdn(H)/ 19-May-1943
Activated: 1-Aug-1943
Redesignated:
795THBombSqdn(VH)/ 20-Nov-1943

Disbanded: 12-Oct-1944

* The 794th BombSqdn opted to replace its originally assigned red color designator with yellow after the 468th BombGp's relocation to Tinian and the disbandment of the 795th BombSqdn on 12 October 1944.

68th BombGp/B-29s
Tactical Markings: c. Apr 1943-Apr 1945

The tactical markings adopted by the 468th consisted of two black bordered diagonal stripes in respective squadron colors applied to rudder surfaces. The last three digits of each B-29 was enlarged and added to the mid-fin area, just above the serial number, and served as the ships call sign.'Shooting Stars', painted in squadron colors and resplendent with comet trails (which generally contained individual aircraft names) came in a variety of patterns, and began appearing on both sides of the nose in October 1944.

Beginning in January 1945, the 468th BombGp's Billy Mitchell emblem began appearing on the tail fins of the group's B-29s. Each of these devices was affixed to the lower fin area and positioned directly below the serial number.

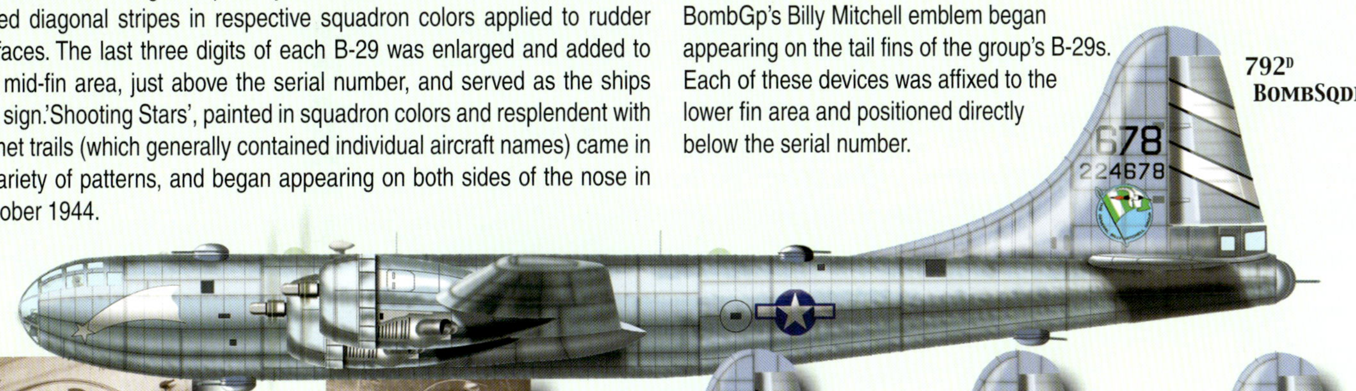

* Following the disbandment of the 795thBS, the 794thBS adopted yellow as its squadron color.

68th BombGp/B-29s
Tactical Markings: c. Apr 1945 through V-J Day

Soon after their transfer to Tinian and the XXI Bomber Command everything on the tail surfaces of the group's B-29s, including the factory applied serial numbers, was replaced with the 468th's new unit designator, the Triangle "I." Tail tips were painted in squadron colors, some with a thin black base line.

Newly assigned call numbers were applied aft the fuselage national emblem, usually in black, but the use of squadron colors was sometimes substituted. In April 1945, the Star/Comet nose applications were replaced with the group's Billy Mitchell unit emblem relocated from its original location on the lower tail fins.

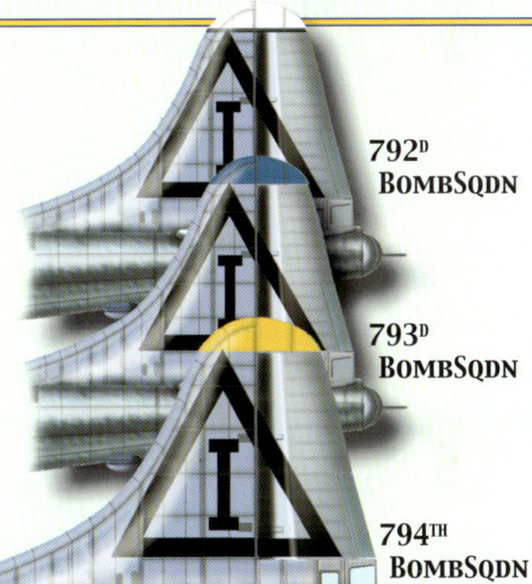

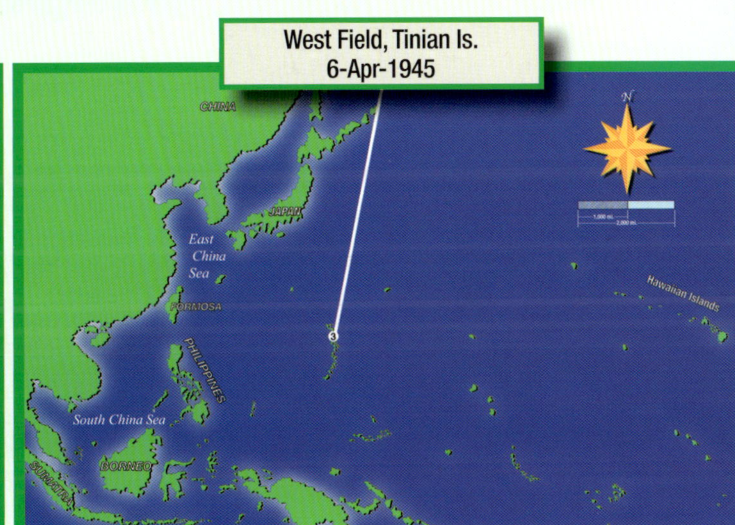

• Assigned Twentieth AF: October 1944 thru V-J Day •

73D Bomb Wg
c.Nov-1943

XXI Bomb Comd
c.Oct-1944

497TH Bombardment Group (VH)

Insignia: (unapproved)

Motto: (unknown)

Sobriquet:
The Long Haulers

Constituted:
497TH Bomb Gp (VH)/ 19-Nov-1943

Activated: 20-Nov-1943

869TH Bombardment Squadron (VH)

Insignia: Approved/ 10-May-1944

Constituted:
869TH BombSqdn(VH)/ 19-Nov-1943
Activated: 20-Nov-1943

870TH Bombardment Squadron (VH)

Insignia: Approved/ 18-Aug-1944

Constituted:
870TH BombSqdn(VH)/ 19-Nov-1943
Activated: 20-Nov-1943

871ST Bombardment Squadron (VH)

Insignia: Approved/ 5-Aug-1944

Constituted:
871STBombSqdn(VH)/ 19-Nov-1943
Activated: 20-Nov-1943

497th BombGp/B-29s
Tactical Markings: c. October 1944-Apr 1945

When the 497th BombGp received orders to prepare for deployment to the island of Saipan a directive regarding tactical markings was issued. As a unit of the 73d BombWg the following recognition elements were to be affixed to the tail surfaces of all group B-29s. An upper case "A" was to be placed near the fin tip as a 497th group indicator. A heavy outlined square representing the 73dBombWg was to be positioned mid-fin, while directly below this geometric image was to be applied each aircraft's individual call number. Factory applied aircraft serial numbers were removed, with the last four digits of each number being reapplied to the mid-rudder area. All of these new devices were uniformly applied with black paint.

At one time the 497th BombGp boasted some of the most colorful and lavish nose art found in the AAF, but sometime in April/May 1945, for reasons still uncertain, all individual nose art was ordered removed and replaced with a standard 73d BombWg emblem.

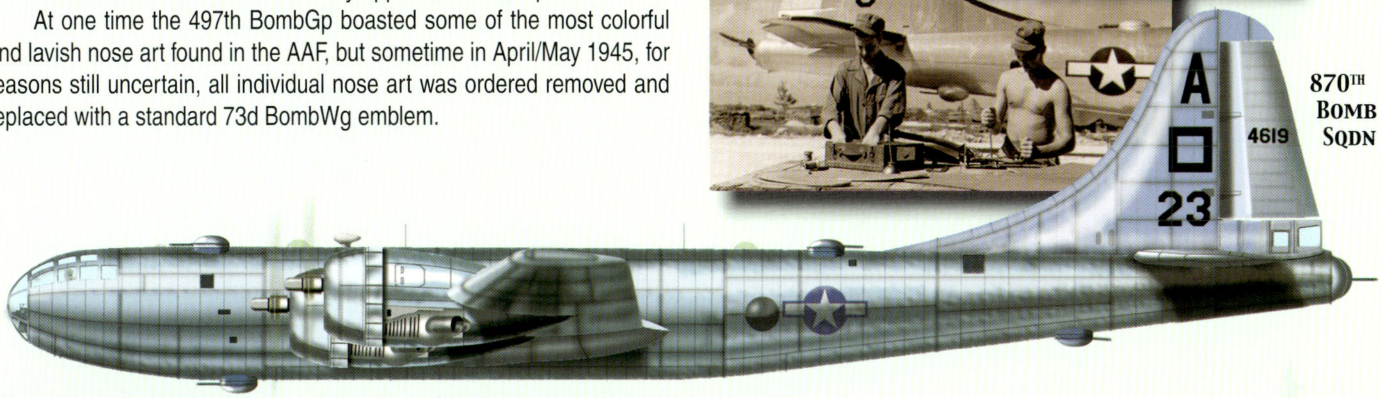

497th BombGp/B-29s
Tactical Markings: c. April 1945 through V-J Day

Second pattern group tactical markings saw the earlier three element devices replaced with a single black upper case "A" that crossed over onto the lower rudder surface. The policy of reapplying the last four digits of an aircraft's serial number in black to the mid-rudder surface continued. Call numbers were relocated to the rear fuselage area and were often repeated on both sides of the forward fuselage nose section.

Pre-approved individual aircraft names were allowed to be applied to the forward "arrow" portion of the new 73d BombWg emblem. Flight leaders were denoted with either a single black band on the dorsal fin or a wide yellow band sided with two thin black bands applied to the forward empennage area.

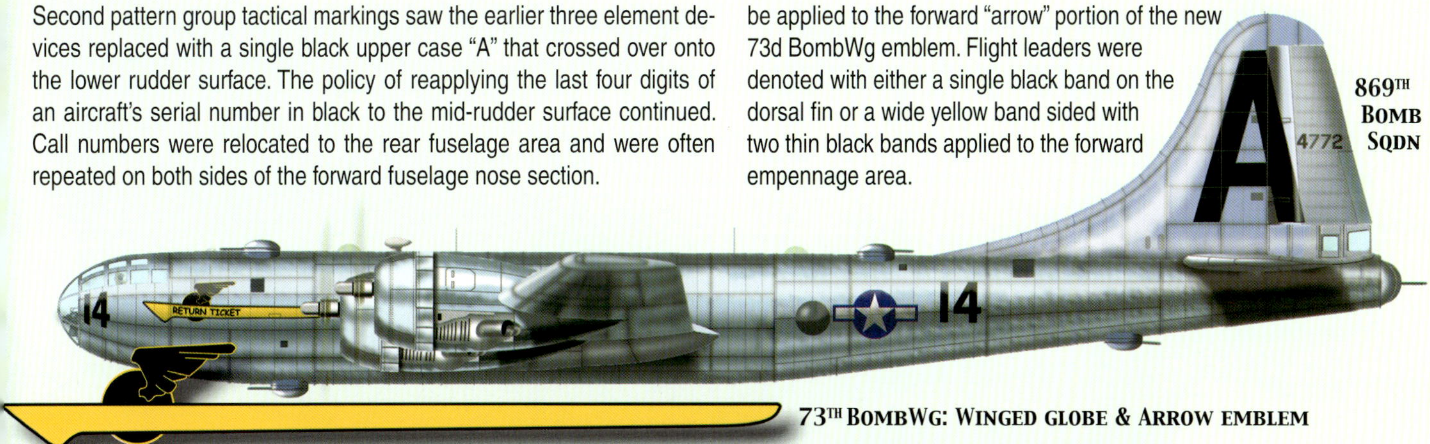

73th BombWg: Winged globe & Arrow emblem

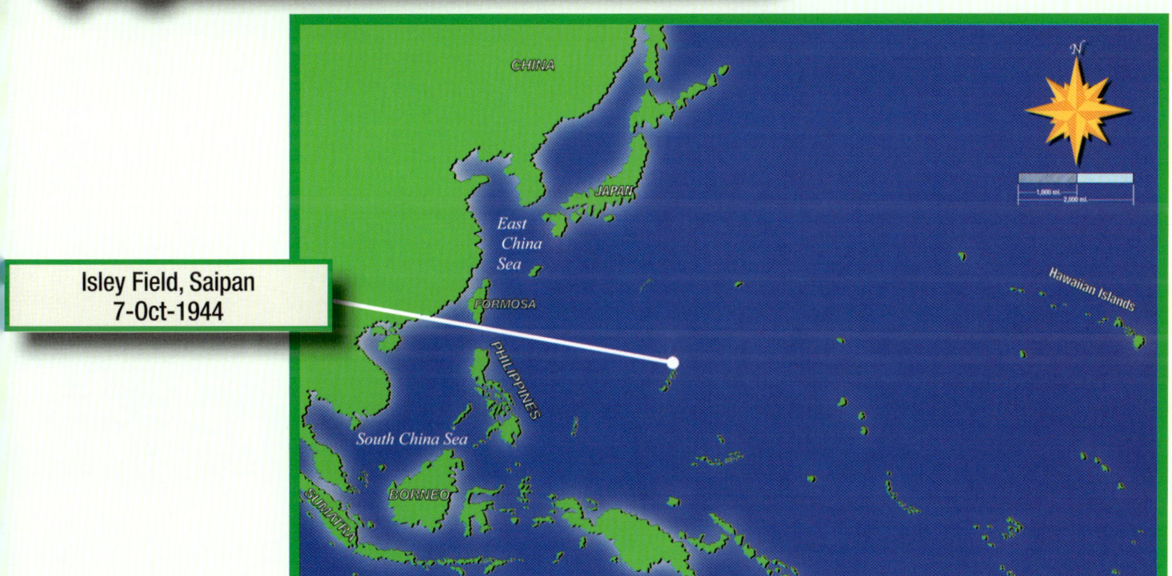

• ASSIGNED TWENTIETH AF: JULY 1944 THRU V-J DAY •

73D BOMB WG c. JUL-1944

XX BOMBER COMD c. JUL-1945

XXI BOMBER COMD c. JUL-1944

498TH BOMBARDMENT GROUP (VH)

INSIGNIA: (UNKNOWN)

MOTTO: (UNKNOWN)

CONSTITUTED:

498TH BOMB GP (VH)/ 19-NOV-1943

ACTIVATED: 20-NOV-1943

873D BOMBARDMENT SQUADRON (VH)

INSIGNIA: APPROVED/ 11-SEP-1944

CONSTITUTED:

873D BOMBARDMENT SQUADRON (VH)/ 19-NOV-1943

ACTIVATED: 20-NOV-1943

874TH BOMBARDMENT SQUADRON (VH)

INSIGNIA: APPROVED/ 10-AUG-1944

CONSTITUTED:

874TH BOMBARDMENT SQUADRON (VH)/ 19-NOV-1943

ACTIVATED: 20-NOV-1943

875TH BOMBARDMENT SQUADRON (VH)

INSIGNIA: APPROVED/ 9-NOV-1943

CONSTITUTED:

875TH BOMBARDMENT SQUADRON (VH)/ 19-NOV-1943

ACTIVATED: 20-NOV-1943

498th BombGp/B-29s
Tactical Markings: c. Sep 1944–Apr 1945

Early 498th BombGp tactical markings adhered to standard 73d Bomb-Wg unit identification: an upper case "T" denoting the group and a heavy outlined square indicating wing affiliation, with numbers indicating an aircraft's number-in-squadron positioned directly below. All of these elements were on the fin. The original factory applied serial numbers were replaced with a duplication of the last four digits of the serial number applied to mid-rudder surfaces.

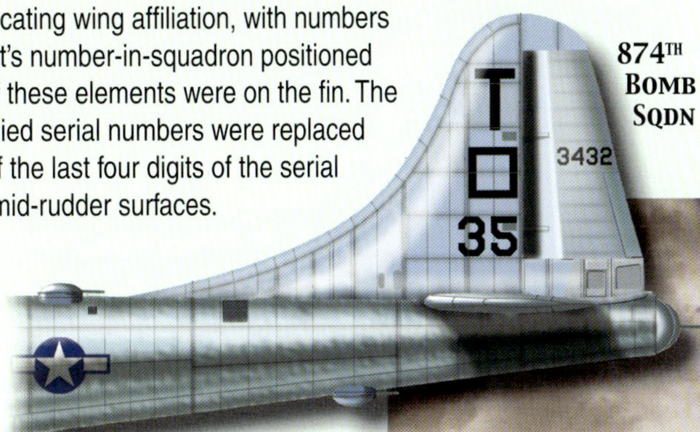

874th Bomb Sqdn

498th BombGp/B-29s
Tactical Markings: c.Apr 1945 through V-J Day

In April 1945, all 73d BombWg groups adopted higher visibility tactical markings. The aircraft call number and geometric square were removed from the fin completely and replaced with a large black uppercase "T" which crossed and overlapped the upper rudder area. The individual call numbers were relocated to the rear fuselage, aft the national emblem.

Unlike other squadrons in the 73d BombWg, the 498th eliminated the last four digits from the rudder and did not duplicate the call number on the nose section. Flight leaders were designated with standard 73d BombWg dorsal fin vertical bands.

875th Bomb Sqdn

Isley Field, Saipan
6-Sep-1944

• Assigned Twentieth AF: July 1944 thru V-J Day •

73D Bomb Wg
c. Jul-1944

XXI Bomb Comd
c. Jul-1944

499TH Bombardment Group (VH)

Insignia: (unknown)
Motto: (unknown)
Constituted:
499TH Bomb Gp (VH)/ 19-Nov-1943
Activated: 20-Nov-1943

The story behind the emblem depicted on the signage board (above) is an unresolved mystery. The only clues relating to the history behind this photo is that it was reputedly taken at Isley Field. Even the configuration of this emblem is questionable, being more consistent with that of a bomb group than a bomb squadron.

877TH Bombardment Squadron (VH)

Insignia: Approved/ 16-May-1945

Constituted:
877THBombSqdn(VH)/ 19-Nov-1943
Activated: 20-Nov-1943

878TH Bombardment Squadron (VH)

Insignia: Approved/ 6-Sep-1945

Constituted:
878THBombSqdn(VH)/ 19-Nov-1943
Activated: 20-Nov-1943

*879TH Bombardment Squadron (VH)

Insignia: (unapproved)

Constituted:
879THBombSqdn(VH)/ 19-Nov-1943
Activated: 20-Nov-1943

* This emblem has not yet been confirmed as representing the 879th BombSqdn.

99TH BOMBGP/B-29S ACTICAL MARKINGS: C. JULY 1944-APR 1945

In keeping with prevailing 73d BombWg directives, all tactical unit markings on 499th BombGp B-29s were painted in black on the vertical tail fin surfaces, beginning with the group's assigned upper case letter "V" near the tail tip. The original aircraft serial numbers were removed, with the last four digits reapplied to the mid-rudder area. The two battle damage photos (right) afford a good close-up of the tactical tail markings application.

99TH BOMBGP/B-29S ACTICAL MARKINGS: C. APRIL 1945 THROUGH V-J DAY

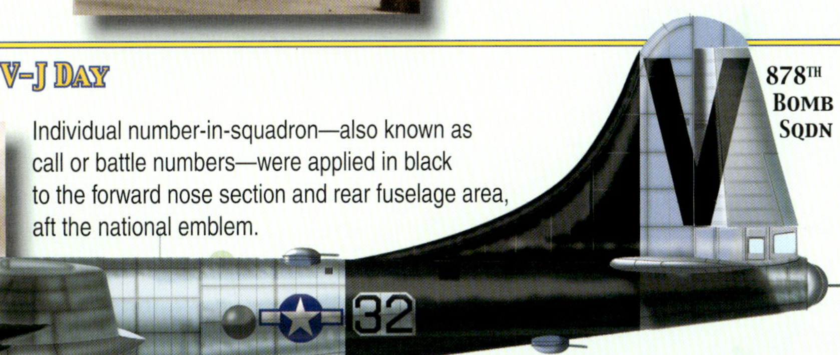

Individual number-in-squadron—also known as call or battle numbers—were applied in black to the forward nose section and rear fuselage area, aft the national emblem.

There is some wartime evidence indicating the 499th developed their own unique method of showing flight leader status. The illustration above depicts one such aircraft (No. 32 of the 878th BombSqdn). Note how the entire forward section of the empennage has been painted in solid black, leaving only the aft fuselage battle number showing through.

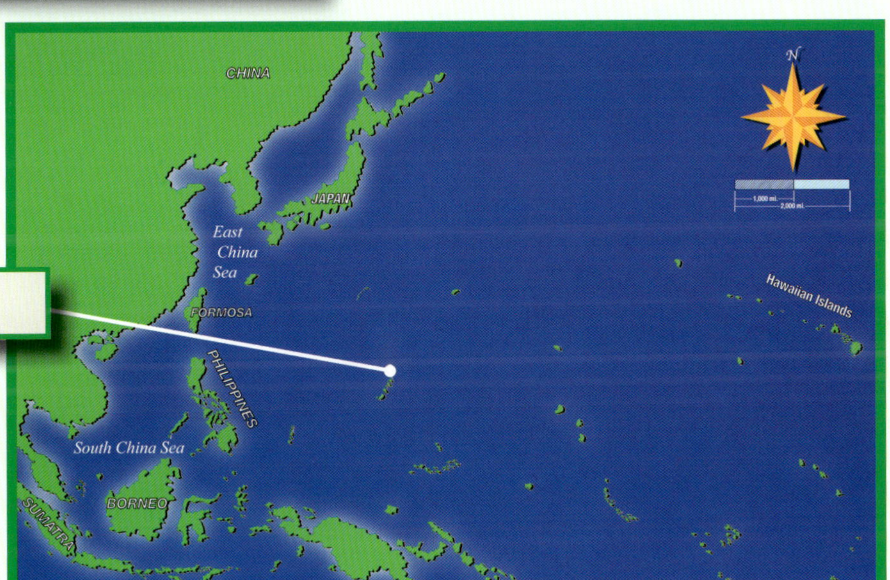

• Assigned Twentieth AF: July 1944 thru V-J Day •

73D Bomb Wg c. Jul-1944 — XX Bomber Comd c. Jul-1945 — XXI Bomber Comd c. Jul-1944

500TH Bombardment Group (VH)

Insignia: (unknown)

Motto: (unknown)

Constituted:

500TH Bomb Gp (VH)/ 19-Nov-1943

Activated: 20-Nov-1943

881ST Bombardment Squadron (VH)

Insignia: (unapproved)

Constituted:

881ST Bombardment Squadron (VH)/ 19-Nov-1943

Activated: 20-Nov-1943

882D Bombardment Squadron (VH)

Insignia: (unknown)

Constituted:

882D Bombardment Squadron (VH)/ 19-Nov-1943

Activated: 20-Nov-1943

883D Bombardment Squadron (VH)

Insignia: (unknown)

Constituted:

883D Bombardment Squadron (VH)/ 19-Nov-1943

Activated: 20-Nov-1943

500th BombGp/B-29s Tactical Markings: c.July 1944–Apr 1945

Assignment to the 73d BombWg brought with it the allocation of an upper case letter "Z" as its group tactical aircraft indicator. In compliance with 73d BombWg directives, this group designator was applied in stack fashion to the vertical tail fins of all 500th BombGp B-29s, with the 73d's geometric square symbol centered between the group device and the individual aircraft's call number.

As with other groups in the 73d BombWg, factory applied tail serial numbers were removed to make room for the new tactical markings. The last four digits of each ship's serial number was reapplied to the mid-rudder area, and as with the fin markings all were applied in black.

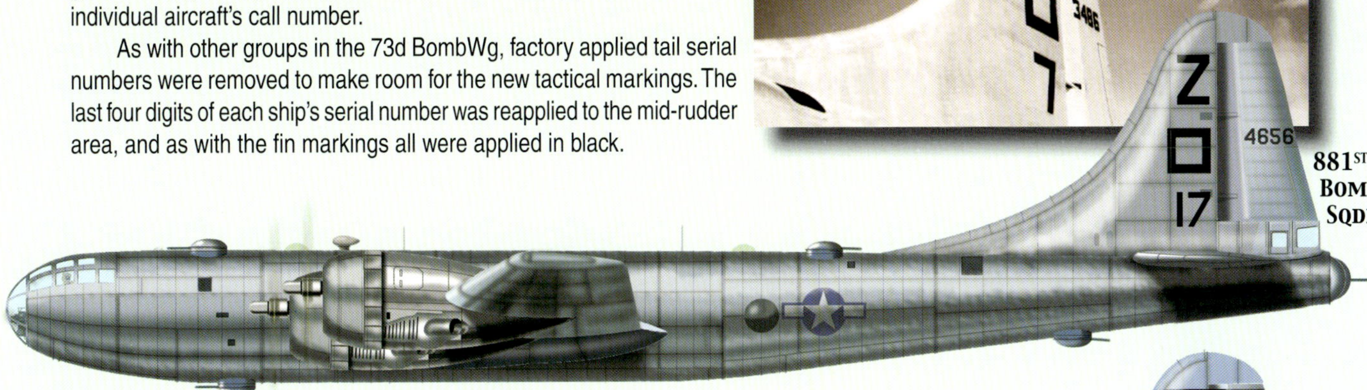

881st Bomb Sqdn

500th BombGp/B-29s Tactical Markings: c.April 1945 thru V-J Day

882d Bomb Sqdn

New tactical markings accompanying a directive to remove all individual nose art from 73d BombWg B-29s resulted in the 500th BombGp letter "Z" designator becoming the sole tactical tail marking device. Aircraft call numbers were relocated to the rear fuselage, with a smaller version placed on the forward nose area.

As with the 497th BombGp, the 500th opted to replace old nose art with the 73d BombWg Winged Globe and Arrow, with many of these applications including preapproved aircraft names in the forward arrow section.

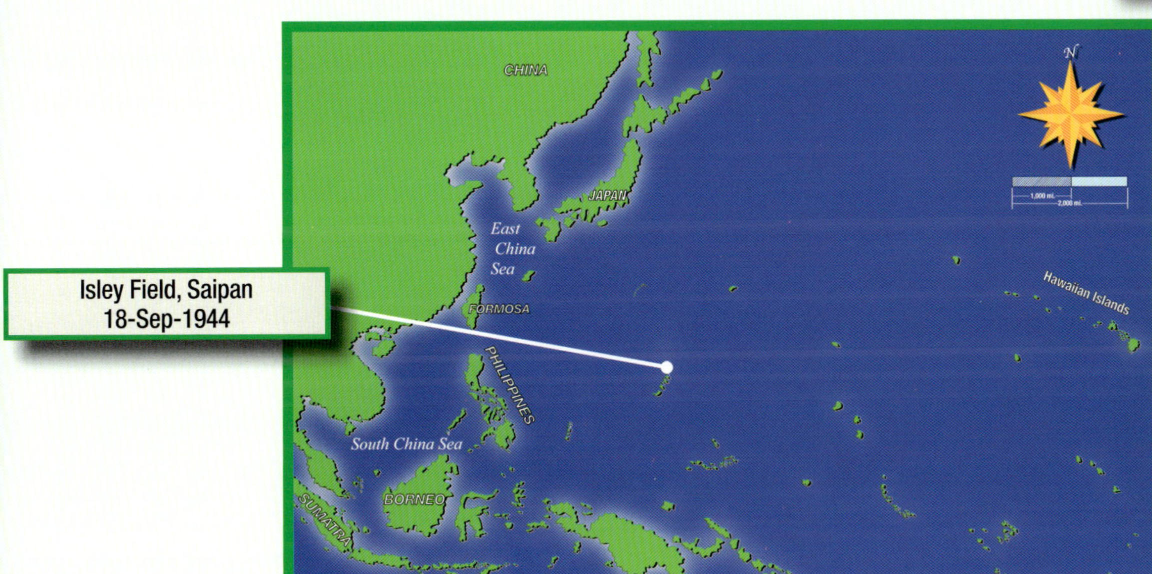

• Assigned Twentieth AF: March 1945 thru V-J Day •

315th Bomb Wg
c. Apr/May-1945

XXI Bomb Comd
c. Apr/May-1945

501st Bombardment Group (VH)

Insignia: (unknown)

Motto: (unknown)

Constituted:

501st Bomb Gp (VH)/ 25-May-1944

Activated: 1-Jun-1944

21st Bombardment Squadron (VH)

Insignia: (unknown)

Constituted:
21st BombSqdn(VH)/ 28-Mar-1944
Activated: 1-Apr-1944

41st Bombardment Squadron (VH)

Insignia: Approved/ 17-Apr-1945

Constituted:
41st BombSqdn(VH)/ 28-Mar-1944
Activated: 1-Apr-1944

485th Bombardment Squadron (VH)

Insignia: Approved/ 26-Jun-1945

Constituted:
73d AeroSqdn/ 14-Aug-1917
Redesignated:
485th AeroSqdn/ 1-Feb-1918
485th BombSqdn/ 31-Mar-1924
485th BombSqdn(VH)/ 28-Jan-1944
Activated: 28-Feb-1944

501st BombGp/B-29s
Tactical Markings: c.March 1945 through V-J Day

Research turned up very few photos on file of the 501st. The group's late arrival to the war, a war-weary public, and lack of unique airframe design elements may have all contributed to this lack of visual record. The 501st BombGp was but one of the most lackluster units serving in the Twentieth Air Force, comprised of aircraft not only void of any colorful unit distinctiveness, but apparently lacking even any vestige of individual nose art. Tactical markings of the 501st BombGp consisted of a large black diamond "Y" affixed to the vertical tail with designated aircraft-in-squadron numbers in twenty-digit sequences applied in black to the rear fuselage, immediately aft the national emblems. Research found no indication these same numbers were duplicated on the aircraft's nose area, as was the case within many other groups.

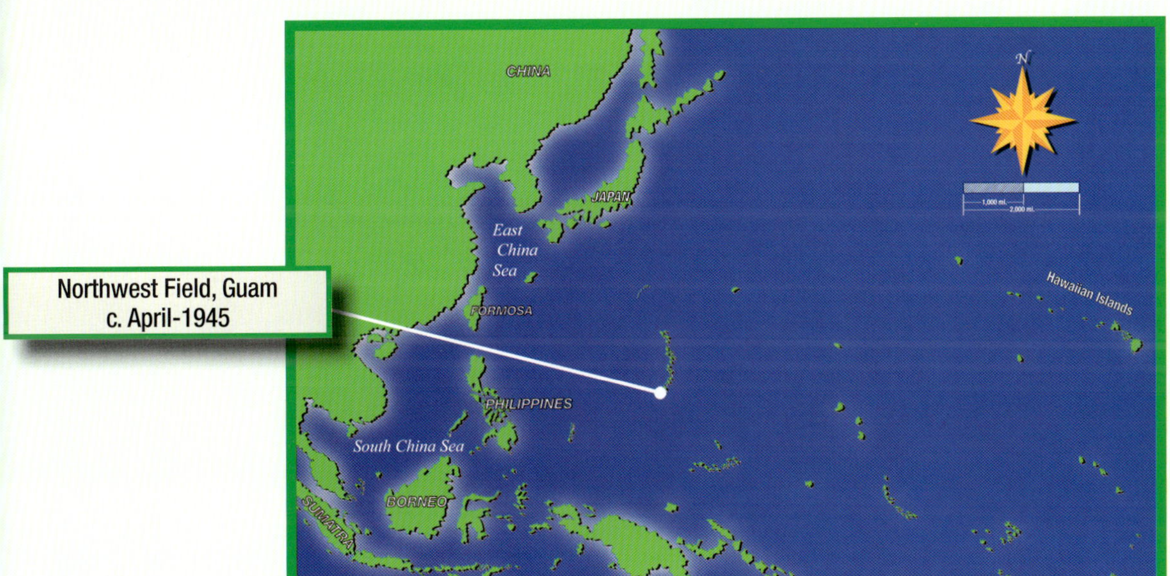

• Assigned Twentieth AF: April 1945 thru V-J Day •

315TH Bomb Wg
c. Apr/May-1945

XXI Bomb Comd
c. Apr/May-1945

20

502D Bombardment Group (VH)

Insignia: (unapproved)

Motto: (unknown)

Constituted:

502D Bomb Gp (VH)/ 25-May-1944

Activated: 1-Jun-1944

402D Bombardment Squadron (VH)

Insignia: Approved/ 23-Oct-1941

Constituted:
12THRcnSqdn(H)/ 20-Nov-1940
Activated: 15-Jan-1941
Redesignated:
402D BombSqdn(H)/ 22-Apr-1942
402D BombSqdn(VH)/ 28-Mar-1944

H 1 THRU 20

411TH Bombardment Squadron (VH)

Insignia: Approved/ 7-Aug-1937

Organized:
16TH AeroSqdn/ May-1917
Redesignated:
21ST AeroSqdn/ 13-Jun-1917
21ST ObsSqdn/ 24-Mar-1923
21ST ObsSqdn(L-R, Amphib)/ 2-Dec-1936
21ST RcnSqdn/ 1-Sep-1936
21ST RcnSqdn(L-R)/ 6-Dec-1939
21ST RcnSqdn(H)/ 20-Nov-1940
411TH BombSqdn(H)/ 22-Apr-1942
411TH BombSqdn(VH)/ 28-Mar-1944

H 21 THRU 40

430TH Bombardment Squadron (VH)

Insignia: Approved/ 20-Jan-1925

H 41 THRU 60

Organized:
44THAeroSqdn/ 30-Jun-1917
Redesignated:
Sqdn "K," Wilbur Wright Fld/ Oct-1918
Sqdn "P," Wilbur Wright Fld/ Nov-1918
44TH Sqdn/ 1923
44TH ObsSqdn/ 25-Jan-1923
44TH RcnSqdn/ 1-Sep-1937
44TH RcnSqdn(MedRange)/ 6-Dec-1939
44TH RcnSqdn(H)/ 12-Apr-1942
430TH BombSqdn(H)/ 22-Apr-1942
430TH BombSqdn(VH)/ 28-Mar-1944

502d BombGp/B-29s
Tactical Markings: c. April 1945 through V-J Day

Another visually lackluster unit in the 315th BombWg virtually ignored by the US press corps and their photographers was the 502d BombGp.

A large, heavily outlined black geometric diamond containing an uppercase letter "H" dominated the vertical tail surface of the 502d's B-29s, serving to identify both group and wing assignment. Each ship bore black call numbers according to its respective squadron affixed to the rear fuselage aft the national emblem.

Research turned up very few wartime photos of this group's aircraft. What makes this image (right) particularly interesting (in addition to the AN/APG-15 radar unit) is the presence of the four-digit numbers applied to the lower leading tail fin. It can be speculated these were the last four digits of each aircraft's original serial numbers, but this is only conjecture, as no field orders make reference to these particular numbers. This image was not dated, so we are left to guess when this photo was taken. It could very well be postwar, taken on Guam sometime before the 502d was inactivated in April 1946.

Additionally, the 502d BombGp is said to have painted the inner part of its tail diamond in a medium blue late in the war, but again, no photos or documentation could be located that factually support this particular application.

In spite of the fact the 502d emblem was never officially approved, it was nevertheless a very attractive design and would have been a visually appealing addition to the forward nose section of this group's B-29s.

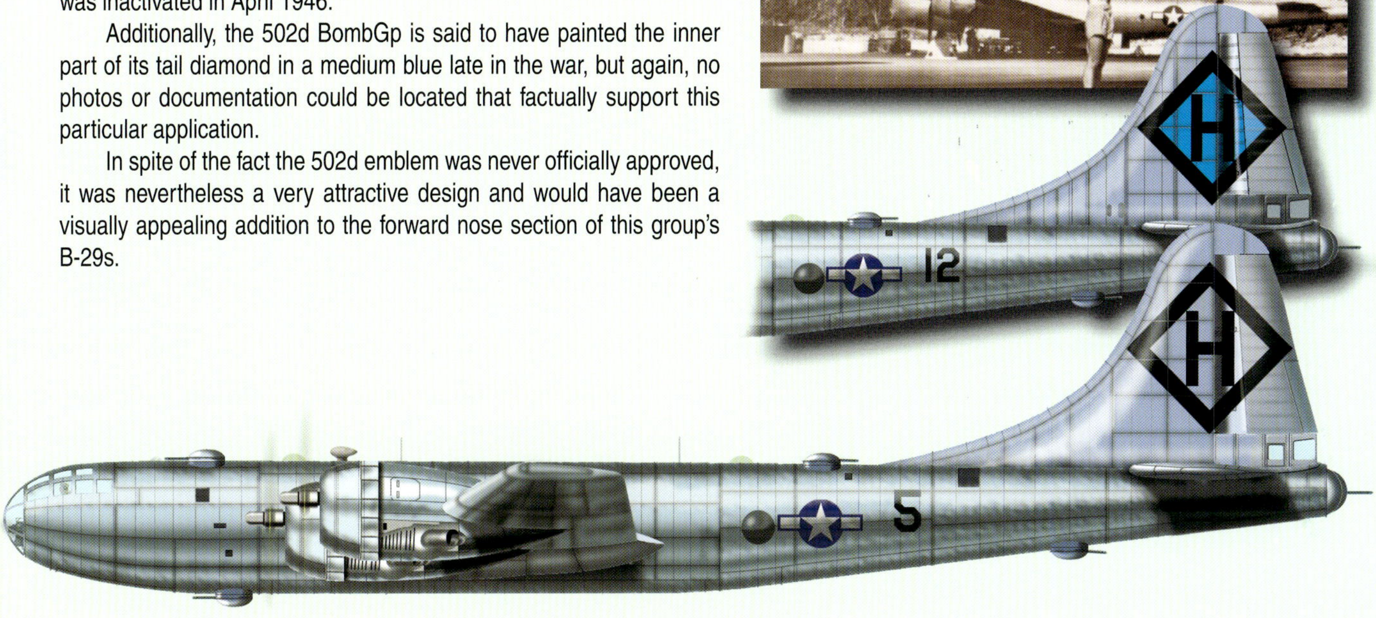

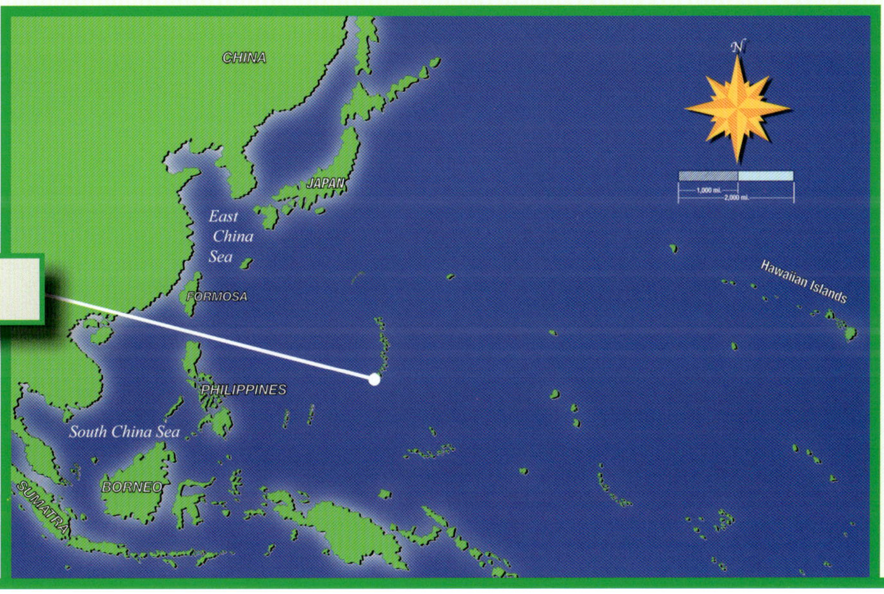

Northwest Field, Guam
c. April-1945

• Assigned Twentieth AF: c.December-1944 thru V-J Day •

313th Bomb Wg
c. Dec-1944

XXI Bomber Comd
c. Dec-1944

504th Bombardment Group (VH)

Insignia: (Unapproved)

Motto:

Those Who Are
Virtuous Command

Constituted:

504th Bomb Gp (VH)/ 28-Feb-1944

Activated: 11-Mar-1944

This simplified version was sometimes used as a substitute for the somewhat more detailed emblem depicted below. Although neither version was ever approved for use, there is no evidence that this insignia was ever submitted to the Heraldic Section for consideration.

398th Bombardment Squadron (VH)

Insignia: Approved/ 20-Sep-1944

Constituted:

398th Bombardment Squadron (VH)/ 28-Feb-1944

Activated: 11-Mar-1944

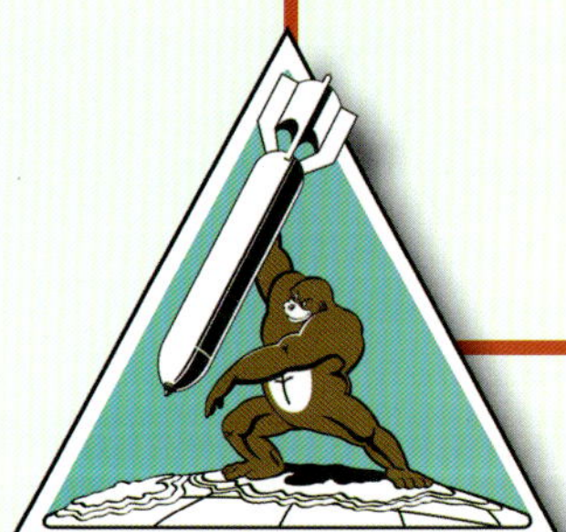

421st Bombardment Squadron (VH)

Insignia: Approved/ 2-Nov-1944

Constituted:

421st Bombardment Squadron (VH)/ 28-Feb-1944

Activated: 11-Mar-1944

680th Bombardment Squadron (VH)

Insignia: (Unapproved)

Constituted:

680th Bombardment Squadron (VH)/ 25-Nov-1944

Activated: 4-Dec-1944

04th BombGp/B-29s
actical Markings: c. January 1945-April 1945

Shortly after arriving at North Field, 504th BombGp B-29s were displaying Triangle "E" tail markings, the uppercase "E" being the group designator, while the geometric triangle represented the 313th BombWg.

Assigned call numbers were positioned directly below the group/wing symbols and were all situated on both sides of the vertical fin in black paint. The factory applied serial numbers were eliminated with apparently no reapplication.

Flight leaders in the squadrons were originally identified with the application of a black band on the dorsal fin, but were later expanded to encircle the entire leading empennage area.

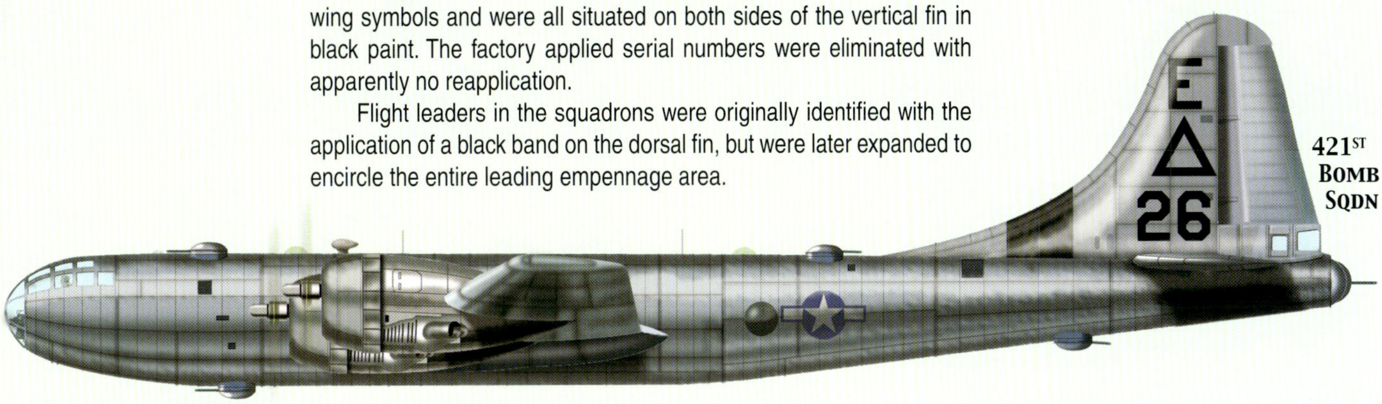

04th BombGp/B-29s
actical Markings: c. April 1945 through V-J Day

In spring 1945, the entire 313th BombWg modified the tactical markings for all of its assigned heavy bomb groups. For the 504th BombGp, this entailed replacing its earlier three component fin markings with a single Circle "E" encompassing the fin and rudder areas of both sides of the vertical tail section. Tail tips were painted a yellow-orange as an additional wing marking; while the call numbers were more often than not relocated to the rear fuselage, there were some aircraft in the group that did not display these devices (i.e., s/n 42-24780 of the 398th BombSqdn below).

Flight leaders during this period were generally identified by yellow-orange and black empennage bands, chordwise wing stripes, and often accompanied with yellow-orange painted inner cowling rings on all four engines.

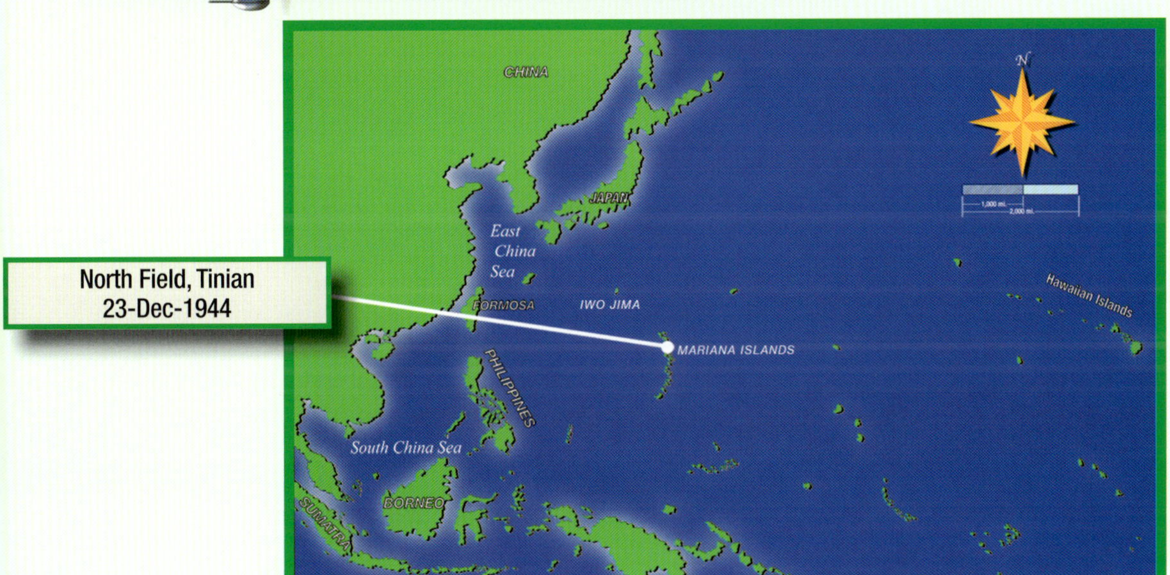

• Assigned Twentieth AF: December 1944 thru V-J Day •

313th Bomb Wg
c.Dec-1944

XXI Bomb Comd
c.Dec-1944

505th Bombardment Group (VH)

Insignia: (unapproved)

Motto:

Either To Conquer Or To Die

Constituted:

505th Bomb Gp (VH)/ 28-Feb-1944

Activated: 11 Mar-1944

The colors used in depicting these 505th BombGp emblems are based upon personal recollections of former unit members. This design was apparently never forwarded to the Heraldic Section for consideration; consequently, there is nothing on file serving as reliable reference when it came to replicating this design. It has been conclusively established that the three large symbols depicted diagonally within the shield proper are intended to represent the Chinese numerals 505.

482d Bombardment Squadron (VH)

Insignia: Approved/16-Dec-1944

Organized:
70th AeroSqdn/13-Aug-1917
Redesignated:
482d Aero Sqdn/1-Feb-1918
482d BombSqdn/ 31-Mar-1924
482d BombSqdn(VH)/ 28-Feb-1944
Activated: 11-Mar-1944

483d Bombardment Squadron (VH)

Insignia: (unapproved)

Constituted:
483d BombSqdn(VH)/ 28-Feb-1944
Activated: 11-Mar-1944

484th Bombardment Squadron (VH)

Insignia: (unapproved)

Organized:
72d AeroSqdn/ 15-Aug-1917
Redesignated:
484th AeroSqdn/ 1-Feb-1918
484th BombSqdn/ 31-Mar-1924
484th BombSqdn(VH)/ 28-Jan-1944
Activated: 28-Feb-1944

04th BombGp/B-29s
actical Markings: c. December 1944 through April 1945

Triangle "K" tail fin markings identified the B-29s of the 505th BombGp shortly after being posted to Tinian Island. Marking devices were stacked on vertical fin surfaces above the aircraft's factory applied serial numbers and were applied with black paint. Immediately below the serial number was each aircraft's assigned call number, also applied with black paint. These tactical markings were confined to both sides of the vertical tail fin surfaces with no additional identifying devices being utilized on any other part of the airframe.

04th BombGp/B-29s
actical Markings: c. April 1945 through V-J Day

Factory applied aircraft serial numbers disappeared from the tail fins of the group's B-29s with the adoption of the new tactical markings. Along with the 6th BombGp, the 505th BombGp was the only other unit in the 313th BombWg that changed its letter designation. In the case of the 505th, the uppercase "K" was replaced with an uppercase "W" in a heavily outlined circle. This new device covered the fin and rudder surface area on both sides of the vertical tail. Individual aircraft call numbers were relocated to the fuselage, immediately aft the national emblem. What few photos there are of this group's B-29s indicate the unit emblem was applied to the forward nose area of numerous ships.

Flight leaders in the group displayed the vertical stripes to the dorsal fin or leading empennage consistent with 313th BombWg directives. Inner engine cowlings and wing stripes were also known to have been applied to some but not all flight leaders in the 505th BombGp.

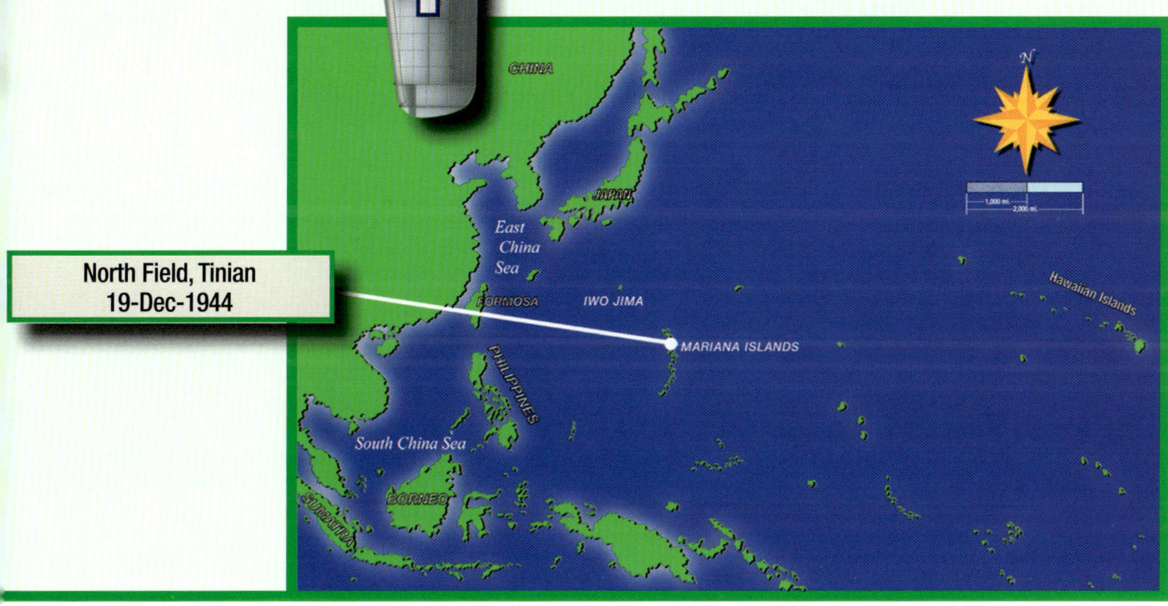

U.S.A.A.F. SPECIAL OPERATIONS UNITS

CHINA-BURMA-INDIA THEATER OF OPERATIONS

Tactical Markings

Those familiar with the Hiroshima mission will recognize the top two photos in this montage—these images might be titled "A Wolf in Wolf's Clothing." The proper tactical emblem for the *Enola Gay* was the Circle Arrow of the 509th Composite Group, but for security purposes these markings were replaced during the first atomic bomb drop. The *Enola Gay* actually carried the Circle "R" tail markings of the 6th Bomb Group into battle—a minor point perhaps, but one that has caused no small amount of confusion ever since with those not altogether familiar with this aspect of history.

Although changing tactical markings on military equipment was by no means a new innovation, the advent of photographic images of this equipment did create a somewhat new problem for the modern researcher. Sometimes a squadron might inherit aircraft from another unit and go into combat before the original squadron's markings could be replaced. Unless such photographs were careful to make note of such discrepancies, this could well lead to mislabeling such photos in the future. Outside B-29s of the 509th BombGp, tactical markings on other AAF specialized units operating in the CBI were more a matter of self protection than anything else. At times the greater threat to US airmen was not the Japanese or weather, but friendly fire incidences with Allied anti-aircraft ground fire; this was especially true with many of the indigenous gun crews, who were grievously under trained in aircraft identification. This seems to have been directly behind the 1st Air Commando Group eventually adopting a series of five thin stripes applied diagonally toward the rear fuselage of their aircraft. These stripes were affixed to the group's medium bombers, transports, fighters, and even L-Birds. This reflects just how close this particular unit operated in relation to the action taking place on the ground.

• Assigned HQ/AAF, c. September-1943 / Tenth AF, c. March-1944 thru V-J Day •

1st Air Commando Group

Insignia: (Unapproved)

Motto:

Anywhere, Anyplace, Anytime

Authorized: 'Project 9' / 13-Sep-1943

Redesignated:

5318 Provisional Air Unit/ c.Jan-1944

1st Air Cmdo Force/ c. Feb-1944

1st Air Cmdo Gp/ 29-Mar-1944

The origins and time frame connected with this emblem are the subject of much discussion, but it is generally agreed this design was connected with the 1st Air Commando Group, with a strong likelihood it belonged to the 5th FtrSqdn.

5th Ftr Sqdn (Cmdo)

Insignia: (unknown)

NO KNOWN SQUADRON INSIGNIA

Constituted:
6th Ftr Sqdn (Cmdo)
9-Aug-1944
Activated: 1-Sep-1044

6th Ftr Sqdn (Cmdo)

Insignia: (unknown)

NO KNOWN SQUADRON INSIGNIA

Constituted:
6th Ftr Sqdn (Cmdo)
22-Sep-1944
Activated: 30-Sep-1944

164th Ln Sqdn (Cmdo)

Insignia: (unknown)

NO KNOWN SQUADRON INSIGNIA

Constituted:
164th Ln Sqdn (Cmdo)
9-Aug-1944
Activated: 1-Sep-1944

165th Ln Sqdn (Cmdo)

Insignia: (unknown)

NO KNOWN SQUADRON INSIGNIA

Constituted:
165th Ln Sqdn (Cmdo)
9-Aug-1944
Activated: 1-Sep-1944

166th Ln Sqdn (Cmdo)

Insignia: (unknown)

NO KNOWN SQUADRON INSIGNIA

Constituted:
166th Ln Sqdn (Cmdo)
9-Aug-1944
Activated: 1-Sep-1944

319th Tr Carr Sqdn (Cmdo)

Insignia: (unofficial)

?

Constituted:
319th Tr Carr Sqdn (Cmdo)
9-Aug-1944
Activated: 1-Sep-1944

The Chindits—a mixed force of British serving units—proudly adopted this emblem (left) during Operation Longcloth, Brig. Orde Wingate's first incursion behind Japanese lines in Burma in early 1943. In later joint operations, members of the 5418th Provisional Air Unit (1stACG) were often presented this emblem by their British counterparts in appreciation for the tremendous support provided to the Chindit ground forces during Operation Thursday. Being made an honorary Chindit was considered a singular distinction by the US airmen.

C-47 Skytrain Transport Section

Very early on, the unit's Transport Section adopted the placement of the "!" unit emblem on the vertical tail fin of their C-47s, immediately above the serial number. This same squadron device was later adopted to represent the entire 1st AirCmdoGp.

Spinners of the unit's P-51As were painted white or left in a natural metal finish.

P-51A Mustang Fighter Section

B-25 Mitchell Bomber Section

In addition to the five fuselage stripes, the twelve B-25s of the 5318th each displayed their respective assigned numbers affixed to both sides of the nose area. These were not standardized and appeared in black or medium blue, sometimes accompanied with a white contour outline.

P-47 Thunderbolt

1st AirCmdoGp Tactical Markings: c. March 1944 Thru V-J Day

The 5418th Provisional Air Unit was withdrawn from front line duty in late May 1945 for rest and reorganization. The exact chronology of the reorganization of this unit is somewhat convoluted during this period, but when the dust finally settled, the 1st Air Commando Group had been constituted. During this transition the bomber section of the original unit was eliminated and the remaining sections reorganized as squadrons, with the P-51s of the 5th FtrSqdn being reequipped with P-47 Thunderbolts. The original fuselage stripes employed by the 5418th ProvAirUnit were discarded for a time during the reorganization phase. These tactical marking devices were revived and continued in use throughout the war.

When these diagonal stripes were readopted they were applied with Insignia Blue to NMF airframes. Additional markings on the 5th FtrSqdn's P-47s were EAC markings applied to the tail fin, cowling ring, and wings in the same blue color. The fin markings were originally confined to the fin area with a number-in-squadron affixed near the cockpit in black. Later the horizontal tail stripe was extended to the rudder surface as well, with the aircraft number painted in white on the horizontal EAC tail band.

Last to adopt the diagonal tactical stripes were the group's light planes and gliders, but the application of these markings were reduced in size and confined to the vertical fin strakes of the aircraft (left).

L-5 'Sentinel'

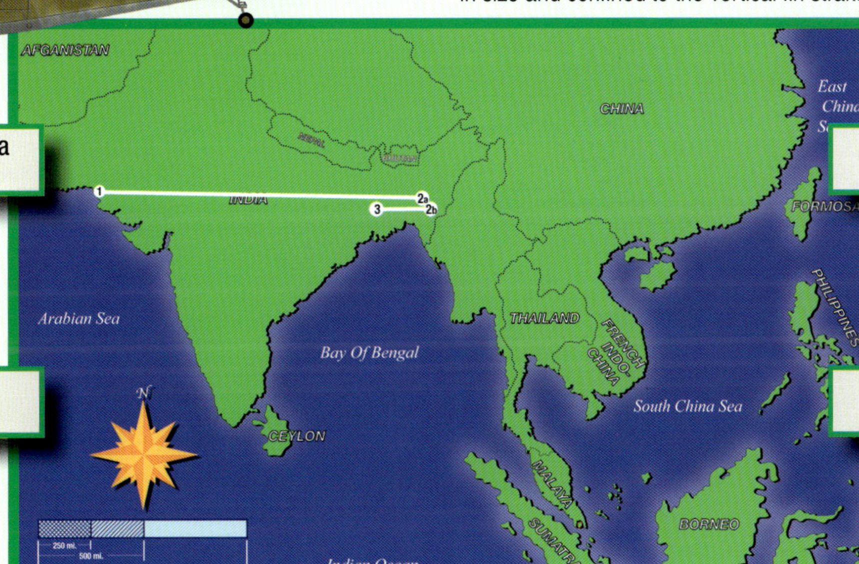

***1) Malir A/F, Karachi, India c.Nov-1943**

* HQ established for transition and training.

***2a) Hailakandi A/F, India c.Jan-1944**

3) Asansol A/F, India 20-May-1944

***2b) Lalaghat A/F, India c.Jan-1944**

* HQ, Fighter, Bomber, and Liaison units were stationed at Hailakandi Airfield. Transport units and gliders were stationed at Lalaghat Airfield

• Assigned AAF, c.12-Nov-1944 / Tenth AF, 10-July-1945 / AAF, c.18-Aug-1945 •

2D Air Commando Group

Insignia: (Unapproved)

Constituted:
2D Air Cmdo Gp/ 11-Apr-1944

Activated: 22-Apr-1944

Group Emblem Note

In keeping with the "?" unit marking device theme started by the 1st AirCmdoGp, the 2d AirCmdoGp selected an exclamation point "!" as their unit marker. This particular punctuation mark was to play a prominent role during this group's existence, being positioned on the vertical tail section of virtually all of its combat aircraft.

The Thunderbolt icons (opposite page) incorporated in the 2d AirCmdoGp's emblem were also adopted for airframe applications.

1ST Ftr Sqdn (Cmdo)

Insignia: (Unofficial)

Constituted:
1ST Ftr Rcn Sqdn/ 11-Apr-1944
Activated: 20-Apr-1944
Redesignated:
1ST Ftr Sqdn (Cmdo)/ 2-Jun-1944

2D Ftr Sqdn (Cmdo)

Insignia: Approved/ 3-Aug-1945

Constituted:
2D Ftr Rcn Sqdn/ 11-Apr-1944
Activated: 20-Apr-1944
Redesignated:
2D Ftr Sqdn (Cmdo)/ 2-Jun-1944

©Walt Disney

127TH Ln Sqdn (Cmdo)

Insignia: Approved/ 16-Jun-1942
(Approved for 127th Observation Squadron)

Designated:
127TH Obs Sqdn/ 30-Jul-1940
Activated: 4-Aug-1941
Redesignated:
127TH Obs Sqdn (Lt)/ 13-Jan-1942
127TH Obs Sqdn/ 4-Jul-1942
127TH Ln Sqdn/ 2-Apr-1943
127TH Ln Sqdn (Cmdo)/ 1-May-1944

155TH Ln Sqdn (Cmdo)

Insignia: Approved/ 10-Jun-1944

Constituted:
155TH Ln Sqdn/ 31-Dec-1943
Activated: 10-Jan-1944
Redesignated:
155TH Ln Sqdn (Cmdo)/1-May-1944

No Known Squadron Insignia

156TH Ln Sqdn (Cmdo)

Insignia: (Unknown)

Constituted:
156TH Ln Sqdn/ 28-Jan-1944
Activated: 10-Feb-1944
Redesignated:
156TH Ln Sqdn (Cmdo)
1-May-1944

317TH Tr Carr Sqdn (Cmdo)

Insignia: (Unknown)

Constituted:
317th Tr Carr Sqdn (Cmdo)
1-May-1944
Activated: 1-May-1944

No Known Squadron Insignia

Unlike its sister unit (1st AirCmdoGp), the 2d AirCmdo was deployed without a bombardment squadron attached to it. Another difference was the fighters assigned to both fighter squadrons. While the 1stACG started and ended operating P-51A and D Mustangs with P-47 Thunderbolts in between, the 2dACG was equipped with P-51D and F6-D Mustangs for its entire wartime deployment. The 1stACG adopted a large "!" incorporated in its emblem, in addition to being affixed in black paint to the vertical tail fin of assigned aircraft. Group EAC markings varied from those specified and were applied with black paint, including tail control surfaces.

The 2dACG's "!" marking device was applied to virtually all operational aircraft. Some L-5s assigned to the group later also displayed the group's signature thunderbolts on their airframes—similar to those affixed to the fighters, but with the fuselage 'bolts running from top to bottom. As a rule these aircraft were also adorned with the same, albeit smaller version of the EAC markings.

Spinners of the group's Mustangs were painted solid black.

As depicted here, all Mustangs in the 2dACG were adorned with black thunderbolts on their airframes. These unit marking devices were also applied to the wing undersurfaces. The 2d FtrSqdn(Cmdo) was the only squadron in the 2d ACG known to have displayed its unit emblem on their aircraft in the form of commercially supplied dry transfer decals positioned on the fuselage, just forward of the wing leading edge.

Around June 1945, the group's exclamation point tail marking, as well as the horizontal EAC band and aircraft serial number (previously positioned on the forward nose area), were replaced on the group's P-51s with large aircraft-in-squadron numerical codes. Other types of aircraft also received these numerical tail codes, but in these cases serial numbers were retained. The new call numbers were painted black on NMF surfaces and white on airframes still painted olive drab.

509th Composite Group

Insignia: (see notation)

Motto:

First Atomic Bombardment

Constituted:

509th Comp Gp/ 9-Dec-1944

Activated: 17-Dec-1944

Group Emblem Note

The design depicted (left), although never officially approved by the Heraldic Section, is nevertheless the design selected to represent the 509thCG by veterans of this unit. Additionally, it is included in memorials at Wendover Field, Tinian Island, and other locations. There are those that believe Col. Paul Tibbits was the creator of this insignia, but to date there exists no hard evidence to conclusively support this position.

Equally uncertain is an exact date connected with this design. If not created prior to V-J Day, it most certainly came into being immediately on the heels of the conclusion of hostilities.

320th Troop Carrier Squadron

Insignia: Approved/ 27-Jun-1945
'The Green Hornet Line (Airline)'

Constituted:
320th Troop Carrier Squadron / 9-Dec-1944
Activated: 17-Dec-1944

*

* This winged device was affixed to the upper tail fin of 320thTCS's transports. It is not certain exactly what the base color used was but it appears to have been a darker shade of green. The individual aircraft call numbers were applied with white, but the full range of the numerical series used by this squadron is uncertain.

393d Bombardment Squadron (VH)

Insignia: Approved/ 19-Dec-1944

Constituted:
393d Bombardment Squadron (VH)/ 28-Feb-1944
Activated: 11-Mar-1944

The *Enola Gay* in actual WWII battle markings as displayed on 6 August 1945. On this mission led by Col. Paul Tibbits' crew, this ship dropped "Little Boy"—the world's first tactical atomic bomb—on Hiroshima, Japan. Of particular note is the absence of the 509th's actual Circle-Arrow tactical tail marking, replaced instead with the Circle "R" of the 6th BombGp.

Circle "R"	Square "P"	Triangle "N"	"A"
6thBG / 313thBW	39thBG / 314thBW	444thBG / 58thBW	497thBG / 73dBW
Tinian	Guam	Tinian	Saipan
Victor Nos:	Victor Nos:	Victor Nos:	Victor Nos:
[a]82, [a, b]89, [b]90, [a]91	83, 94, 95	[b]77, [a]85, 86, 88	71, 72, 73, 84

Of the fifteen Silverplates assigned to the 509thCG, the *Enola Gay* (V-82) was the only B-29 in the group to display any type of nose art until Japan's surrender. This and other measures were implemented for security reasons. The prevailing opinion for these security measures was because the only defensive capabilities extant in the Silverplates were twin fifty caliber M-2 machine guns in the tail, a commonly known fact even at the time. It can be logically argued that displaying the 509th's Circle Arrow tail marking was tantamount to advertising this defensive vulnerability to enemy fighters.

The display of tail markings (above) shows the allocation of other group tactical tail markings as displayed by all Silverplates prior to the formal surrender of Japan. Footnotes show the "V" Nos. of ships in both phases of Operation Centerboard—the two atomic bomb missions:

a = Hiroshima Strike Force • b = Nagasaki Strike Force

These numbers were affixed in black to the rear fuselage, aft the national emblem, with a smaller version on the nose.

Although sometimes mistakenly used in conjunction with the wartime history of the 509th CombGp, this emblem did not come into existence until well after the end of hostilities.

The 320th TrCarrSqdn displayed its unit emblem with the addition of a large dark green wing on the forward nose area of its transport aircraft, as evidenced in this period photo showing Col. Tibbits at the controls of one of the squadron's C-54 Skymasters.

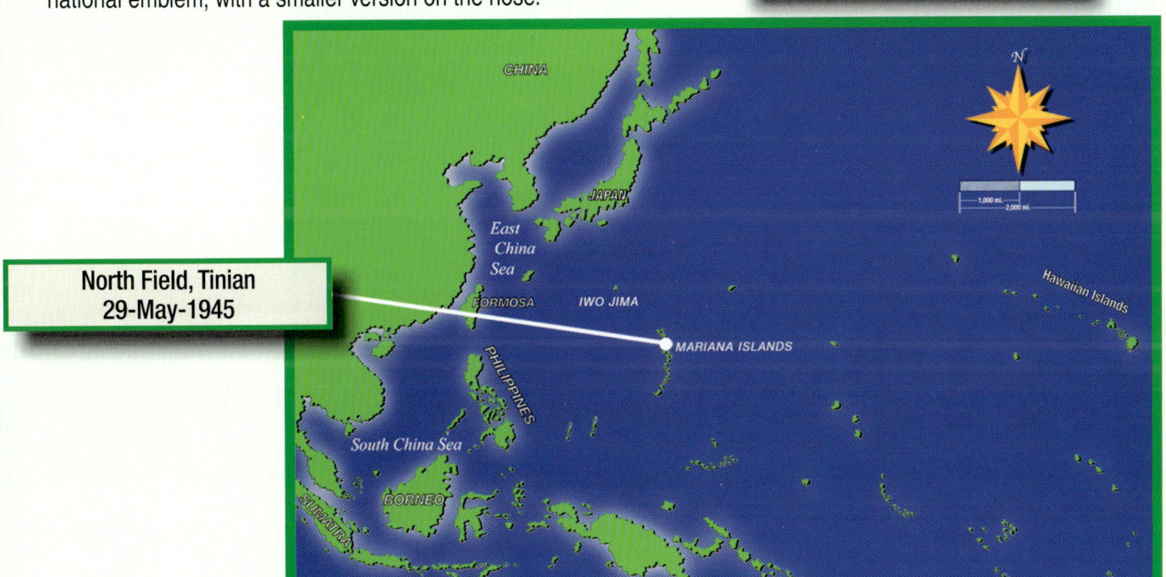

• Assigned Tenth AF, c. February-1944 thru V-J Day •

8th Photographic Reconnaissance Group

Insignia: (unknown)

Constituted:

8th Photo Rcn Gp/ 15-Sep-1943

Activated: 1-Oct-1943

Redesignated: 8th Rcn Gp: Jun-1945

• Mission Panel •

Although not a tactical marking, this mission tally score on the side of one of the 8th PhotoRcnGp's NMF F-5s is worthy of note. Above each of the camera images is carefully lettered the last name of the individual pilot that flew that particular mission.

*9th Photographic Squadron

Insignia: (unapproved)

Constituted:

9th Photo Sqdn/19-Jan-1942

Activated: 1-Feb-1942

Redesignated:

9th Photo Rcn Sqdn/ 9-Jun-1942

9th Photo Sqdn (Lt)/ 6-Feb-1943

9th Photo Sqdn/ 13-Nov-1943

*20th Reconnaissance Squadron

Insignia: Approved: 31-Oct-1942

Constituted:

20th Obs Sqdn (Lt)/ 5-Feb-1942

Activated: 2-Mar-1942

Redesignated:

20th Obs Sqdn/ 4-Jul-1942

20th Rcn Sqdn (Ftr)/ 2-Apr-1943

20th Tac Rcn Sqdn/ 11-Aug-1943

*24th Combat Mapping Squadron

Insignia: Approved: 2-Apr-1945

Constituted:

24th Photo Mpng Sqdn/ 14-Jul-1942

Activated: 2-Sep-1942

Redesignated:

24th Photo Sqdn (H)/ 6-Feb-1943

24th Cmbt Mpng Sqdn/ 11-Aug-1943

40th Photographic Reconnaissance Squadron

Insignia: Approved: 10-Apr-1931

Activated:

103d Obs Sqdn/ 27-Jun-1924

Redesignated:

103d Obs Sqdn (M)/ 13-Jan-1942

103d Obs Sqdn/ 4-Jul-1942

103d Rcn Sqdn (Ftr)/ 2-Apr-1943

103d Tac Rcn Sqdn/ 11-Aug-1943

40th Photo Rcn Sqdn/ 21-Oct-1943

* The 9th PhotoSqdn, 20th RcnSqdn, and 24th CmbtMpngSqdn were already deployed and operational in the CBI prior to subsequently being assigned to the 8th PhotoRcnGp.

Aircraft assigned to the squadrons of the 8th PhotoRcnGp varied considerably, but the primary inventory consisted of P-40s, F-4s, F-5As, F-7s, and F-10s.

There were few tactical markings employed by any of the assigned squadrons, with the exception of the 9th PhotoSqdn. This unit did make use of its unapproved Baby Bengal Tiger emblem. This image was applied to the nose area of a number of the squadron's aircraft. With the arrival of NMF F-5Es in the summer of 1944, a few of these ships also displayed three red stripes on the rear boom area and several of the squadron's B-25s carried single digit call numbers on their tails. These few markings were an exception within the structure of the 8th PRG.

9TH PHOTO SQDN

This emblem was an early war design developed for the 9th PS by Disney Studios. Although originally accepted to represent the group, this image was ultimately replaced with the Bengal Tiger Cub design (facing page) due to the highly complex nature of the dragon motif, which was not only time consuming to replicate, but required a skill set not always readily available in every aviation unit.

20TH PHOTO RCN SQDN

Little is known about this emblem variation, other than it began showing up on flight jackets shortly after the 20th PhotoRcnSqdn's CBI deployment.

40TH PHOTO RCN SQDN

An unapproved late war alternate emblem (right) depicting an F-5 in silhouette over a partial contour map of Indochina.

Until NMF finishes were authorized later in the war, all F-4 and F-5A aircraft operating with the 8th PhotoRcnGp were painted with a haze paint. The use of call numbers in the 9th PhotoSqdn appears to have been sporadic, but those ships that did display such markings were applied in black to the outer engine nacelles. Some ships carried the squadron emblem on the center fuselage pod nose. Individual spinner colors and patterns were common with all squadrons equipped with the F-4 and F-5A Lightning.

In compliance with an AAF recommendation dated 16 October 1943, all F-7s serving with the 8thPRG were painted in a two-color haze blue camouflage. The 24th CmbtMpng was the only squadron to display any tactical markings: the application of the unit emblem to the outside vertical tail fin surfaces.

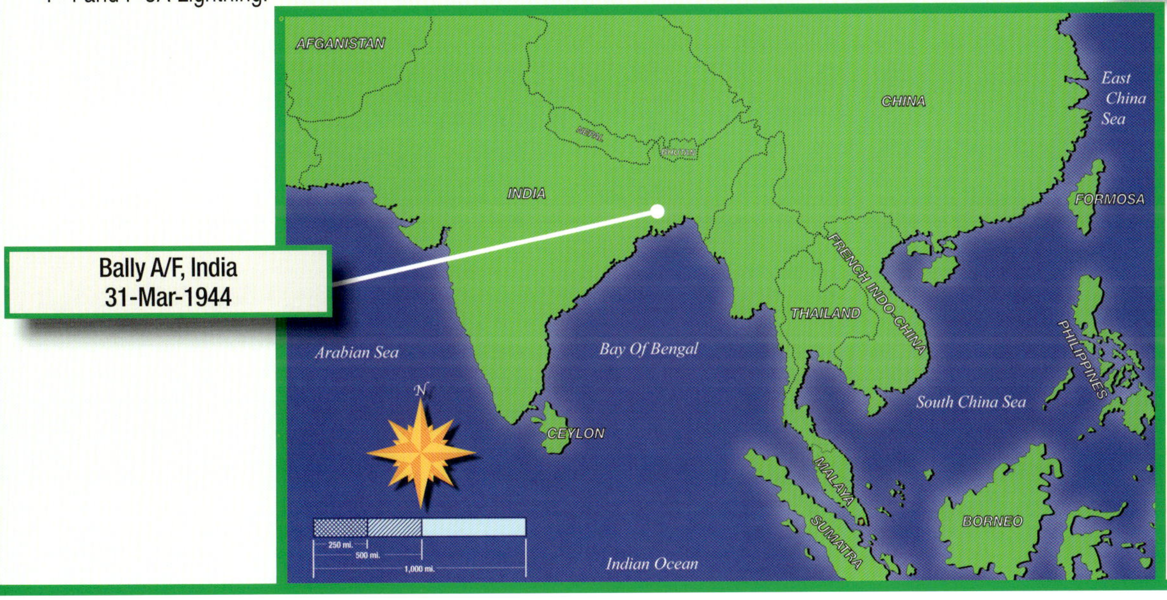

8thPhotoRcnGp Stations

As was so often the case with numerous CBI serving units, this stations map is somewhat deceiving. While its true the 8th PRG / HQ remained anchored in Bally, India, during the unit's entire CBI tour, all of its assigned squadrons operated at various times from a vast number of additional bases in eastern India, Burma, and even as far as China.

1ST PHOTOGRAPHIC RECONNAISSANCE SQUADRON (FLT "C")

ASSIGNMENTS:
311TH RCN WG, 1944
(DETACHED DUTY;
CBI/WPAC)
STATIONS:
OKINAWA, 19-JUL-1945

INSIGNIA: APPROVED/ 3-OCT-1941
CONSTITUTED:
1ST PHOTO RCN SQDN/ 22-DEC-1939
ACTIVATED: 1-FEB-1940
REDESIGNATED:
1ST MPNG SQDN/ 13-JAN-1942
1ST PHOTO MPNG SQDN/ 9-JUN-1942
1ST PHOTO CHRTNG SQDN/ 11-AUG-1943
1ST PHOTO RCN SQDN (VH)/ 10-NOV-1944

3D PHOTOGRAPHIC RECONNAISSANCE SQUADRON

ASSIGNMENTS:
311TH PHOTO (LATER RCN) WG, 5-OC-1944
ATTACHED TO:
A) TWENTIETH AIR FORCE,1-NOV-1944
B) XXI BOMBER COMMAND, DEC-1944
C) TWENTIETH AIR FORCE, 16-JUL-1945
STATIONS:
SAIPAN, 18-SEP-1944
GUAM, 11-JAN-1945

INSIGNIA: APPROVED/ 24-JUL-1943
CONSTITUTED:
3D PHOTO SQDN/ 15-MAY-1941
ACTIVATED: 10-JUN-1941
REDESIGNATED:
3D MPNG SQDN/ 13-JAN-1942
3D PHOTO MPNG SQDN/ 9-JUN-1942
3D PHOTO RCN SQDN (VH)/ 19-MAY-1944

3D PhotoMpngSqdn
This original emblem was designed by Disney Studios at the request of the squadron (c. 1941) prior to the unit's deployment to the CBI, but was subsequently replaced by the approved design (left).

21ST PHOTOGRAPHIC RECONNAISSANCE SQUADRON

ASSIGNMENTS:
FOURTEENTH AIR FORCE, JUN 1943-6 JAN 1946
STATIONS:
BISHNUPUR, INDIA, 27-JUN-1943
KUNMING, CHINA, 22-AUG-1943
LIANGSHAN, CHINA, 1-APR/18-OCT-1944
KANCHOW, CHINA, AUG/20-NOV-1944
LIUCHOW, CHINA, 10-SEP/6-NOV-1944
HANCHUNG, CHINA, 18-OCT-1944/13 AUG-1945
LULIANG, CHINA, C. 26-NOV-1944/13-MAY-1945
LAIFENG, CHINA, 7-MAY/16-AUG-1945)
SHWANGLIU, CHINA, 14-MAY-1945

INSIGNIA: APPROVED/ 29-APR-1944
CONSTITUTED:
21ST PHOTO RCN SQDN/ 14-JUL-1942
ACTIVATED: 2-SEP-1942
REDESIGNATED:
21ST PHOTO SQDN (LT)/ 6-FEB-1943
21ST PHOTO RCN SQDN/ 13-NOV-1943

35TH PHOTOGRAPHIC RECONNAISSANCE SQUADRON

INSIGNIA: APPROVED/ 23-OCT-1944
DESIGNATED:
123D OBS SQDN/ 30-JUL-1940
ACTIVATED: 18-APR-1941
REDESIGNATED:
123D OBS SQDN (LT)/ 13-JAN-1942
123D OBS SQDN/ 4-JUL-1942
123D RCN SQDN (BOMB)/ 2-APR-1943
35TH PHOTO RCN SQDN/ 11-AUG-1943

ASSIGNMENTS:
AAF, INDIA-BURMA SECTOR, 5-MAY-1944
FOURTEENTH AIR FORCE, C.SEP-1944
TENTH AIR FORCE, 1-AUG-1945
FOURTEENTH AIR FORCE, 25-AUG/7-NOV-1945
STATIONS:
GUSKHARA, INDIA, 13-JUN-1944
KUNMING, CHINA, 1-SEP-1944
CHANYI, CHINA, 17-SEP-1944

41st Photographic Reconnaissance Squadron

Assignments:
* 7th Fighter Wing, 18-Apr-1945
AAF, Pacific Ocean Area
(attached to XXI Bomber Command, 13-Jun-1945)
United States Army Forces, Middle Pacific
(attached to Twentieth Air Force, 16-Jul-1945)
Stations:
Kualoa Field, TH, 18-Apr/31 May-1945
Northwest Field, Guam, 13-Jun-1945
(detachment at Iwo Jima, 9-Aug/c.15-Sep-1945)
* Refer to *Battle Colors / Vol. V*

Insignia: Approved/ 3-Jan-1933
Organized:
Co. 'A', 4th Bln Sqdn/ 13-Nov-1917
Redesignated:
9th Bln Co./ 25-Jul-1918
9th Arshp Co./ 30-Aug-1921
9th Arsp Sqdn/ 26-Oct-1933
1st Obs Sqdn/ 1-Jun-1937
1st Obs Sqdn (M)/ 13-Jan-1942
1st Obs Sqdn/ 4-Jul-1942
1st Rcn Sqdn (Spcl)/ 25-Jun-1943
41st Photo Rcn Sqdn/ 25-Nov-1944

*118th Tactical Reconnaissance Squadron

* Refer to pp. 25–26

655th Reconnaissance Squadron (LR)

Insignia: Approved/ 16-Feb-1945
Designated:
655th Bomb Sqdn (H)(WR)/ 30-Jul-1940
Activated: 21-Aug-1944
Redesignated:
55th Rcn Sqdn (LR)(Wea)/ 16-Jun-1945

Assignments:
Twentieth Air Force, XXI Bmr Comd/ 11-Apr-1945
Stations:
Harmon Field, Guam, 18-Apr/31 May-1945
Northwest Field, Guam, 8-Mar-1945
(Detachment operated from Okinawa, 24-Jul-1945)

5306th Photographic Reconnaissance Group (Prov)

Squadrons: 9th PhotoRcnSqdn / 20th TacMpngSqdn / 24th CmbtMpngSqdn
(Refer to 8th PhotoRcnGp, pp. 122–124)

• ASSIGNED: CHINESE AIR FORCE, (OP/CON) FOURTEENTH USAF, C. JUL-1943 THRU 1-AUG-1945 •

CHINESE-AMERICAN COMPOSITE WING

INSIGNIA: (UNAPPROVED)
ESTABLISHED:
CHINESE-AMERICAN COMPOSITE WING (PROVISIONAL)
13-JUL-1943
ACTIVATED: 1-OCT-1943
REDESIGNATED:
CHINESE-AMERICAN COMPOSITE WING
C.APR-1945

Initially created with the establishment of the 1stBombGp(P) and 3dFtrGp(P) on 31 July 1943, these two units would ultimately evolve into the Chinese American Composite Wing (Prov), and would later be joined by the 5thFtrGp. The CAW was the culmination of a vision and the efforts of Gen. Claire L. Chennault to create a comprehensive pilot training program for Chinese nationals that would eventually result in an operational joint Anglo/Sino air combat unit. The CACW was actually a unit of the Chinese Air Force under the operational control of the US Fourteenth AF.

1ST BOMBARDMENT GROUP (PROVISIONAL)

INSIGNIA: (UNAPPROVED)

ESTABLISHED:
1ST BOMB GP (PROV)/ 31-JUL-1943
REDESIGNATED:
1ST BOMB GP/ C.APR-1945

3D FIGHTER GROUP (PROVISIONAL)

INSIGNIA: (UNAPPROVED)

ESTABLISHED:
3D FTR SQDN (PROV)/ 31-JUL-1943
REDESIGNATED:
3D FTR SQDN/ C.APR-1945

5TH FIGHTER GROUP (PROVISIONAL)

INSIGNIA: (UNAPPROVED)

ESTABLISHED:
5TH FTR SQDN (PROV)/ 13-JAN-1944
ACTIVATED: 13-JAN-1944
REDESIGNATED:
5TH FTR SQDN/ C.APR-1945

h) Peishiyi A/F, China
g) Suichwan A/F, China
f) Hengyang A/F, China
e) Lingling A/F, China
d) Kwelin A/F, China
c) Liuchow A/F, China
b) Chihkiang A/F, China
a) Chanti A/F, China

i) Liangshan A/F, China
j) Enshih A/F, China
k) Hanchung A/F, China
l) Ankang A/F, China
m) Haian A/F, China
n) Laohokow A/F, China
o) Valley Field A/F, China

• Assigned: Chinese-American Composite Wing, c. Jul-1943 thru 1-Aug-1945 •

1st Bombardment Group (Provisional)

Insignia: (unapproved)

Established:
1st Bombardment Group (Provisional)
31-Jul-1943

Activated: 1-Oct-1943

1st Bombardment Squadron (Provisional)

Insignia: (unapproved)

Established
1st Bomb Sqdn (Prov)/ 31-Jul-1943
Activated: 1-Oct-1943

2d Bombardment Squadron (Provisional)

Insignia: (unapproved)

Established
2d Bomb Sqdn (Prov)/ 31-Jul-1943
Activated: 1-Oct-1943

3d Bombardment Squadron (Provisional)

Insignia: (unapproved)

Established
3d Bomb Sqdn (Prov)/ 31-Jul-1943
Activated: 1-Oct-1943

4th Bombardment Squadron (Provisional)

(*Insignia:* (unapproved)

Established
4th Bomb Sqdn (Prov)/ 31-Jul-1943
Activated: 1-Oct-1943

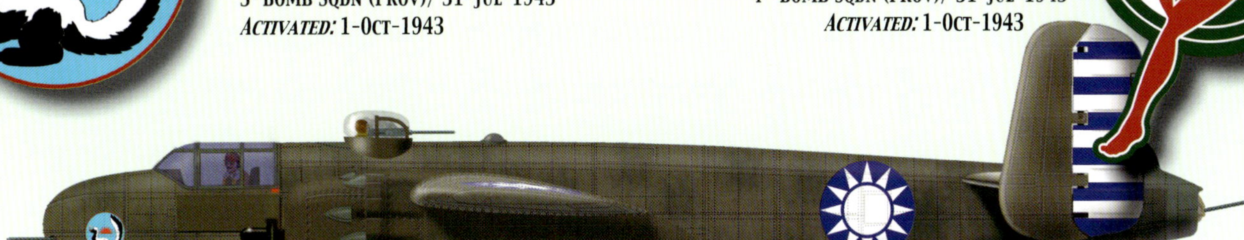

During its tour of duty, the 1stBombGp operated the B-25 Mitchell D, H, and J series medium bombers. Original markings on the two-color camouflaged airframes consisted of a rough over paint of US markings with the application of the Kuomintang emblem to under wings and CAF serial numbers applied in yellow to tail fins. In early 1944, the numbers 601–610 were applied to 2dBS ships. The 1stBS originally started with numbers in the 700 series, but soon changed to 610–620, with the 3dBS adopting a 710–711 series and the practice of affixing its Stinky emblem to the nose area.

Call numbers were likewise affixed to the nose area with either yellow or white paint. The 4thBS may have used a letter "B" with a five-digit code on their tail surfaces, but this is unconfirmed. CAF emblems were eventually applied to upper and lower wing surfaces, and US markings also appeared on ships in standard AAF locations. Rudders often displayed twelve horizontal stripes of alternating blue and white colors on camouflaged and NMF airframes, and this same pattern was often duplicated on inboard rudder surfaces.

• Assigned: Chinese-American Composite Wing, c. Jul-1943 thru 1-Aug-1945 •

3D Fighter Group (Provisional)

Insignia: (unapproved)

Established:
3D Fighter Group (Provisional)
31-Jul-1943

Activated: 1-Oct-1943

In January 1945, the 3dFG began receiving "C" model Mustang hand-me-downs from the 51stFG. Most of these ships were NMF, displaying USAAF markings with three-digit tactical tail codes and adorned with the distinctive sharks mouth on the nose. Newer D and K model Mustangs began arriving in the group in the spring of 1945, but these new arrivals lacked the classic sharks mouth nose pattern of the earlier C models.

7th Fighter Squadron (Provisional)

Insignia: (unapproved)

Established:
7th Ftr Sqdn (Prov)/ 31-Jul-1943
Activated: 1-Oct-1943

8th Fighter Squadron (Provisional

Insignia: (unapproved)

Established:
8th Ftr Sqdn (Prov)/ 31-Jul-1943
Activated: 1-Oct-1943

28th Fighter Squadron (Provisional)

Insignia: (unapproved)

Established:
28th Ftr Sqdn (Prov)/ c.Aug-1943
Activated: 9-Oct-1943

32D Fighter Squadron (Provisional)

Insignia: (unapproved)

Established:
32D Ftr Sqdn (Prov)/ c.Aug-1943
Activated: 9-Oct-1943

All P-40Ns of the group displayed the CAF emblem on under wings and most fuselages. These emblems called for the use of Chinese Medium Royal Blue, but there were many color variations in the entire wing. All ships were of a standard USAAF two-color camouflage, with some ships receiving a medium green edging on leading and trailing wing surface edges. As a rule, most P-40s in the squadron had rudders painted in the standard CAW twelve band pattern. Sharks mouth designs were prevalent throughout the group, with variants in configuration and eye placement.

Unit tac markings until early 1944 were three-digit numbers approximately 10 in. high applied mid-fin with either white or yellow paint. In the spring of 1944, each squadron adopted the following markings: 7thFS/Nos. 660–670 and letters I, J, K, and L; 8thFS/Nos. 678–689 and letters M, N, O, and P; 28thFS/Nos. 631–639 and letters E, F, G, H; and the 32dFS/Nos. 640–657 with letters A, B, C, and D. These new markings were applied as per the above illustration. The exception to these markings were inter-squadron swaps and a number of existing 700 series P-40s in the 28thFS from the 51st FtrGp.

• Assigned: Chinese-American Composite Wing, c.Jan-1944 thru 1-Aug-1945 •

5th Fighter Group (Provisional)

Insignia: (unapproved)

Established:

5th Fighter Group (Provisional)

13-Jan-1944

Activated: c.Jan-1944

The above emblem has been attributed to the 26th FtrSqdn, but the time frame is unknown. Equally unknown is the significance of all of the individual and collective imagery depicted in this design.

17th Fighter Squadron (Provisional)

Insignia: (unapproved)

Established:

17th Ftr Sqdn (Prov)/ c.Mar-1944

Activated: c.Mar-1944

(attached to 26th Ftr Sqdn thru late Aug-1944)

26th Fighter Squadron (Provisional)

Insignia: (unapproved)

Established:

26th Ftr Sqdn (Prov)/ c.Jan-1944

Activated: c.Mar-1944

27th Fighter Squadron (Provisional)

Insignia: (unapproved)

Established:

27th Ftr Sqdn (Prov)/ c.Mar-1944

Activated: 22-Jun-1944

(attached to 29th Ftr Sqdn thru late Aug-1944)

29th Fighter Squadron (Provisional)

Insignia: (unapproved)

Established:

29th Ftr Sqdn (Prov)/ c.Jan-1944

Activated: 17-Mar-1944

The original P-40Ns assigned to the 26th and 29th FtrSqdn were painted in an experiential overall Haze camouflage. Although effective, this paint was short lived, reportedly due to a significant increase in friendly-fire incidents due to AA gunners having difficulty distinguishing friend from foe. Aircraft spinners retained the Haze paint, thus becoming an ad hoc group tactical marking. Three-digit numbers were applied in ten-inch black numerals to the tail fins:

17thFS/ Nos. 760–770 • 26thFS/ Nos. 730–740

27thFS/ Nos. 730–740 • 29thFS/ Nos. 750–760

Some higher numbers are known to have been used, as evidenced in rare photos of this group.

Standard CAF emblems were present on all ships and distinctive sharks mouths were a predominate addition to the noses of most of the group's P-40s, as was the distinctive twelve band rudder pattern. These latter devices were not applied to the group's replacement P-40s.

P-51 Mustangs began arriving at the 5thFtrGp in late February 1945, and eventually included C, D, K, and F-6 models. The same black ten inch numerical blocks of the group's P-40s was carried over to the P-51s. Other Mustang squadron markings are too complex to be adequately covered here. The book *Wing To Wing* by Carl Molesworth is recommended for anyone interested in the history of the CACW.

U.S.A.A.F. LIAISON UNITS

CHINA-BURMA-INDIA THEATER OF OPERATIONS

In contrast to their counterparts in the ETO, there was only one liaison group posted to the CBI, and that unit was not officially constituted, but formed in India as a provisional unit. That is not to say this was the sole liaison representation in the CBI during WWII; although not an overwhelming presence by ETO standards, in addition to the 1st LnGp(P) there were an additional six squadrons permanently assigned to the 1st and 2d Air Commando Groups, plus one additional attached squadron.*

The nature of operations conducted by liaison pilots varied widely and took them into sometimes remote and hostile terrain, often alone. From a practical perspective, tactical markings were not a necessary component of the daily operations conducted by liaison squadrons. In spite of this, those aircraft operating with the liaison squadrons of the 1st and 2d Air Commando Groups did display a similar type of unit tactical marking as carried on other types of aircraft assigned to their respective group, albeit in a much smaller version.

Perhaps due to its provisional status, the 1st LnSqdn(P) is not known to have adopted any type of tactical markings on their assigned L-1, L-4, or L-5 aircraft.

Of the eleven Liaison squadrons that served in the CBI only five had known emblems, all of which were officially approved. The oldest of these emblems dated to 1929, with the newest receiving approval in February 1945.

* The 163d Liaison Squadron served briefly in the CBI (16 May–3 November 1945). There are no known tactical markings or emblem.

• Attached Tenth AF, 29-Aug-1944 thru 30-Apr-1945 •

1st Liaison Group (Provisional)

Insignia: (unknown)

Organized:

1st Ln Grp (Prov)/ 29-Aug-1944

Activated: 29-Aug-!944

To date, there is no indication the 1st LnGp(P) ever developed a group emblem, a situation not uncommon with provisional units.

The 1st LnGp(P) operated several types of aircraft—primarily the Stinson L-1 Vigilant, Piper L-4 Grasshopper, and Stinson L-5 Sentinel—but in spite of some claims to the contrary, research to date has found nothing conclusive to indicate any group/ squadron tactical airframe markings were ever employed while serving in the CBI.

5th Liaison Squadron

Insignia: Approved/ 22-Dec-1944

Constituted:

5th Obs Sqdn (Spcl)/ 28-Jan-1942

Activated: 7-Feb-1942

Redesignated:

5th Obs Sqdn/ 28-Aug-1942

5th Ln Sqdn/ 2-Apr-1943

19th Liaison Squadron

Insignia: Arrroved/ 11-Oct-1943

Constituted:

19th Obs Sqdn (Lt)/ 5-Feb-1942

Activated: 6-Mar-1942

Redesignated:

19th Obs Sqdn/ 4-Jul-1942

19th Ln Sqdn/ 2-Apr-1943

71st Liaison Squadron

Insignia: Approved/ 20-Feb-1945

Constituted:

71st Ln Sqdn/ 17-Jun-1943

Activated: 15-Jul-1943

115th Liaison Squadron

Insignia: Approved/ 26-Dec-1929

Organized:

115th Aero Sqdn/ 28 Aug 1917

Redesignated

636th Aero Sqdn/ 1 Feb 1918

115th Obs Sqdn/ 16 Jun 1924

115th Obs Sqdn (L)/ 13-Jan-1942

115th Obs Sqdn/ 4-Jul-1942

115th Ln Sqdn/ 2-Apr-1943

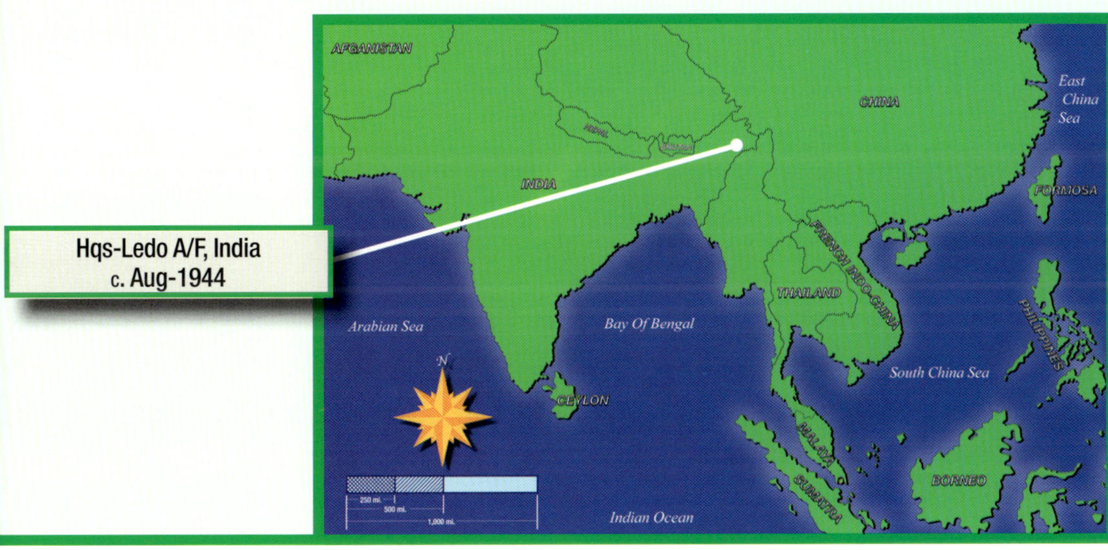

• Tenth USAF: Groups/Squadrons •

China Air Task Force	11th BombSqdn(M)	16th FtrSqdn	74th FtrSqdn	75th FtrSqdn
				76th FtrSqdn
India Air Task Force (P)				
	7th BombGp(H)	9th BombSqdn(H)	436th BombSqdn(H)	492d BombSqdn(H)
				493d Bomb Sqdn (H)
	51st FtrGrp	16th FtrSqdn	25th FtrSqdn	
	341st BombGp	11th BombSqdn(M)	22d BombSqdn(M)	490th BombSqdn(M)
				491st BombSqdn(M)
1st Air Cmdo Grp	5th FtrSqdn(Cmdo)	6th FtrSqdn(Cmdo)	164th LnSqdn(Cmdo)	165th LnSqdn(Cmdo)
			319th TrCarrSqd(Cmdo)	166th LnSqdn(Cmdo)
1st Ln Gp (Prov)	5th LnSqdn(P)	19th LnSqdn(P)	71st LnSqdn(P)	115th LnSqdn(P)
2d Air Cmdo Gp	1st FtrSqdn(Cmdo)	2d FtrSqdn(Cmdo)	127th LnSqdn(Cmdo)	155th LnSqdn(Cmdo)
			317th Tr Carr Sqdn (Cmdo)	156th Ln Sqdn (Cmdo)
3d Cmbt Crgo Gp	9th CmbtCrgoSqdn	10th CmbtCrgoSqdn	11th CmbtCrgoSqdn	12th CmbtCrgoSqdn
7th Bomb Gp (H)	9th BombSqdn(H)	436th BombSqdn(H)	492d BombSqdn(H)	493d BombSqdn(H)
8th Photo Rcn Gp	9th PhotoSqdn	20th RcnSqdn	24th CmbtMpgSqdn	40th PhotoRcnSqdn
12th Bomb Gp	81st BombSqdn(M)	82d BombSqdn(M)	83d BombSqdn(M)	434th BombSqdn(M)
64th Tr Carr Gp	16th TrCarrSqdn	17th TrCarrSqdn	18th TrCarrSqdn	35th TrCarrSqdn
311th Ftr Gp	385th BombSqdn(Dive)	528th FtrSqdn	529th FtrSqdn	530th FtrSqdn
341th Bomb Gp (M)	11th BombSqdn(M)	22d BombSqdn(M)	490th BombSqdn(M)	491st BombSqdn(M)
443d Tr Carr Gp	1st TrCarrSqdn	2d TrCarrSqdn	27th TrCarrSqdn	315th TrCarrSqdn
	10th CmbtCrgoSqdn	426th NgtFtrSqdn	427th NgtFtrSqdn	

• Fourteenth USAF: Groups/Squadrons •

23d FtrGp	74th FtrSqdn	75th FtrSqdn	76th FtrSqdn	
33d FtrGp	58th FtrSqdn	59th FtrSqdn	60th FtrSqdn	
51st FtrGp	16th FtrSqdn	25th FtrSqdn	26th FtrSqdn	449th FtrSqdn
80th FtrGp	88th FtrSqdn	89th FtrSqdn	90th FtrSqdn	459th FtrSqdn
81st FtrGp	91st FtrSqdn	92d Ftr Sqdn	93d Ftr Sqdn	
311th Ftr Gp	385th Bomb Sqdn (Dive)	528th Ftr Sqdn	529th Ftr Sqdn	530th Ftr Sqdn
443d TrCarrGp	1st TrCarrSqdn	2d TrCarrSqdn	27th TrCarrSqdn	315th TrCarrSqdn
308th BombGp(H)	373d BobSqdn(H)	374th Bomb(H)	375th BombSqdn(H)	425th BombSqdn(H)
341th BombGp(M)	11th BombSqdn(M)	22d BombSqdn(M)	490th BombSqdn(M)	491st BombSqdn(M)
	426th NgtFtrSqdn	427th NgtFtrSqdn	21st PhotoRcnSqdn	35th PhotoRcnSqdn

• Chinese Air Force/Fourteenth USAF: Groups/Squadrons •

Chinese-American Composite Wing (Prov)

1st BombGp(P)	1st BombSqdn(P)	2d BombSqdn(P)	3d BombSqdn(P)	4th BomnSqdn(P)
3d FtrGp(P)	7th FtrSqdn(P)	8th FtrSqdn(P)	28th FtrSqdn(P)	32d FtrSqdn(P)
5th FtrGp(P)	17th FtrSqdn(P)	26th FtrSqdn(P)	27th FtrSqdn(P)	29th FtrSqdn(P)

• Twentieth AF: Groups/Squadrons •

15th FtrGp	45th FtrSqdn	47th FtrSqdn	79th FtrSqdn	
21st FtrGp	46th FtrSqdn	72d FtrSqdn	531st FtrSqdn	
413th FtrGp	1st FtrSqdn	21st FtrSqdn	34th FtrSqdn	
414th FtrGp	413th FtrSqdn	437th FtrSqdn	456th FtrSqdn	
506th FtrGp	457th FtrSqdn	458th FtrSqdn	462d FtrSqdn	
507th FtrGp	463d FtrSqdn	464th FtrSqdn	465th FtrSqdn	
6th BombGp(VH)	24th BombSqdn(VH)	39th BombSqdn(VH)	40th BombSqdn(VH)	
9th BombGp(VH)	1st BombSqdn(VH)	5th BombSqdn(VH)	99th BombSqdn(VH)	
16th BombGp(VH)	15th BombSqdn(VH)	16th BombSqdn(VH)	17th BombSqdn(VH)	21st BombSqdn(VH)
19th BombGp(VH)	28th BombSqdn(VH)	30th BombSqdn(VH)	93d BombSqdn(VH)	
29th BombGp(VH)	6th BombSqdn(VH)	43d BombSqdn(VH)	52d BombSqdn(VH)	
39th BombGp(VH)	60th BombSqdn(VH)	61st BombSqdn(VH)	62d BombSqdn(VH)	
40th BombGp(VH)	25th BombSqdn(VH)	44th BombSqdn(VH)	45th BombSqdn(VH)	395th BombSqdn(VH)
330th BombGp(VH)	457th BombSqdn(VH)	458th BombSqdn(VH)	459th BombSqdn(VH)	
331st BombGp(VH)	355th BombSqdn(VH)	356th BombSqdn(VH)	357th BombSqdn(VH)	
444th BombGp(VH)	676th BombSqdn(VH)	677th BombSqdn(VH)	678th BombSqdn(VH)	679th BombSqdn(VH)
462d BombGp(VH)	768th BombSqdn(VH)	769th BombSqdn(VH)	770th BombSqdn(VH)	771st BombSqdn(VH)
468th BombGp(VH)	792d BombSqdn(VH)	793d BombSqdn(VH)	794th BombSqdn(VH)	795th BombSqdn(VH)

• Twentieth AF: Groups/Squadrons (cont) •

497th BombGp(VH)	869th BombSqdn(VH)	870th BombSqdn(VH)	871st BombSqdn(VH)
498th BombGp(VH)	873d BombSqdn(VH)	874th BombSqdn(VH)	875th BombSdn(VH)
499th BombGp(VH)	877th BombSqdn(VH)	878th BombSqdn(VH)	879th BombSdn(VH)
500th BombGp(VH)	881st BombSqdn(VH)	882d BombSqdn(VH)	883d BombSdn(VH)
501st BombGp(VH)	21st BombSqdn(VH)	41st BombSqdn(VH)	485th BombSdn(VH)
502d BombGp(VH)	402d BombSqdn(VH)	411th BombSqdn(VH)	430th BombSdn(VH)
504th BombGp(VH)	398th BombSqdn(VH)	421st BombSqdn(VH)	680th BombSdn(VH)
505th BombGp(VH)	482 BombSqdn(VH)	483d BombSqdn(VH)	484th BombSdn(VH)
509th CompGp	320th TrCarrSqdn	393d BombSqdn(VH)	

• USAAF/CBI: Groups/Squadrons •

1st Cmbt Crgo Gp	1st CmbtCrgoSqdn	2d CmbtCrgoSqdn	3d CmbtCrgoSqdn	4th CmbtCrgoSqdn
4thCmbt Crgo Gp	13th CmbtCrgoSqdn	14th CmbtCrgoSqdn	15th CmbtCrgoSqdn	16th CmbtCrgoSqdn
1st Air Cmdo Gp	5th FtrSqdn(Cmdo)	6th FtrSqdn(Cmdo)	64th LnSqdn(Cmdo)	165th LnSqdn(Ln)
			319th TrCarrSqdn(Cmdo)	166th LnSqdn(Cmdo)
2d Air Cmdo Gp	1st FtrSqdn(Cmdo)	2d FtrSqdn(Cmdo)	127th LnSqdn(Cmdo)	155th LnSqdn(Ln)
			317th TrCarrSqdn(Cmdo)	156th LnSqdn(Cmdo)
	35th PhotoRcnSqdn	41st PhotoRcnSqdn	426th NgtFtrSqdn	427th NgtFtrSqdn

SUMMING UP

From time to time the question invariably arises why one would dedicate so much time and effort to a subject so obscure as unit insignia and tactical markings. The source of this type of query is generally "big picture" advocates—those individuals who prefer to view history from the perspective of cause and effect, and while there is nothing wrong with this approach to the study of history, it is often the smaller elements comprising the whole that afford us insight into the human aspect of any given point in historical study.

The organizational or practical side of tactical markings has already been addressed earlier in this text; what remains is the subject of wartime unit insignia. Like the study of USAAF aircraft nose art during WWII, much of the individual character of the men actually tasked with carrying out day-to-day operations of war can be gleaned from the images they created. Several things become obvious when these images are viewed as a whole: even lacking supportive information, the men of the USAAF at this moment in history were little more than boys—perhaps a more apt description would be young men.

As such, they were preoccupied with the opposite sex, a fact reflected through their nose art; but what we learn through the study of their unit insignia tells even more about these young men. It tells us that taken as a whole, in addition to their youth, they were somewhat unsophisticated by European standards, but possessed a keen sense of humor which, given the dire circumstances they were subjected to, equated directly with confidence, and confidence in war is often a major determining factor between ultimate victory and defeat.

Interest in the subject of unit insignia was not confined to the respective units themselves; the full reality concerning these images was quite the opposite during the war years. Those on the home front expressed a great deal of interest in these symbols.

Virtually anyone could design and submit a concept for a squadron and even group insignia. To become officially authorized for display by a unit, a design concept had to be submitted to the US Army's Heraldic Department, where it would subsequently be scrutinized by a review board. The regulations governing Army Air Force insignia at the time stated a submission, "may be of caricature design, not necessarily classic or heraldic, but must be in good taste and of composition to enable painting on airplanes by simple stencil." If a design met these basic guidelines it was forwarded up the line for the next phase. There were several additional prerequisites a proposed insignia had to meet. Each design had to be sufficiently concise to be distinguishable at a maximum distance of 150 yards. The general submission criteria further prohibited the following specific data from inclusion in a design format: numerals of any kind; the flag or coat of arms of the United States; the letters "U.S."; geographical maps; military decorations; and mottos or coat of arms of any state, country, or United States service branch.

Many units elected to request the services of professionals in the civilian sector to assist in the development of their respective insignia designs. Those within this art profession who gladly contributed their services included such notable names as Al Capp, Walter Lantz, Milt Canniff, and V. T. Hamlin. By far the largest contributor to this design pool was Disney Studios. Walt Disney designed his first unit insignia for the US Naval Reserve Squadron in 1933, and by the end of WWII, Disney had created over 1,200 pro bono designs for virtually every branch of government service. Requests for these designs reached such a large scale that a special five-man department was created to meet overwhelming demand.

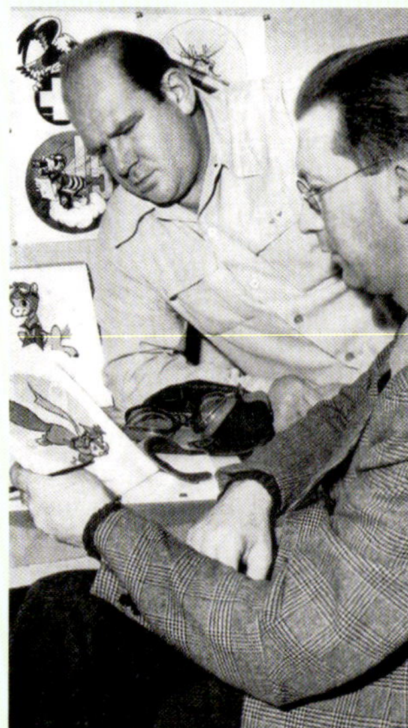

The majority of this effort seems to have gone into designing insignia for the US Army Air Forces, and this effort was not to be totally forgotten.

A special exhibit commemorating Disney Studios' contribution to America's war effort exists at the National Museum of the United States Air Force at Wright-Patterson Air Force Base, Ohio. Perhaps due to the rapidly changing nature of American society, these contributions made on behalf of US servicemen by Disney, Warner Brothers, and all the other artists during WWII are now largely a seldom acknowledged footnote in the history of this conflict.

Interest in the subject of unit or combat insignia was by no means confined to active duty personnel. Pearl Harbor had galvanized the country and the home front stood unified in the war effort and expressed great interest in a wide variety of subjects connected with their servicemen overseas—unit insignia among them. The interest in combat insignia was so keen that entire marketing/advertising campaigns and promotional programs were developed utilizing these insignia as their central theme.

Not Just For Kids! Lest those unfamiliar with this period in American history go away with the wrong idea, it was not only youngsters who were attracted to the cartoon images of combat insignia. The popularity of these designs among adults is perhaps best illustrated by a lengthy ad campaign launched in 1943 by the Oldsmobile Division of General Motors. This series of full page, full color ads featured a different unit insignia each month for almost two years, and while the series depicted insignia of all service branches, for some reason those of the Army Air Force dominated the campaign. Although General Motors had ceased manufacturing civilian transportation during the war years, like all other automobile manufacturers in the United States, this campaign was designed to foster patriotism while simultaneously keeping the product name before the buying public until that time when the company was again in the business of manufacturing cars.

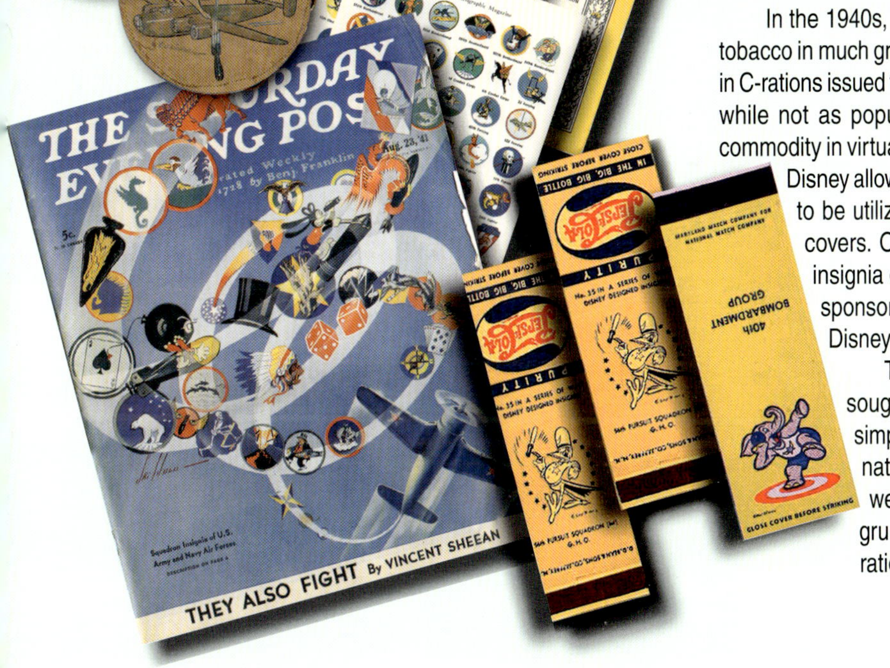

In the 1940s, a large portion of Americans indulged in the use of tobacco in much greater quantities than today. Cigarettes were included in C-rations issued to troops until as late as 1975. Pipe and cigar smoking, while not as popular as cigarettes, were nevertheless a common commodity in virtually every sector of American life. Throughout the war Disney allowed many of the unit insignias his studio had designed to be utilized as the central theme for a series of matchbook covers. One series of these covers depicted only a single insignia design and very little text copy. Later Pepsi-Cola Co. sponsored a similar licensed series incorporating additional Disney designs.

Today these free give-away items of the 1940s are a sought-after collectors item, but at the time they were simply an everyday utility used as a subtle reminder of a nation's young fighting men. These and other reminders were intended to curb, among other things, civilian grumbling about shortages of many items due to war rationing.

USAAF MARKINGS

THE EVOLUTION OF US NATIONAL AIRCRAFT INSIGNIA

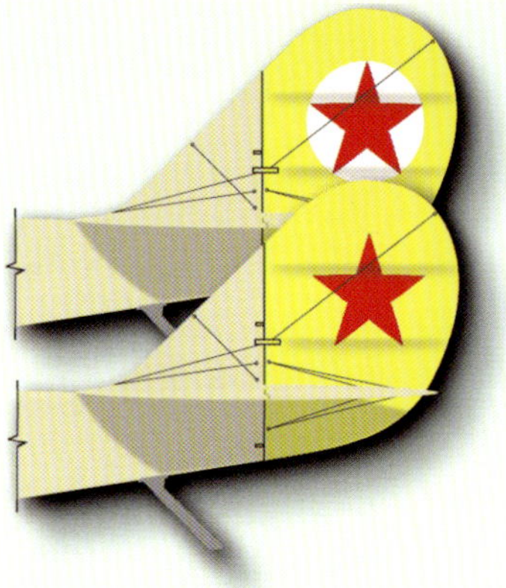

Circa 1916: The first national identification markings applied to US aircraft appeared at the North Island Aviation School, California. Neither design was ever officially adopted by the Army Signal Corps. These applications appeared on the tail section only, with no other images applied to the surface area of the wings (top or bottom), nor the fuselage.

May 17, 1917: These represent the first authorized combination of national recognition insignia on US military aircraft. During this period there were no standards regulating color uniformity, and as a result many applications varied from one aircraft to another, and tended to be governed solely by those color shades currently on hand.

January 11, 1918: For reasons that may have been as much political as practical, star-and-circle insignia was replaced with the cockade pattern depicted at left. This modification affected only those AEF aircraft serving on the Western Front. The tail color configuration was itself modified from reading red-white-blue (right to left) to blue-white-red.

No documentation has been located to explain the logic behind these changes, but the Army officially dropped this combination and reverted to the original 1917 configuration on all its aircraft in May 1919.

Circa 1924–1927: The "U.S. Army" designator was adopted for under wing surface application on all Army Air Corps aircraft in 1924. The alternating pattern of horizontal red and white tail stripes came into existence three years later. The red emblem disk was to disappear permanently from all United States warplanes shortly after the outbreak of WWII.

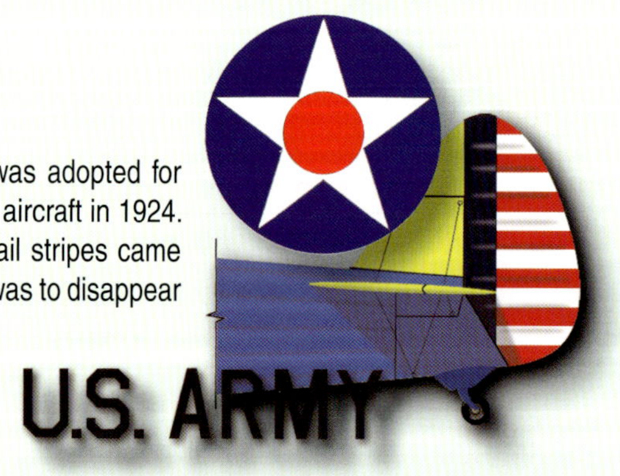

Elgin Field Military Reservation, 18 June 1943

A series of tests were held under authority of the Army / Navy Aeronautical Board featuring a selection of Allied and Axis national markings applied to several US aircraft, principally the P-47 Thunderbolt. A series of fly-bys were conducted and photographed at varying altitudes and distances to establish the optimum image for recognition of US aircraft. The overall favorite was a new design recently added to the mix that included a set of horizontal white bars on each side of the circle and star configuration. The entire design was originally enclosed with a red outline, but this was soon converted to the now familiar Insignia Blue contour line which, except for the addition of a red horizontal bar, remains in use by the United States military.

This was the standard national marking on virtually all US military aircraft at the time the Japanese offensive in the Pacific began. In some instances these devices were removed on an individual basis in the 49th Pursuit Group already in Australia. This action was due to friendly fire incidences when Allied gunners mistook this marking for the Japanese hinomaru (Meatball) emblem. 29 June 1943 saw the first revised emblem pattern derived from the Elgin Field tests. Although patriotic in nature with its red, white, and blue color theme, the red outline presented a problem. It seems the mere presence of this color in any form in conjunction with aircraft insignia was akin to waving a red flag at a bull, so this new design was modified shortly following its debut.

War Department Circular No. 141 of 28 May 1942 officially revised the US national insignia in a straightforward manner by simply directing the removal of the center red disc. The directive further ordered the removal of the prewar tricolored rudders, an order that was in some cases ignored by some units of the Fifth AF. Always the innovators and acting independent of higher approval, fighter units in the Fifth AF took it upon themselves to eliminate the threat caused by the recently approved red-bordered US national insignia by simply white washing over the offending red outline. These modifications ran the gambit from being masked prior to repainting to hastily freehanded overpainting with a brush.

Although at times mistaken as a tactical marking similar to that employed in the European Theater, such is not the case. P-40E-1 series Kittyhawks originally intended for delivery to the UK were painted in a standard RAF three color paint scheme and roundels, but many were diverted for service with the 49th Fighter Group. AAF personnel immediately affixed US insignia over the existing roundels, but being slightly smaller in diameter than their RAF counterparts, these left a small outer yellow ring exposed, many of which remained throughout the entire service life of the aircraft.

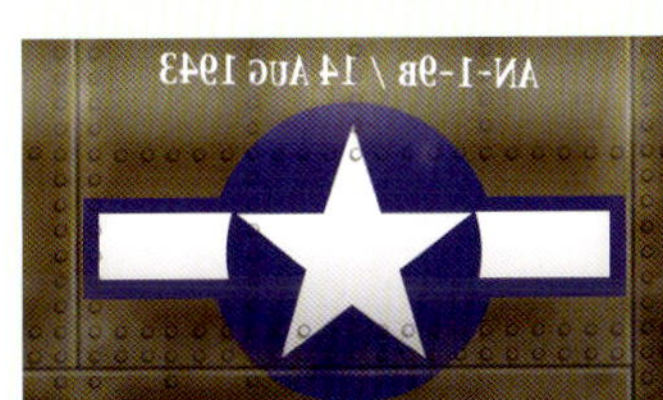

The final results of the Elgin Field tests as approved 14 August 1943.

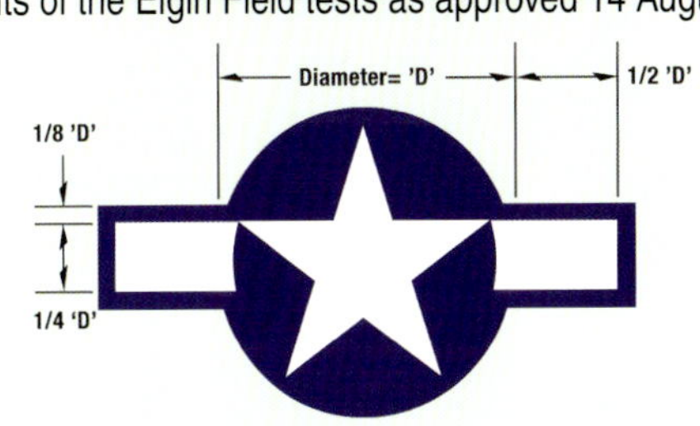

The following diagrams show the official WWII / USAAF specifications for placement of national insignia and tail numbers as they applied to the fighter aircraft depicted. A combat aircraft might undergo any number of surface modifications, some of which would alter the original size and placement of the factory applications depicted in these diagrams. To those interested in a specific aircraft at a specific time in WWII, it is strongly suggested that a thorough study and comparative analysis of actual wartime photographs pertaining to the subject be conducted. Such research will often reveal variations in positioning, color, and configuration of markings and paint schemes differing from those detailed in official USAAF or ANA directives. The two photographs in the adjacent column are included to address a marking scheme employed by the AAF prior to the outbreak of hostilities in 1941. These were colored cowling bands and fuselage command stripes. These devices were used to denote group, squadron, and flight leaders, but were not much used overseas. A few fighter units did utilize some form of command stripe during their wartime deployment, but these were rare. When applicable, and also confirmable, reference is made within this text to those groups/squadrons that employed such devices overseas regardless of how briefly.

LOCKHEED P-38 LIGHTNING

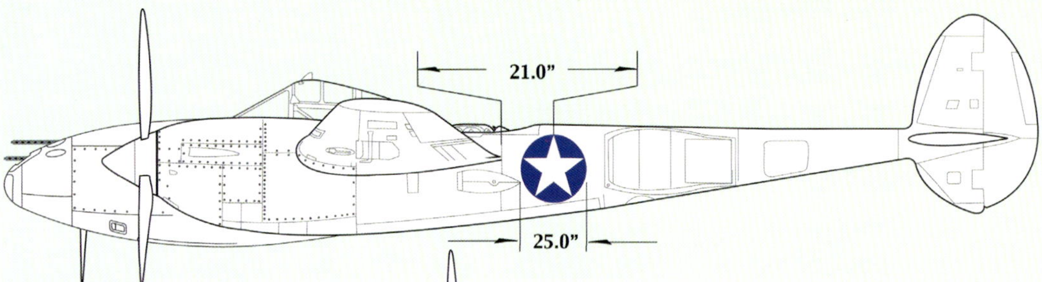

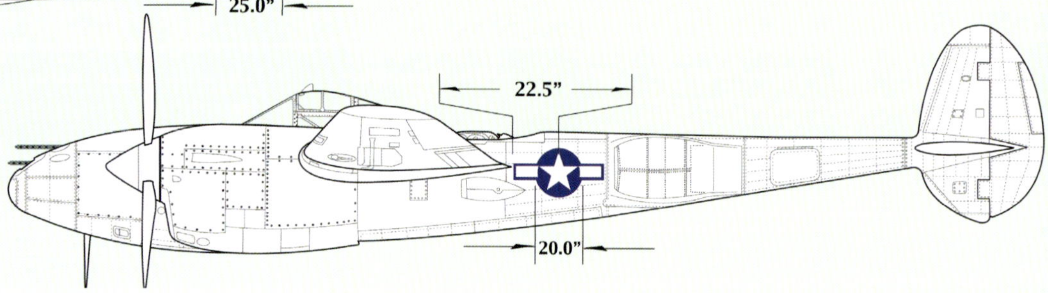

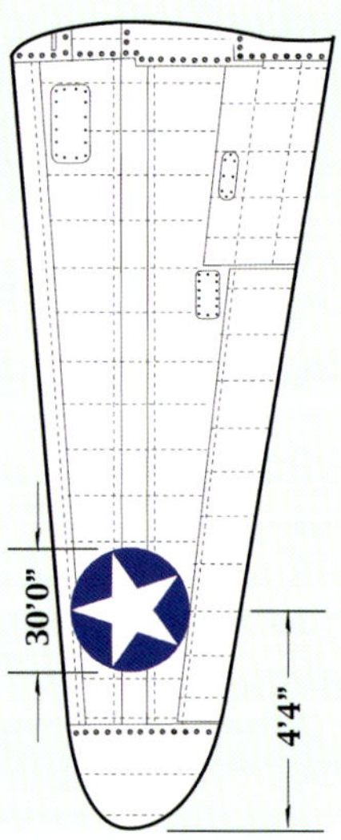

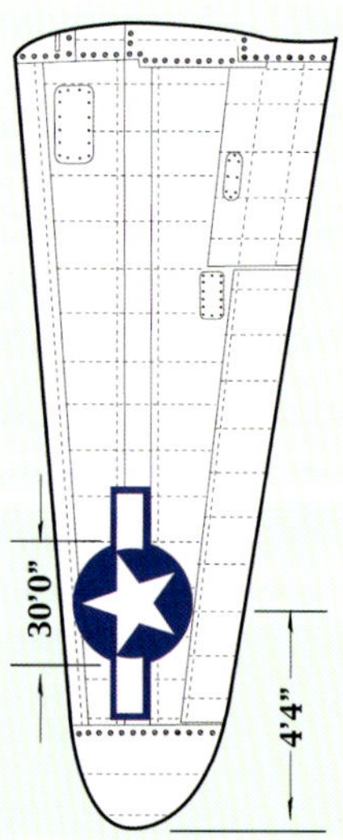

Tail, or serial numbers, were factory applied and varied from an 8 in. height on early applications to a 9 in. height later in the war. The numerals were stenciled on using Insignia Yellow on camouflaged aircraft and Black on metal finished surfaces. Factory applied numerals invariably had the stencil lines filled while in-the-field reapplications often omitted this final step.

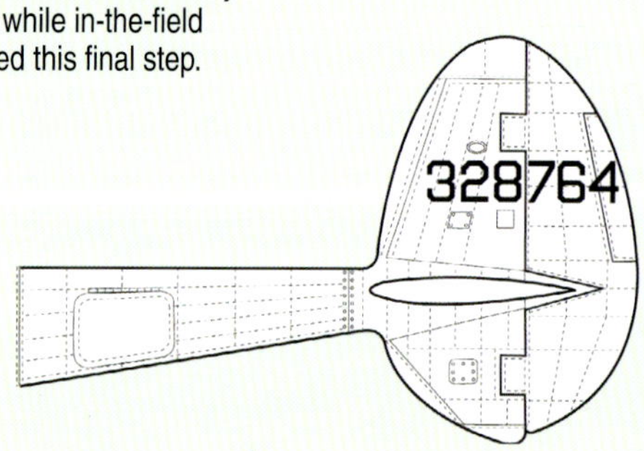

NORTH AMERICAN P-51 MUSTANG

FACTORY APPLIED TAIL NUMBERS ON P-51S WERE 8 IN. HIGH.

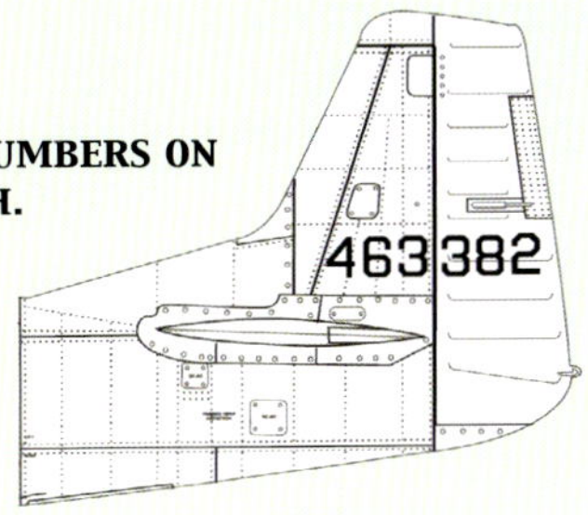

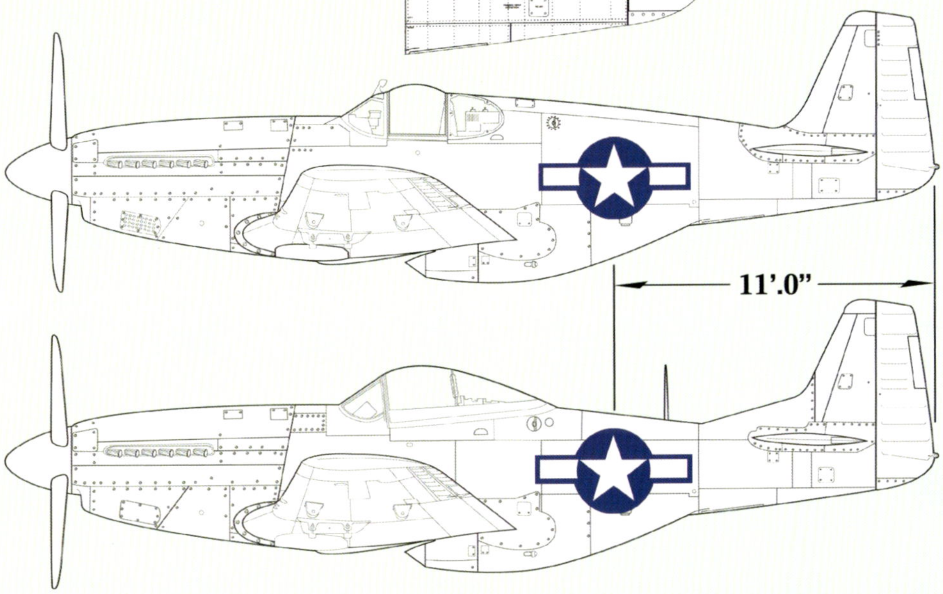

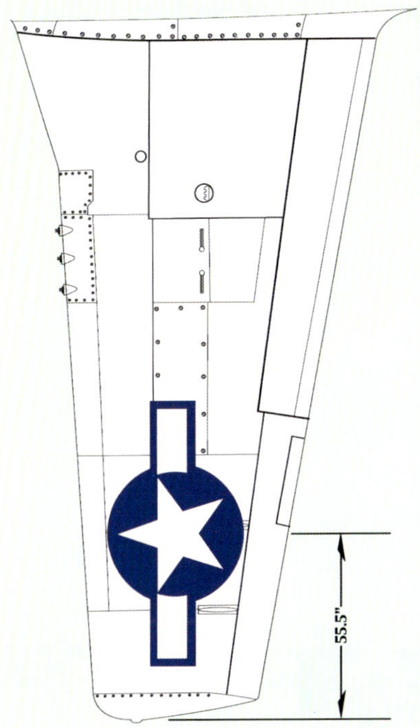

REPUBLIC P-47 THUNDERBOLT

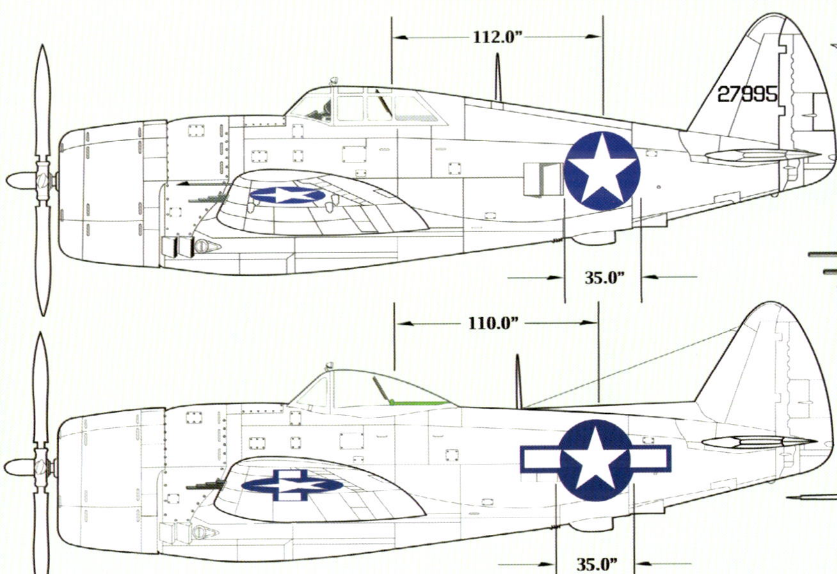

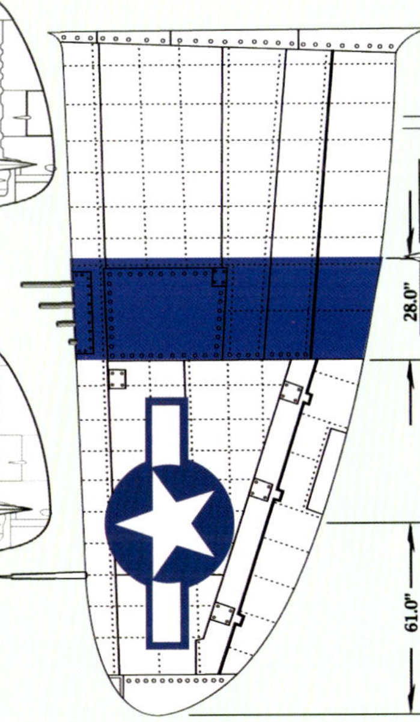

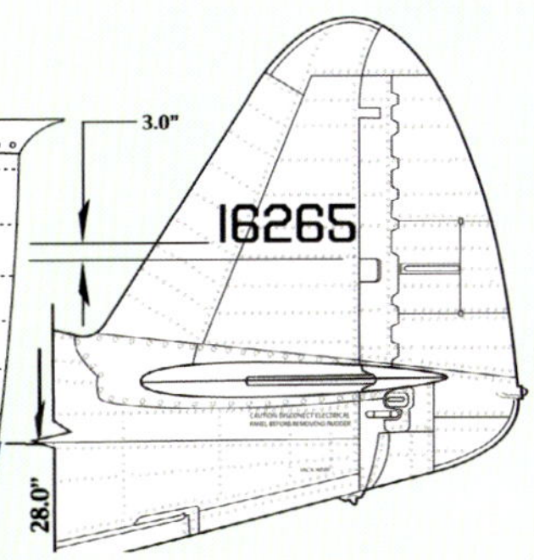

(1) EARLY TAIL SERIAL NO. POSITIONING

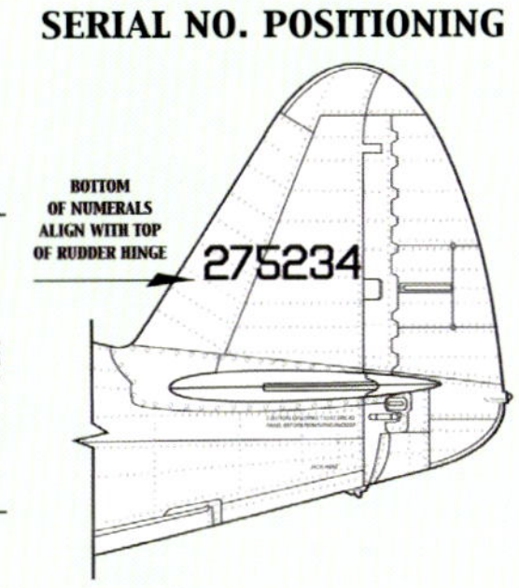

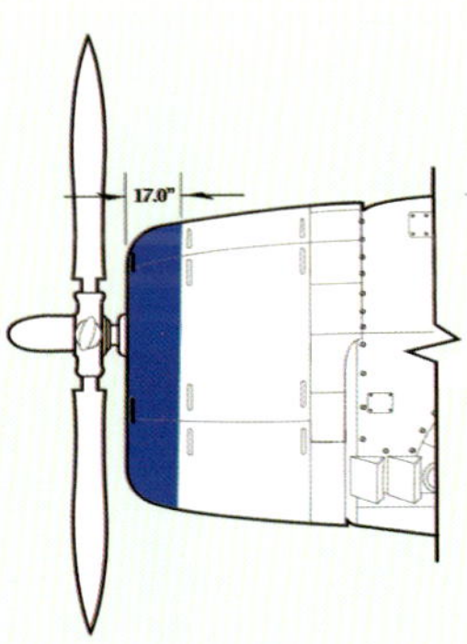

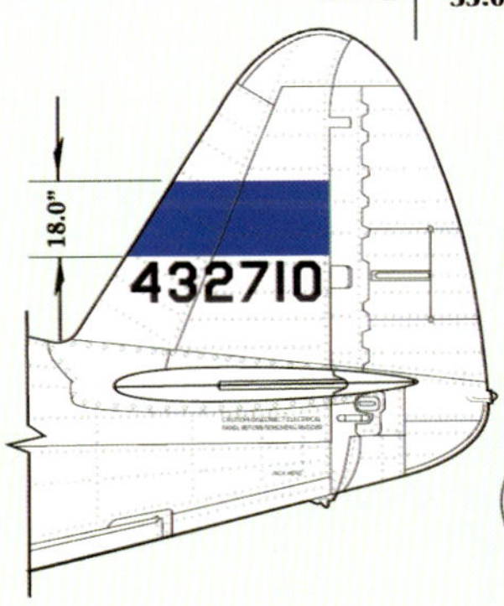

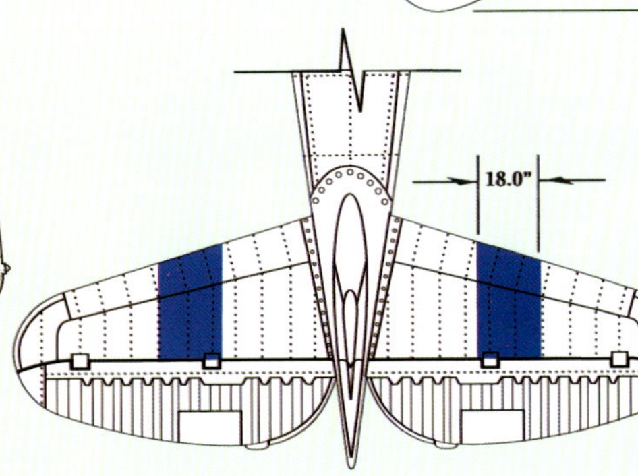

(2) LATER TAIL SERIAL NO. POSITIONING

Placement of US national emblems and EAC tactical stripes as they applied to the Tenth AF beginning November 1944. This directive also applied to P-51 Mustangs assigned in the EAC-A/O.

Japanese wartime map of conquest in the Pacific

Chronology of Events/Pacific Theater

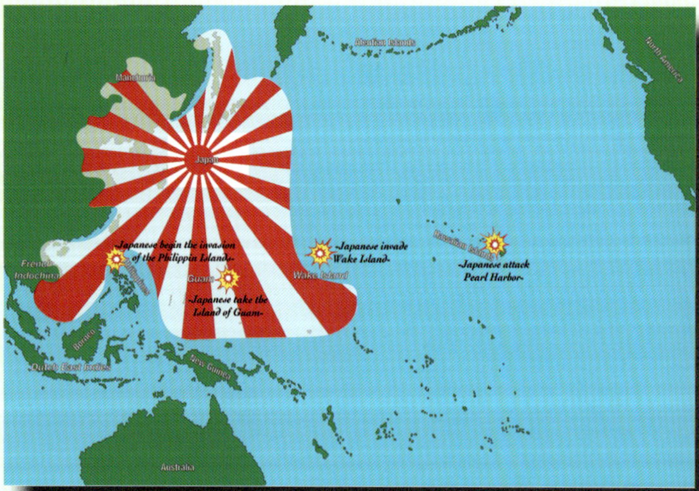

1941

December 7: Japanese bomb Pearl Harbor, Hawaii, Guam, Philippines, Wake Island, Malaya, Thailand, Shanghai and Midway.

December 8: U.S. and Britain declare war on Japan. Japanese land near Singapore; invade Thailand.

December 9: China officially declares war on Japan.

December 10: Japanese invade Philippines and capture Guam.

December 11: Japanese invade Burma.

December 15: First Japanese MARU sunk by a U.S. submarine.

December 16: Japanese invade British Borneo.

December 18: Japanese invade Hong Kong.

December 22: Japanese invade Luzon Island, Philippines.

December 23: Gen. Douglas MacArthur begins a withdrawal from Manila to Bataan; Japanese capture Wake Island.

December 25: British forces surrender Hong Kong.

December 26: Manila declared open city.

December 27: Japanese bomb Manila.

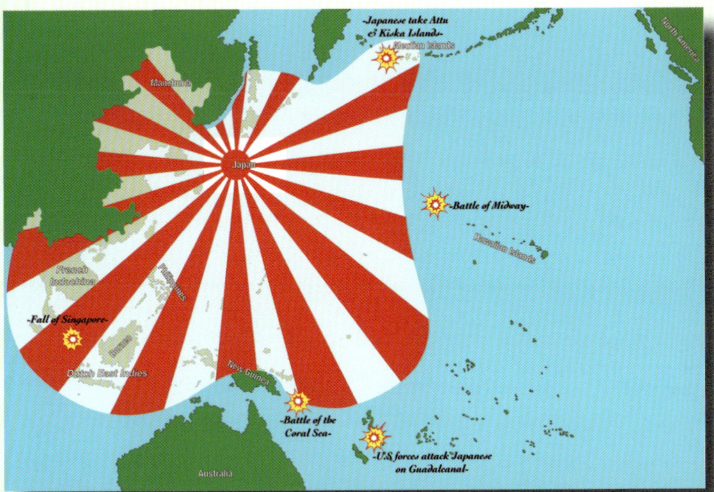

1942

January 2: Manila, U.S.N. base at Cavite captured.
January 7: Japanese attack Bataan in the Philippines.
January 11: Japanese invade Dutch East Indies, Dutch Borneo.
January 16: Japanese begin advancing into Burma.
January 18: Axis Treaty signed in Berlin.
January 19: Japanese overrun North Borneo.
January 23: Japanese take Rabaul, New Britain in the Solomons chain; invade Bougainville.
January 27: First Japanese warship sunk by a U.S. submarine.
January 30-31: The siege of British held Singapore begins.
February 1: USS *Yorktown* and *Enterprise* conduct first U.S. carrier based air raids on Japanese bases; Gilbert & Marshall Is.
February 2: Japanese invade Java, Dutch East Indies.
February 8/9: Japanese invade Singapore.
February 14: Japanese invade Sumatra in the Dutch East Indies.
February 15: British surrender at Singapore.
February 19: Largest Japanese air raid since Pearl Harbor against Darwin, Australia; Japanese invade Bali.
February 22: President Franklin D. Roosevelt orders General MacArthur out of the Philippines.
February 23: First Japanese attack on the US mainland when submarine *I-17* shells Ellwood Oil Field near Santa Barbara, California.
February 24: USS *Enterprise* attacks Japanese forces on Wake Island.
February 26: USS *Langley* sunk by Japanese bombers.
February 27- March 1: Japanese naval victory in the Battle of the Java Sea; USS *Houston* sunk.
March 4: Two Japanese flying boats bomb Pearl Harbor; USS *Enterprise* attacks Marcus Island 1,000 miles from Japan.
March 7: British evacuate Rangoon in Burma; Japanese invade Salamaua and Lae on New Guinea.
March 8: Dutch forces and civilians on Java surrender.
March 11: Gen. MacArthur departs Corregidor for Australia; Gen. Jonathan Wainwright appointed US commander.
March 18: President Roosevelt names Gen. MacArthur as Supreme Commander, Southwest Pacific Area.
May 3: Japanese take Tulagi in the Solomon Islands.
May 5: Japanese prepare to invade Midway and Aleutians.
May 6: Japanese take Corregidor; Gen. Wainwright unconditionally surrenders all US/Filipino forces.
May 7-8: Japan suffers its first defeat at the Battle of the Coral Sea off New Guinea.
May 12: Mindanao; last US troops surrender.
May 20: Japanese complete capture of Burma; reach India.
June 4-5: Decisive US naval victory at the Battle of Midway
June 7: Japanese forces invade the Aleutian Islands.
June 9: Japanese postpone further plans against Midway.
June 20: Japanese *I-25* shells Estevan Point, Vancouver.
July 21: Japanese land troops near Gona, New Guinea.
August 7: The first US amphibious landing of the Pacific War at Tulagi and Guadalcanal.
August 8: US Marines take Lunga Point (later Henderson) airfield on Guadalcanal.
August 8/9: USN suffers a disastrous defeat off Savo Island.
August 17: US Marine raiders attack Makin Atoll.
August 24: Battle of the Eastern Solomons; USN victory.
August 30: Troops of the US Army's 7thInfDiv invade Adak; Aleutian Islands.
September 9: A Japanese floatplane launched from *I-25* drops incendiary bombs on US forests in Oregon state.
September 12-14: Battle of Bloody Ridge; Guadalcanal.
September 15: Japanese submarine torpedo attack near Solomon Islands sinks USS *Wasp* and USS *O'Brien*.
September 27: British launch Burma offensive.
October 11/12: USN victory at the Battle of Cape Esperance.
October 13: US Army's 164th Inf Regiment land on Guadalcanal.
October 18: Vice Admiral William F. Halsey named new commander of the South Pacific Area.
October 26: USS *Hornet* lost at the Battle of Santa Cruz.
November 14/15: Five Sullivan brothers lost on USS *Juneau*.
November 23/24: Japanese launch aerial attack on Darwin, Australia.
November 30: Battle of Tasafaronga off of Guadalcanal.
December 20-24: Japanese launch air strikes; Calcutta, India.
December 31: Emperor Hirohito authorizes withdrawal of Japanese forces from Guadalcanal.

1943

January 2: Allied forces take Buna in New Guinea.

January 22: Sananda, New Guinea; Japanese defeated.

February 1: Japanese troops begin evacuation of Guadalcanal.

February 8: British-Indian forces begin guerrilla warfare campaign against Japanese in Burma.

February 9: Guadalcanal is officially declared secure.

March 2-4: USN victory at the Battle of the Bismarck Sea.

April 18: P-38 pilots of the 339thFS/347thFG intercept and shoot down Japanese Admiral Yamamoto near Bougainville.

April 21: Japanese announce the execution of several captured crewmen from the Doolittle Raid.

April 22: Japan declares that captured Allied pilots will be given "one way tickets to hell."

May 10: Troops of the 17thInfDiv, US Army, land on Attu Island, the Aleutians beginning a vicious two week long battle against occupying Japanese forces.

May 31: Japanese evacuate the Aleutian Islands.

June 1: USN initiates submarine warfare against Japanese merchant shipping.

June 21: Allied offensive advances to New Georgia in the Solomon Islands.

July 8: Midway based USAAF bombers launch an attack against the Japanese garrison on Wake Island.

August 2: *PT-109*, commanded by Lt. John F. Kennedy, sunk by Japanese cruiser *Amagiri* in Blackett Strait near Kolombangra Island, Solomons.

August 6/7: Battle of Vella Gulf; Solomon Islands.

August 25: Allies complete the occupation of New Georgia.

September 4: Allied forces retake Lae-Salamaua, New Guinea.

October 7: Wake Island; Japanese troops execute approximately 100 American POWs.

November 1: US Marines invade Bougainville.

November 2: The Battle of Empress Augusta Bay.

November 20: US Troops invade Makin and Tarawa.

November 23: Makin and Tarawa declared secure.

December 15: US Troops land on the Arawe Peninsula, New Britain, in the Solomon Islands.

December 26: Allied forces launch an attack on New Britain.

1944

January 9: Maungdaw, Burma retaken by British forces.

January 31: US forces land on Kwajalein, Marshall Islands.

February 1-7: US forces capture Kwajalein and Majura Atolls in the Marshall Islands.

February 17/18: USN carrier-based planes attack and decimate the Japanese naval base at Truk, Caroline Islands.

February 20: USN carrier and land-based planes devastate the Japanese garrison at Rabaul.

February 23: USN carrier-based planes strike at the Mariana Is.

February 24: The 5307th CmpUnit(P), Merrill's Marauders, begin an offensive ground campaign in Northern Burma.

March 5: Gen. Wingate's Chindits begin guerilla operations behind Japanese lines in Burma.

March 15: Japanese launch an offensive drive toward Imphal and Kohima.

April 17: Japanese forces begin final offensive in China. USAAF airfields in eastern China are primary targets.

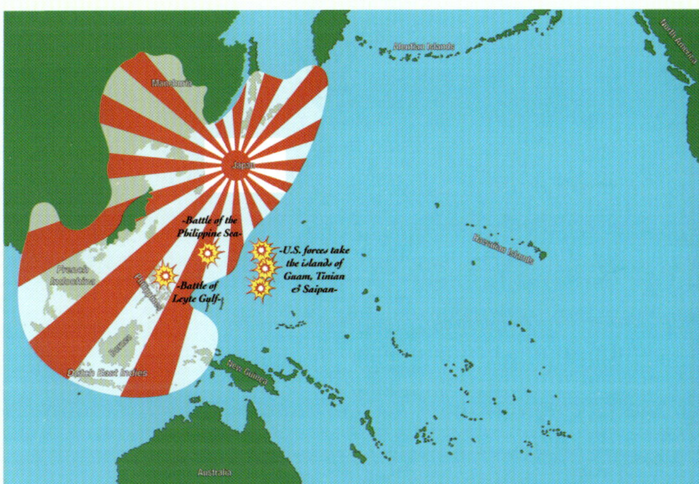

April 22: Allied forces invade Aitape and Hollandia in Papaua New Guinea.

May 27: Allies invade Biak Island, Papua New Guinea.

June 5: First mission by 77 B-29 bombers of the Twentieth AF dispatched in raid against Japanese railway facilities at Bangkok, Thailand.

June 15: US Marines invade Saipan, Mariana Islands.

June 15/16: 47 USAAF B-29s based in Bengal, India, strike the steel works at Yawata, Japan. First attack on home islands since Doolittle's Tokyo Raid.

July 24: US Marines invade Tinian Island.

July 27: American troops complete liberation of Guam.

August 3: US and Chinese troops take Myitkyina airfield.

August 8: US forces complete capture of Mariana Islands.

September 15: US troops invade Morotai and Paulaus.

October 11: USAAF and USN air raids begin against Okinawa.

October 18: USAAF Marianas based B-29s attack the Japanese stronghold on Truk Island.

October 20: The US Sixth Army invades the island of Leyte in the Philippines.

October 23-26: Battle of Leyte Gulf; decisive USN victory.

October 25: Japanese launch the first organized Kamikaze attacks against USN warships in the Leyte Gulf.

November 11: The USN and USMC aviators initiate the first in a series of attacks against Japanese defenses on Iwo Jima.

November 24: B-29s of the Twentieth AF bomb Nakajima Aircraft Factory near Tokyo.

December 15: Philippines; US Troops strike at Mindoro.

December 17: The 509th Composite Group, Twentieth AF, is constituted in preparation for dropping the atomic bomb on targets in Japan.

1945

January 3: Gen. MacArthur placed in command of all Pacific based US ground forces. Adm. Nimitz to command naval forces in all future offensive operations.

January 4: British occupy Akyab, in Burma.

January 9: US Sixth Army lands at Lingayen Gulf, on Luzon.

January 11: Indochina; USN planes attack Japanese bases.

January 28: The reopening of The Burma Road.

February 3: The US Sixth Army attacks Japanese in Manila.

February 16: US Army troops recapture Bataan.

February 19: US Marines invade the island of Iwo Jima.

March 1: USS *Greenfish* sinks the *Awa Maru* in Taiwan Strait, creating international incident resulting in a court martial which ultimately clears sub's captain of charges.

March 2: US Army paratroops of the 3dBn/503dPIR recapture the island Corregidor.

March 3: US Army and Filipino troops retake Manila.

March 9/10: Fifteen square miles of Tokyo consumed by flames after incendiary bombing strike by 279 B-29s belonging to the Twentieth AF.

March 10: US Eighth Army launches amphibious landing on Zamboanga Peninsula, Mindanao, in the Philippines.

March 20: British troops liberate Mandalay, Burma.

March 27: Twentieth AF B-29s begin deploying mines in Japan's Shimonoseki Strait to disrupt shipping.

April 1: US Army and Marine troops launch what turns out to be the final amphibious landing of the war on the island of Okinawa.

April 7: B-29s conduct their first fighter escorted mission against Japan with Iwo Jima based P-51 Mustangs.

April 7: Battleship *Yamato* along with several escort vessels sunk by USN carrier based aircraft while en route to assist Japanese forces in the defense of Okinawa.

April 12: President Franklin D. Roosevelt dies.

May 8: V-E Day.

May 20: Japanese begin withdrawal of forces from China.

May 25: US Joint Chiefs of Staff approve Operation Olympic, the proposed invasion of Japan, on November 1, 1945.

June 18: Organized Japanese resistance ends on Mindanao in the Philippines.

June 22: US Tenth Army forces an end to all organized Japanese military resistance on Okinawa.

June 28: Gen. MacArthur's HQ announce the end of all formal Japanese resistance in the Philippines.

July 5: Philippines Islands officially declared liberated.

July 10: Massed 1,000 plane bomber raids against Japan begin.

July 14: USN opens first naval bombardment of Japanese home islands.

July 16: First atomic bomb is successfully tested at Alamogordo Test Range, New Mexico.

July 26: Components of the atomic bomb "Little Boy" are off-loaded at Tinian Island.

July 29: USS *Indianapolis* sunk by Japanese sub *I-58* after delivering "Little Boy" to the 509th CmpstGp on Tinian.

August 6: "Little Boy" is dropped on Hiroshima from the B-29 *Enola Gay* flown by Col. Paul Tibbets.

August 8: The USSR decides to declare war on Japan.

August 9: A second atomic bomb "Fat Man" is dropped on Nagasaki from *Brockscar*, a B-29 flown by Maj. Charles Sweeney of the 509th CmpstGp..

August 14: Japanese accept unconditional surrender; Gen. MacArthur appointed to head occupation forces in Japan.

August 16: Gen. Wainwright, a POW since May 6, 1942, is released from POW camp in Manchuria.

August 29: First US occupation troops land near Tokyo.

August 30: British troops reoccupy Hong Kong.

September 2: The Japanese formally surrender in a ceremony aboard USS *Missouri* in Tokyo Bay. President Truman declares this date the official V-J Day.

September 3: Gen. Yamashita, aka "The Tiger of Malaya" and the Japanese commander in the Philippines, surrenders to Gen. Wainwright at Baguio.

September 4: The Japanese garrison on Wake Island surrenders.

September 5: British troops land in Singapore.

September 8: Gen. MacArthur enters Tokyo.

September 9: Japanese forces in Korea surrender.

September 13: Japanese in Burma surrender.

USAAF / AREA OF OPERATIONS
CHINA-BURMA-INDIA & WESTERN PACIFIC

Major Campaigns Of The Pacific War

Battle of the Philippines: (1941–42)
Battle of Bataan: 7 January – 9 April 1942
Battle of Corregidor: 5–6 May 1942
Dutch East Indies Campaign: 1941–42
Battle of Badung Strait: 19–20 February 1942
Battle of the Java Sea: 27 February 1942
Battle of Sunda Strait: 28 February – 1 March 1942
Second Battle of the Java Sea: 1 March 1942
Guadalcanal Campaign: 1942–43
Battle of Savo Island: 9 August 1942
Battle of the Eastern Solomons: 24–25 August 1942
Battle of Cape Esperance: 11–12 October 1942
Battle of the Santa Cruz Islands: 26 October 1942
Naval Battle of Guadalcanal: 12–15 November 1942
Battle of Tassafaronga: 30 November 1942
Solomon Islands Campaign: 1943–45
Battle of Kula Gulf: 6 July 1943
Battle of Kolombangara: 13 July 1943
Battle of Vella Gulf: 6–7 August 1943
Naval Battle of Vella Lavella: 6–7 October 1943
Battle of Empress Augusta Bay: 2 November 1943
Battle of Cape St. George: 25 November 1943
New Guinea Campaign: 1942–45
Battle of the Coral Sea: 4–8 May 1942
Kokoda Track Campaign: 1942
Battle of Buna-Gona: 1942
Battle of the Bismarck Sea: 2 March 1943
Landing at Nassau Bay: 1943
Salamaua-Lae Campaign: 1943
Huon Peninsula Campaign: 1943
New Britain Campaign: 26 December 1943
Admiralty Islands Campaign: 29 February 1944
Aitape-Wewak Campaign: 22 April 1944
Invasion of Hollandia: 22 April 1944
Battle of Biak: 27 May 1944
Battle of Noemfoor: 2 July 1944
Battle of Morotai: 15 September 1944
Battle of Timor: 1942–43
Philippines Campaign: 1944–45
Battle of Leyte Gulf: 20 October 1944
Borneo Campaign: 1945

Note on V-J Day: This label has been applied to two separate dates: 15 August 1945 (actually 14 August in the US) and 2 September 1945. The first date refers to the day Japan's surrender was officially announced, the latter being the actual date a formal surrender document was signed in Tokyo Bay aboard the USS *Missouri*. For the purposes of this work, 2 September 1945 is the date indicated in all reference to VJ-Day.

USAAF ABBREVIATIONS & ACRONYMS

AAA	Anti-Aircraft Artillery
AAF	Army Air Forces
AB	Air Base
AAB	Army Air Base
A/C	Aircraft
AD	Air Division
Air.Div	Air Division
A/D	Air Depot
AF	Air Force
A/F	Airfield
ANA	Army-Navy Aeronautical
A/O	Area of Operations
AS / Antisub	Anti-Submarine
A/S	Airstrip
AUS	Australia
ATO	American Theater of Operations
Avn.	Aviation
BD	Bombardment (later Air) Division
BG	Bombardment (Bomb) Group
BG(H)	Bomb Group (Heavy)
BG(M)	Bomb Group (Medium)
BG(L)	Bomb Group (Light)
Bmr.	Bomber
Bomb	Bombardment
BS	Bombardment (Bomb) Squadron
BW	Bombardment (Bomb) Wing
c.	circa (approximate time period)
Carr.	Carrier
CBI	China-Burma-India (Theater of Operations)
Cmbt.	Combat
Cmd.	Command
Cmdo.	Commando
CO	Commanding Officer
Cmpst.	Composite
Crgo.	Cargo
CW	Combat Wing
DB	Dive Bomber
Det	Detachment
EAC(Markings)	Eastern Air Command
ERS	Emergency Rescue Squadron
F/B	Fighter-Bomber
FEAF	Far East Air Force(s)
FG /FtrGp / FtrGrp	Fighter Group
FLAK	Anti-Aircraft Fire
Fld.	Field
Flt.	Flight
Ftr.	Fighter
FO	Flight Officer
FS / FtrSqdn	Fighter Squadron
FW / FtrWng	Fighter Wing
GB	Great Britain
GHQ	General Headquarters
Gp / Grp	Group
HQ	Headquarters
Incpt.	Interceptor
LN	Liaison
JP	Japan
Mpng.	Mapping
PS	Photographic Squadron
OBS	Observation
OPS	Operations
OSS	Office Of Strategic Services (US)
NMF	Natural Metal Finish
(P) (Prov)	Provisional
PG	Photographic Group
Photo	Photographic
POM	Preparation for Overseas Movement
POW	Prisoner Of War
PR	Photographic Reconnaissance
PRG	Photographic Reconnaissance Group
PS	Photographic Squadron
PSYOPS	Psychological Operations
PTO	Pacific Theater of Operations
Pur.	Pursuit
RAF	Royal Air Force
RAAF	Royal Australian Air Force
RCM	Radio Counter Measures
Rcn.	Reconnaissance
RG	Reconnaissance Group
RS	Reconnaissance Squadron
SF	Scouting Force
Spt.	Support
Sq / Sqdn.	Squadron
Srch.	Search
Stn.	Station
SWP	South West Pacific
TA	Territory of Alaska
Tac.	Tactical
TDY	Temporary Duty Assignment
TH	Territory of Hawaii
Trng.	Training
Tr.	Troop
Trnsp.	Transport
T/O	Theater Of Operations
TRG	Tactical Reconnaissance Group
TRS	Tactical Reconnaissance Squadron
Triple-A	Anti-Aircraft Artillery
US	United States
USA	United States Army
USAAF	United Stated Air Forces
UK	United Kingdom
USN	United States Navy
V-J Day	Victory over Japan
WR	Weather Reconnaissance
Wthr.	Weather
Wg.	Wing
X/O	Executive Officer
ZI	Zone of the Interior

BASIC AIRCRAFT NOMENCLATURE

The following diagrams have been included to assist those readers unfamiliar with certain aircraft terminology used frequently within this text.

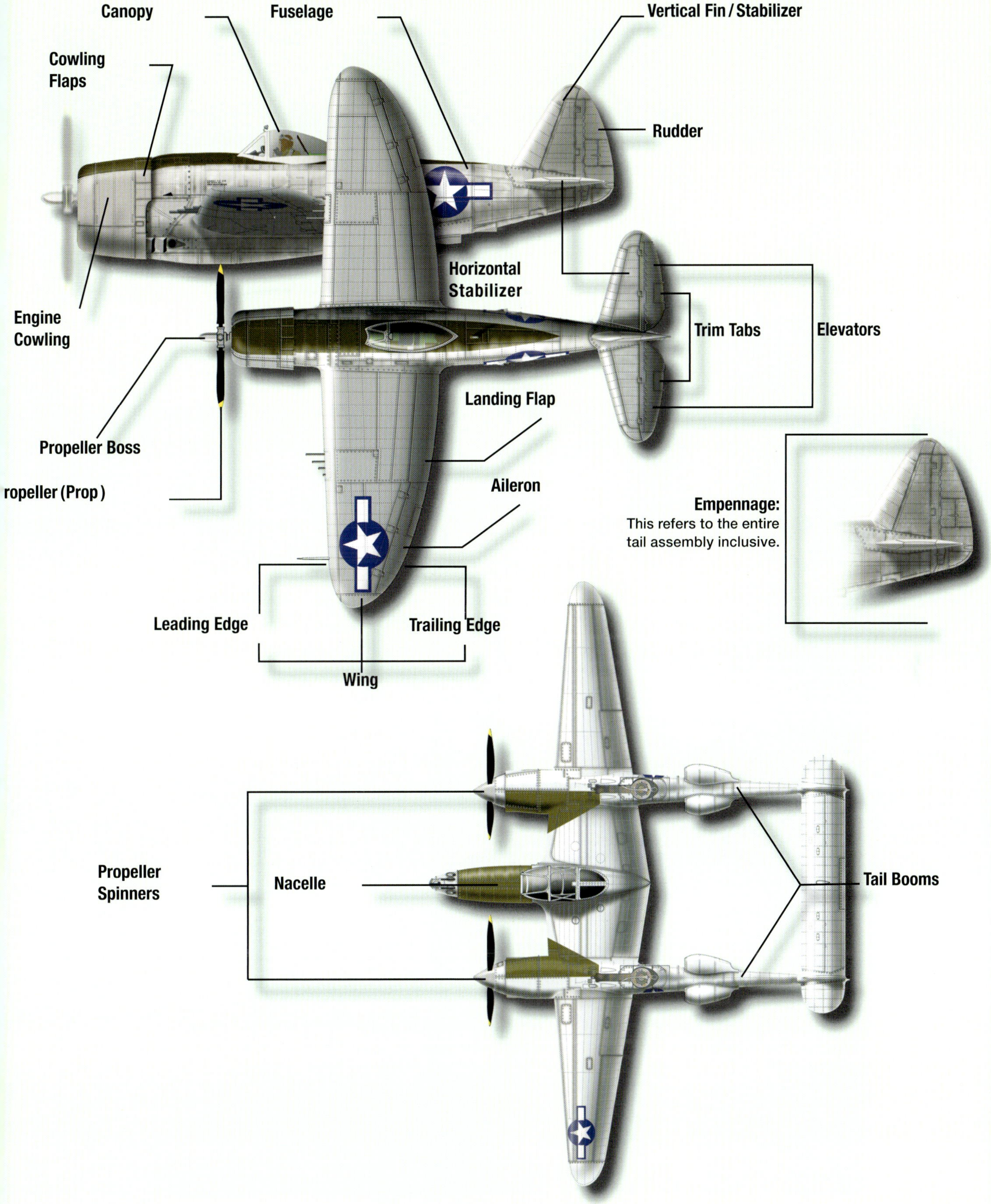

TACTICAL MARKINGS-VISUAL INDEX

This section is for the benefit of those who have ever experienced the frustration of attempting to establish the unit origin of an AAF aircraft viewed in wartime film footage, a postwar documentary, or a photo in a reference book where the assignment of that particular aircraft was not specified.

Not all groups or squadrons adopted distinctive tactical markings, and those units that did often underwent modifications to those markings. Given the limitations of space, the following examples represent the more visual examples adopted by a given USAAF/CBI unit during the course of the war, and these generally appeared in the latter phase of deployment. Earlier markings, if they existed, are included in each respective unit's section.

If a particular group is not featured in this index this does not necessarily mean no markings were ever adopted, but may simply be a case where the tactical devices displayed were so common in nature (e.g., two-digit numbers on tail fin) that these markings did not fall within the "distinctive" unit marking category.

It is hoped this index will prove a useful tool for those readers who share a fascination with this subject.

• FIGHTERS •

(1ST) AMERICAN VOLUNTEER GROUP P. 10

CHINA AIR TASK FORCE (CATF) P. 12

3D FTRGP(P) (CACW) P. 128

5TH FTRGP(P) (CACW) P. 129

15TH FTR GP P. 10

21ST FTRGP P. 22

23D FTRGP P. 24

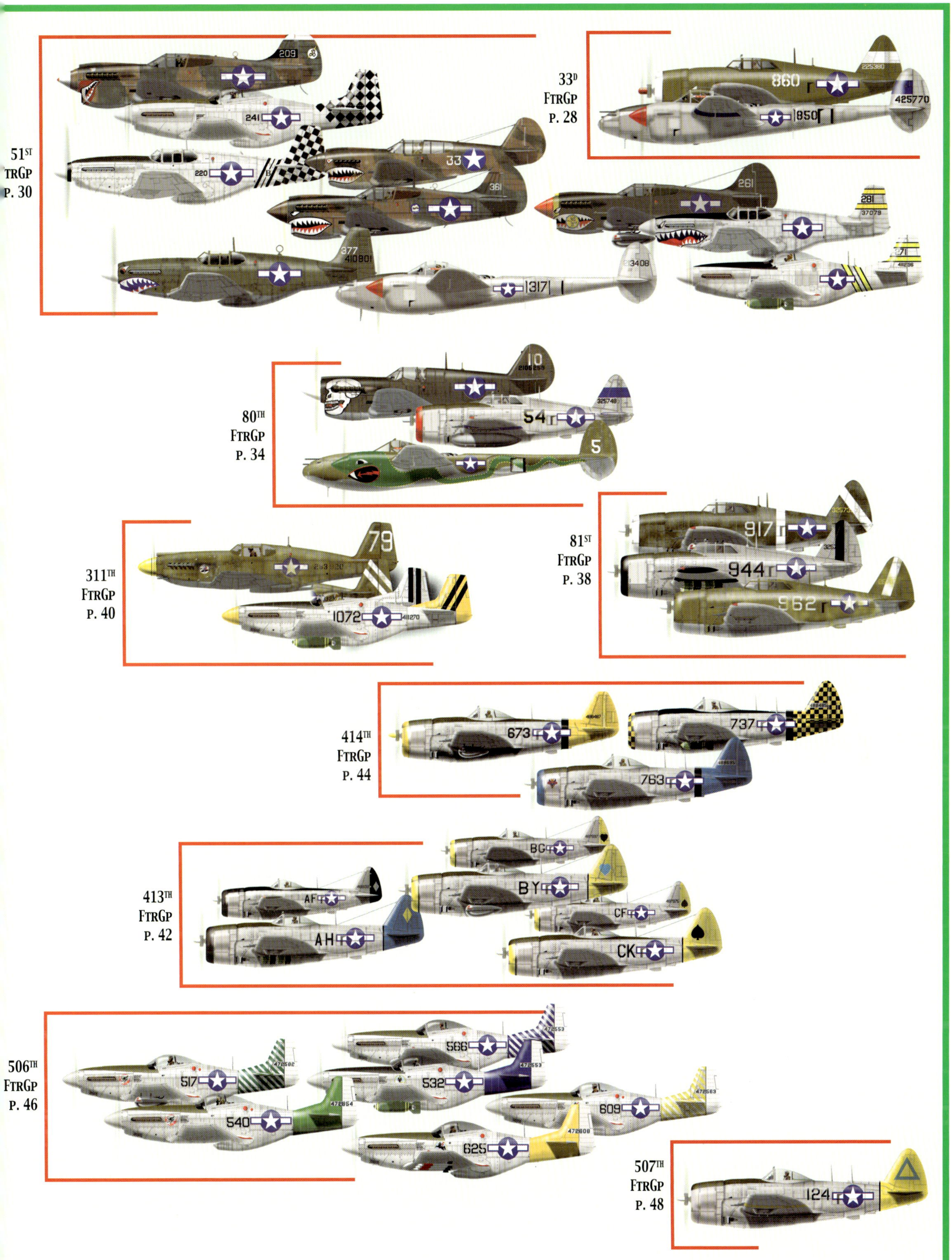
51st FtrGp p. 30
33d FtrGp p. 28
80th FtrGp p. 34
81st FtrGp p. 38
311th FtrGp p. 40
414th FtrGp p. 44
413th FtrGp p. 42
506th FtrGp p. 46
507th FtrGp p. 48

• BOMBERS •

1ST
BOMBGP(P)
(CACW)
P. 127

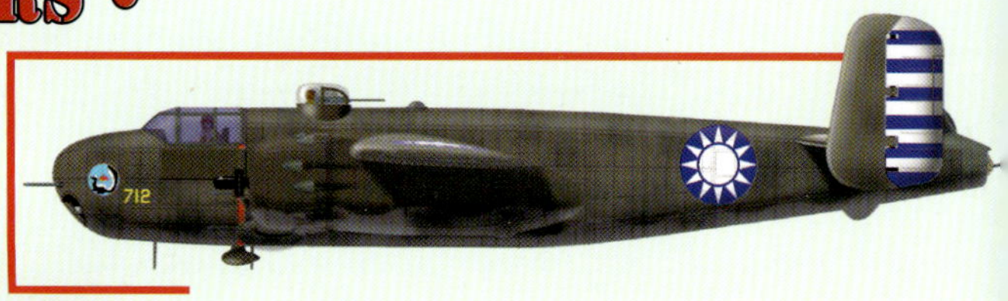

6TH
BOMB
GP(VH)
P. 66

7TH
BOMB
GP(H)
P. 68

9TH
BOMB
GP(VH)
P. 70

12TH
BOMB
GP(H)
P. 72

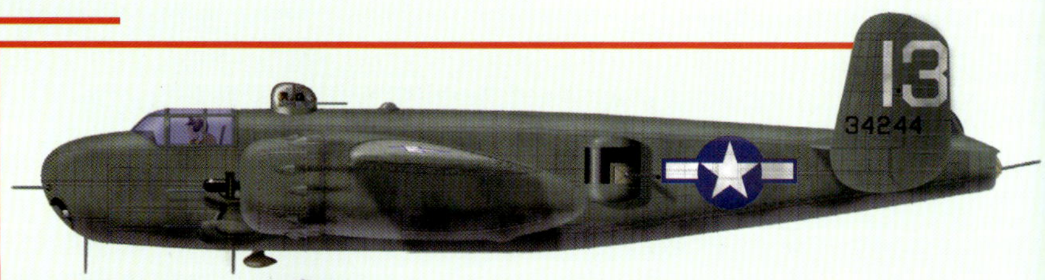

16TH
BOMB
GP(VH)
P. 74

19TH
BOMB
GP(VH)
P. 76

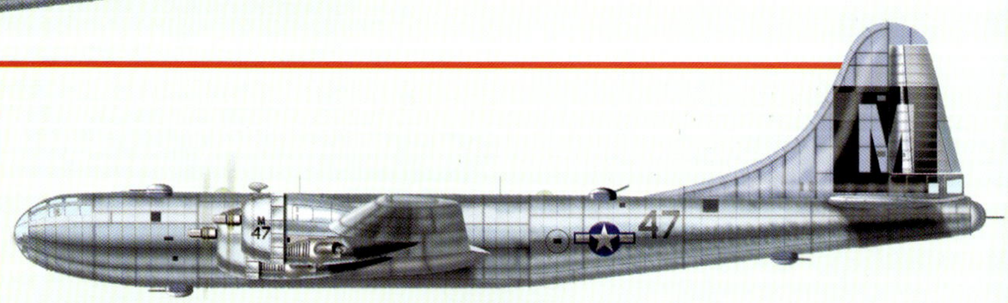

29TH
BOMB
GP(VH)
P. 78

39th Bomb Gp(VH) p. 80

40th Bomb Gp(VH) p. 82

308th Bomb Gp(H) p. 84

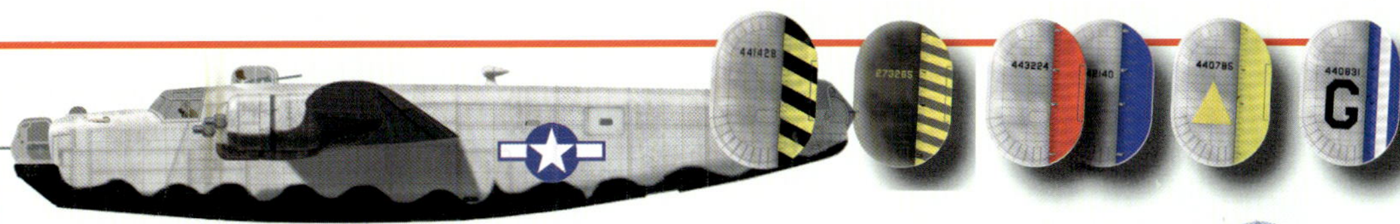

330th Bomb Gp(VH) p. 86

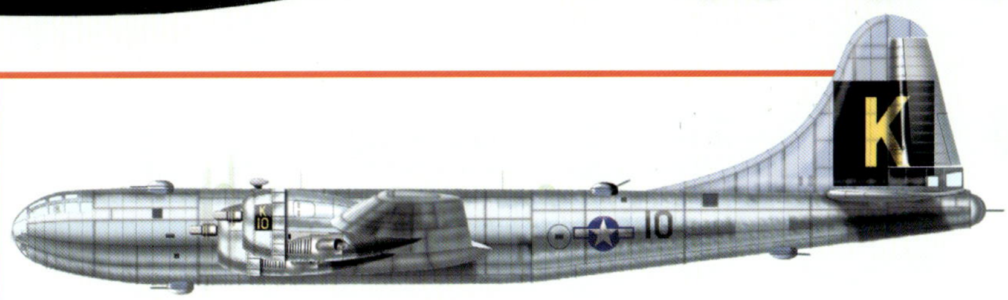

331st Bomb Gp(VH) p. 88

444th Bomb Gp(VH) p. 92

462d Bomb Gp(VH) p. 94

414th FtrGp p. 44

497th Bomb Gp(VH) p. 98

498th Bomb Gp(VH) p. 100

499th Bomb Gp(VH) p. 102

500th Bomb Gp(VH) p. 104

501st Bomb Gp(VH) p. 106

502d Bomb Gp(VH) p. 108

504th Bomb Gp(VH) p. 110

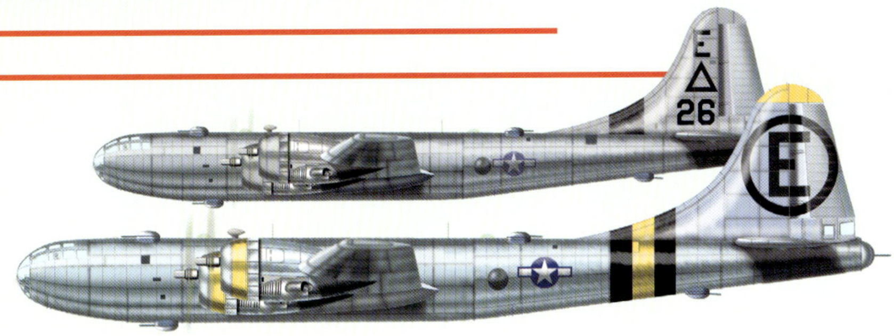

505th Bomb Gp(VH) p. 112

• SPECIAL OPERATIONS •

1st Air CmndoGp p. 116

2d Air CmndoGp p. 118

509th CompGp p. 120

BIBLIOGRAPHY / ACKNOWLEDGMENTS

• *Air Force News; 'Chinese-American Composite Wing'*
Capt. Robert V. Guelich
• *Air Heraldry*
Carl Mann
• *Aircraft Insignia-Spirit Of Youth:*
National Geographic, June 1943 / Gerard Hubbard
• *Air Force Colors/Vol.3:*
Dana Bell
• *Air Force Units Of World War II:*
Dr. M. Maurer
• *China Airlift/The Hump*
Hump Pilots Association
• *Combat Insignia Stamps Of The United States Army & Navy:*
Hearst Publications
• *Combat Squadrons Of The Air Force, World War II:*
Dr. M. Maurer
• *Command And Employment Of Air Power:*
War Department Field Manual / FM 100-20
• *Concise Historical Atlas of World War Two/ The Geography Of Conflict*
Ronald Story
• Days Of The Ching Pao
Malcom Rosholt
• *Distinctive Insignia Of The U.S. Army Air Forces/1924-1947:*
Joseph M. Massaro
• *Insignia & Decorations Of The US Armed Forces:*
National Geographic, 1944
• *Journey Of The Giants/The Story Of The B-29 Superfort*
Maj. Gene Gurney, USAF
• *Mission To Tokyo/The Americal Airmen Who Took The War To The Heart Of Japan*
Robert F. Dorr
• Sharks Over China/The 23rd Fighter Group in WWII
Carl Molesworth
• *The Army Air Forces In World War II-Combat Chronology / 1941-1945:*
Kit C. Carter / Robert Mueller
• *The Official Guide To The Army Forces:*
Army Air Forces Aid Society
• *The Organization And Lineage Of The United States Air Force:*
Charles A. Ravenstein
• *The Silverplate Bombers/A History & Registry of the Enola Gay & Other B-29's Configured to Carry Atomic Bombs*
Richard H. Campbell
• *USAAF Aircraft Markings And Camouflage/1941-1947*
Robert D. & Victor G. Archer
• *USAAF Heavy Bomb Group Markings & Camouflage 1941-1945-Consolidated B-24 Liberator:*
E.A. Munday & Richard Ward
• *War Maps of World War II From Sept.1939-Aug. 1945*
Simon Goodenough
• *Whirlwind/The Air War Against Japan*
Barrett Tillman
• *Wing To Wing/Air Combat In China*
Carl Molesworth & Steve Moseley
• *Victory Report-On the Winning of WWII in Europe and the Pacific:*
Gen. George C. Marshall
• *War Insignia Stamp Album / Volumes 1, 2, 3, 4 & Vol. 1/Series 2*
Robert L. Robbins

-Aircraft Illustration Reference-

• American Volunteer Group Flying Tigers Aces
Terrill Clements
• B-25 Mitchell In Detail:
Bert Kinzey
• B-29 Superfortress Walkaround
Col. Dennis M. Savage, USA (Ret.)
• B-29 Superfortress In Action:
Larry Davis, Don Greer, and Joe Sewell
• Scale Aircraft Drawings Vol. II:
Peter M. Bowers
• National Museum of the US Air Force/Wright-Patterson AFB

Grateful appreciation is extended to the following institutions and individuals for providing much of the invaluable historical data and images used in the creation of this work:

• American Military Insignia Collectors Association (ASMIC)
• American Battle Monuments Commission
• Bomber Command Museum of Canada: Bill Cowan
• Disney Worldwide, Inc.
• National Air and Space Museum
• P-38 National Association
• United States Air Force Museum / Wright-Patterson AFB
• United States National Archives and Records
• 3d Attack (Bomb) Group: Gerry Kersey
• 9th Bomb Group (VH): Rick Feldman
• 41st Bomb Group Association: Rolf Grandstaff
• 307th Bomb Group Association
• 505th Bomb Group: Nancy Stamp & Tom Morris

- Individual Contributors -

• C/Wo James Chastain • Dave Kaufman • Gerry Kersey •
• Hal Kiena • Nick King • Roland Swank • Jim McCabe •
• Don Rinehart • Mark W. Nelson, Lt.Col, USAFR Ret)
A special thanks goes out to fellow insignia enthusiast
• Johnny "Siggy" Signor - WeBeEmblems@aol.com •

- Internet Research Sites -

• ArmyAirForces.com • B24BestWeb.com • ThirdAttackGroup.org •
• ToonsAtWar.blogspot.com/ "Disney" Dave Lesjack •
• USAFPatches.com • U.S.Militaria.com •

And last, but far from least, a very special note of appreciation to the terrific, invaluable research staff of the
- Air Force Historical Research Agency (AFHRA) -
• Mr. Daniel L. Haulman, PhD/GS-13:
Chief, Organizational History Branch •
• Ms. Margaret "Peggy" Ream, GS-12 •
• Mr. Carl Baily, GS-12 •
• Ms. Patsy Robertson (Ret.)•

The Angry Skies

In Honor of Those That Served

From our farms, towns and cities they came,
these were not mystic warriors of legends fame.
Together they banded one and all,
together in answer to freedoms call.
Their boyish dreams they set aside
to fight in distant angry skies.

- R. A. Watkins / 2003

INDEX

INDEX

Current
Battle Colors
Volumes in the
Schiffer Military Library
BattleColors
Insignia and Aircraft Markings of the Eighth Air Force in World War II
Volume I: (VIII) Bomber Command
Robert A. Watkins
Battle Colors
Insignia and Aircraft Markings of the Eighth Air Force in World War II
Volume II: (VIII) Fighter Command
Robert A. Watkins
Battle Colors
Volume III
Insignia and Aircraft Markings of the Ninth Air Force in World War Two
Robert A. Watkins
The Orphan Air Force of the ETO
Battle Colors
Volume IV
Insignia and Aircraft Markings of the U.S. Army Air Forces in WWII
Mediterranean Theater of Operations
Robert A. Watkins
Battle Colors
Volume V
Insignia and Aircraft Markings of the U.S. Army Air Forces in WWII
Pacific Theater of Operations
Robert A. Watkins
Battle Colors
Volume VI
Insignia and Aircraft Markings of the U.S. Army Air Forces in WWII
China-Burma-India & The Western Pacific
Robert A. Watkins
A Schiffer Military History Book